# Fantasies of Empire

## STUDIES IN THEATRE HISTORY AND CULTURE

*edited by Thomas Postlewait*

# Fantasies of Empire

THE EMPIRE THEATRE OF VARIETIES

AND THE LICENSING CONTROVERSY OF 1894

**JOSEPH DONOHUE**

University of Iowa Press    Iowa City

University of Iowa Press, Iowa City 52242

http://www.uiowa.edu/uiowapress

The University of Iowa Press is a member of Green Press Initiative and is committed to preserving natural resources.

Printed on acid-free paper

Library of Congress Cataloging-in-Publication Data

Donohue, Joseph W., 1935–.

Fantasies of Empire: the Empire Theatre of Varieties and the licensing controversy of 1894 / by Joseph Donohue.

p.     cm.—(Studies in theatre history and culture)

Includes bibliographical references and index.

ISBN 0-87745-960-6 (cloth)

1. Empire Theater (London, England).    2. Performing arts—England—London—History—19th century.

I. Title.   II. Series.

PN2596.L7E463   2005

791'.09421—dc22          2005041945

05  06  07  08  09  C  5  4  3  2  1

*For Sharon, Maura, and Sheila*

# CONTENTS

# ACKNOWLEDGMENTS

This book began life as a footnote for another book. Several years ago, I was preparing an annotated edition of Oscar Wilde's *The Importance of Being Earnest* and needed to find out what Algy Moncrieff had in mind when, toward the end of Act 1, discussing with his friend Jack Worthing what they might do after dinner — the theatre and the club having been summarily rejected — he suggested that they "trot round to the Empire at ten." In pursuit of that intriguing reference, I discovered enough about the various kinds of spectacle on view at the Empire, onstage and off, to annotate the line; but the implications of Algy's knowing remark continued to hold my attention. The result, after a long, circuitous journey over highways and down bypaths of fact, event, and significance, is a slim book grown out of a salient paragraph. Along the way, I have incurred a number of debts for help, advice, kindness, and generosity from librarians, archivists, colleagues, and friends. To the extent that verbal thanks may serve as recompense, I am pleased to repay them here.

My first thanks must go to David Cheshire, whose book *Music Hall in Britain* (1974), which began my quest, was one of the first modern critical studies of a subject that, apart from much earlier writings by such first-hand students as William Archer, Percy Fitzgerald, H. G. Hibbert, John Hollingshead, Selwyn Image, Elizabeth Robins Pennell, Bernard Shaw, and Arthur Symons, supplemented by the fearless perspective of the Reverend Stewart Headlam, had remained for too long largely the province of undocumented biography, lively anecdote, and fond reminiscence. A few years later Cheshire collaborated with Lawrence Senelick and Ulrich Schneider to publish *British Music Hall, 1840–1923* (1981), a comprehensive bibliography and guide to sources, which set an admirable factual and contextual standard for further studies and which now, nearly a quarter century later, begs for updating. From these stalwart beginnings much useful work on the music hall and popular theatre has followed, by scholars (too many to name here) whose wide-ranging, reflective scrutiny has demarcated both centers and margins of a multivalent, complex subject and whose writing has substantially informed the present study. From them, and from other scholars too — historians of the theatre, of society, of art and architecture, of dance, and of ideas, along with historians of Victorian life and institutions and of sexuality and empire, among them Richard Altick, Peter Gay, John Stokes, Keith Thomas, and Judith Walkowitz — I have learned more than I can say; it is a heady and precarious perch, standing on all their shoulders at once.

My thanks are extensive and heartfelt. I am particularly grateful, in London, to the staffs of the British Library, including the old reading rooms in Bloomsbury and the new rooms in Euston, as well as the Newspaper Library in Colindale; the British Architectural Library of the Royal Institute of British Architects; the Westminster Archives and Local History Collection (Westminster Area) and the Central Reference Library of the Westminster City Libraries; the art library of the Victoria and Albert Museum; the Mander and Mitchenson Theatre Collection; the Theatre Museum; the Public Record Office in Chancery Lane and in Kew (now the National Archives); the National Portrait Gallery Heinz Archive and Library; the National Monument Record, Royal Commission on Historical Monuments; the Fawcett Library of London Guildhall University; and, especially, the Greater London Record Office and History Library and London Metropolitan Archives, the major repository of records of the London County Council. In the United States and Canada, thanks are due to the Houghton Library of Harvard University and the Harvard Theatre Collection; the University of Massachusetts Amherst, both the Du Bois Library and Photographic Services; Smith College, and particularly its Josten Library; Forbes Library, Northampton, Massachusetts; the New York Public Library, including the main branch at Fifth Avenue and Forty-second Street and the Billy Rose Collection at Lincoln Center; Yale University Library; the Library of Congress; the Sterling and Francine Clark Art Institute, Williamstown, Massachusetts; and the Theatre Collection of the Metropolitan Toronto Library.

David Mayer and Heidi Holder read earlier versions of the manuscript and gave helpful advice and encouragement, and Helen Day-Mayer and David Mayer provided a photograph of a rare print in their collection and granted kind permission to reproduce it. James Ellis, colleague and friend, allowed me to photograph images of Leicester Square and the Empire promenade in his collection and to reproduce them here. My Canadian colleague Heather McCallum surprised and delighted me with a photograph of a painting depicting the subterranean gentlemen's room at the Empire. David Mayer spotted a clue in a Manchester newspaper that enabled me to track down Marjory Lester, the youngest granddaughter of Laura Ormiston Chant. I am deeply grateful to Mrs. Lester for sharing with me images and stories of her illustrious grandmother and the text of her unpublished biographical account of Mrs. Chant, which corrects and amplifies the public record, and for allowing me to reproduce one of those images and to quote from and cite her biography.

Finally, it is a special pleasure to record my debt to the editor of the University of Iowa Press series in which this book is published, Thomas Postlewait, who read and commented on a seemingly endless succession of drafts; his relentless critical eye and unfailing encouragement have contributed in no small way to whatever shapeliness and coherence this work may be said to possess.

There are, no doubt, others who have aided or speeded the completion of this study but whom I have omitted to name; I thank them in absentia and apologize for my imperfect memory. Notwithstanding the assistance I have had from all those, named and otherwise, who had a part in the preparation of this book, all of its shortcomings and errors of fact, omission, and judgment remain entirely my own responsibility.

## Prologue

### A VISIT TO THE CAFE DU GLOBE

One evening in the summer of 1859, a seasoned journalist headed toward Leicester Square to cover the tableaux vivants currently on view at the notorious Cafe du Globe. On assignment from a new weekly journal of town life bearing the ingenuous title *Peeping Tom*, the reporter was planning a piece that would escort a select group of would-be "swells" on a vicarious expedition into the great, mirrored expanse of the cafe. Once there, he would describe the special entertainment available under the Nordic-romantic sobriquet of "Walhalla," revealing its risqué character for the delectation of present and future men-about-town (fig. 1). Evidently familiar with the varied amenities of the square, the journalist brought to his task an intimate knowledge of this licentious, Frenchified territory and its checkered history, together with an eagerness, qualified by no little cynicism, for navigating its disreputable byways. What he did not yet quite know about himself was his readiness to invoke moral judgments on the transgressive character of whatever might meet his eye.

If his experience had stretched back as little as ten or fifteen years from 1859, the *Peeping Tom* journalist would have been well aware of the surge of popularity in tableaux and poses in the London of the late 1840s — "tableau mania," the *Athenaeum* called it, in 1849[1] — and their widespread emergence in the less respectable houses of entertainment and libation in the vicinity of Leicester Square and the Strand, and perhaps most notoriously in "Lord Chief Baron" Renton Nicholson's Coal Hole. Nicholson claimed he had himself introduced the *poses plastiques* entertainments at the Garrick Head tavern in 1846, where some singers billed as "Female American Serenaders" posed while Nicholson gave an "illustrated lecture" on poetry and song.[2] A bill for Nicholson's "Judge and Jury Society" at the Coal Hole Tavern, Fountain Court, in the Strand, offering "Poses Plastiques Every Evening, at Half-Past Seven, and After the Theatres,"[3] indicated that Nicholson was adding poses to his usual "Mimic Court of Law"

# WALHALLA.

*Late Miss Linwoods, Gallery, Leicester Square.*

## MADAME WARTON'S
### Unequalled
# TABLEAUX VIVANS

**Open every Morning at Half-past Two, and every Evening at Eight.**

## MADAME WARTON
**Will have the honour of appearing in her original personation of**

# VENUS
## RISING from the SEA,
# SAPPHO,
# Innocence, &c.

**With her talented Troupe of Male and Female Artistes.**

*Stalls, 3s. Reserved Seats, 2s. Promenade, 1s.*

J..., Printer, &c. 31, Ward Street, Lambeth.

1. *"Walhalla. Late Miss Linwoods, Gallery, Leicester Square."*
*Undated playbill, ca. 1847. Author's collection.*

*2. "The Coal Hole, Strand." Photograph of woodcut, ca. 1854.*
*Harvard Theatre Collection, Houghton Library.*

entertainments — mock trials whose subjects were often related to seduction or "crim. con." (that is, "criminal connection," or adultery) — proceedings in which men dressed as women were cross-examined, producing much "*double entente*" and immoral language.[4] A French critic scoffed at the pretentiousness of a Coal Hole tableau representing the judgment of Paris, whose personages, three large women and a black-bearded fourth, "who it was difficult to say was male or female," turned slowly on a revolving stage, "mute and fixed in the fitful glimmer of bluish-purple light."[5] A contemporary woodcut, datable as 1854 (fig. 2), captures the seedy ambiance of Nicholson's establishment and anticipates the comparable amenities and aura of the more elegant Cafe du Globe. In a mirrored room men in tall hats, some standing, some seated at tables with drinks and cigars, pretend indifference to a couple posed on a raised stage beyond an archway. The two figures are an ostensibly mostly nude woman, with a skirt wrapped loosely around her hips below the waist, exposing her navel, who half embraces another, winged woman whose only clothing is a sash wrapped around one leg and hip, terminating between the legs; perhaps they represent Cupid and Psyche. The same tawdry atmosphere is captured in a bill for Nicholson's Cider Cellars, in Maiden Lane, Covent Garden, to which Nicholson had repaired in January 1858, featuring "Poses Plastiques" and "Tableaux Vivans," along with a new "Judge and Jury Society" case, "The Great Social Evil" — the by now universal euphemism for the chronic problem of prostitution in modern society. The top of the bill is embellished with a drawing of a woman posing with hands clasped behind her head, unclothed except for a V-shaped loincloth.[6]

The *Peeping Tom* reporter would almost surely have known of such attractions, alluded to in all their midcentury shabbiness in plate 3 of George Cruikshank's *The Drunkard's Children*, a pictorial moral narrative in the Hogarthian genre depicting the sad downfall of the son and daughter of a drunkard whose demise had been immortalized in Cruikshank's earlier series *The Bottle*. The plate depicts a tawdry dancing room with liquor sold at a counter; on the walls and against the counter are placards advertising attractions, including "Les Poses Plastiques Every Evening before Le Bal." In his section on prostitution in Henry Mayhew's exhaustive investigation of Victorian lower-class society, *London Labour and the London Poor*, Bracebridge Hemyng explained that the notorious Argyll Rooms in Great Windmill Street, Piccadilly, had once been a small public house called the Hall of Rome, "where *tableaux vivants* and *poses plastiques* found a home and an audience."[7] An advertisement from the period for a tableau, "The Birthday of Bacchus," at the Hall illustrates what had become, by the 1850s, the prevailing tone of exhibitions of this kind (fig. 3). What was drawing the *Peeping Tom* journalist to the Cafe du Globe was the generally risqué reputation of the genre, but his interest was evidently piqued by the upscale ambiance, greater size, and more exclusive clientele of the cafe.

Alighting from an omnibus in the Strand, south of the square and near the Thames, or from a more northerly point in Oxford Street, or perhaps from a more westerly destination in Regent Street or Piccadilly, in walking into Leicester Square the *Peeping Tom*'s correspondent was setting foot in an internationally known pleasure ground, situated advantageously in the middle of London's West End, a place whose denizens and visitors, and whose rewards and risks, he would have known exceedingly well. By day the square exhibited a fragile patina of respectability, and a businesslike aura prevailed; shop fronts beckoned, goods carts mingled with two-wheelers, and tourist attractions like Wyld's Globe did a brisk trade (fig. 4).

3. *"The Birthday of Bacchus." Advertisement for the Hall of Rome, Great Windmill Street, ca. 1850. Collection of Helen Day-Mayer and David Mayer.*

But as the sun went down the square began to assert its essentially nocturnal character (frontispiece). A considerable range of pleasure seekers, some not even local to London, others visiting from the provinces or returning from the outposts of the British Empire, were drawn nightly to the sights, sounds, and smells of this district ringed and dotted by theatres, music halls, variety houses, commercial shops, high-priced eating and drinking places (some populated partly by demurely gloved and respectably veiled demimondaines), murky, gas-lit lounges guarded by expressionless, bowler-hatted toffs, public houses, like the Crown in Charing Cross Road, ablaze with light and crammed with a predictable mix of ungenteel and bohemian patrons, and smoke-filled gambling dens ranged side by side with bland-fronted houses of assignation. These establishments were themselves complemented by the posh, pretentious, or tawdry resorts, in or near the square, of the well-heeled, the ambitious, and the naïve, where drink flowed freely, after-closing-time life pulsed unregulated, and willing or desperate women were easy for men so inclined to find, some of them persuadable to dancing naked on a table. Here, a respectable

4. *Empire Theatre, looking west from the top of Leicester Square.*
*Colored engraving, signed "C. J. Lauder R.S.W.," 1897.*
*Corporation of London, London Metropolitan Archives.*

but reckless professional man had once been seduced, beaten and robbed, and arrested, and in a fit of shame over the loss of his reputation had committed suicide. An already burgeoning mass of resident humanity was further swollen by the influx of visitors from more respectable or less promising environs, some having come only to gape at the throngs of prostitutes on the pavement to the west of the square in Regent Street and the Haymarket — cheek by jowl with top-hatted playgoers in evening dress and their much bejeweled ladies or paramours. Others with less well-defined pleasures in mind came with practiced anonymous faces, ignoring grim-visaged clergymen bellowing at sinners above the din, and reluctantly rubbing shoulders with ragged transients and occupants of the poverty-stricken slums of Seven Dials, just to the east and north, where raw-voiced street vendors vied for custom and where pornographers on the move catered to a knowing trade. Here, in the rapidly gentrifying Regent Street, not far to the west, would appear, in 1865, the greatest of all magnets for royals, celebrities, and celebrity gazers, the Café Royal. About that same time, a cavernous house for grand ballet and spectacular entertainment called the Alhambra (among other successive aggrandizing names) would appear on the east side of the square, to be followed two decades later by an even grander though smaller competitor on the north side called the Empire Theatre of Varieties. Beginning in 1893, the district would become symbolically dominated by a statue intended to represent the angel of Christian charity but that ended up standing for Eros, the god of love, bow in hand and arrow at the ready.[8] Presiding over the junction of Piccadilly and Shaftesbury Avenue, it looked out as if by inspiration over the entire pleasure-loving precinct at whose center stood the fabled, disreputable Xanadu of Leicester Square itself.

Exactly in the center of the north side of the square lay the pleasure dome that was the *Peeping Tom* reporter's destination on this promising summer evening. The Cafe du Globe had probably taken its name from the structure that now dominated the entire place from its lofty central position: a great globe, some sixty feet in diameter, erected in 1851 in the round roof of a large, imposing building in the leafy, symmetrical garden of Leicester Square by James Wyld, geographer to the queen, and maintained there over the next decade.[9] The cafe, licensed by the Middlesex justices in 1858, just a year before the *Peeping Tom*'s emissary paid it a visit, was functioning somewhat eccentrically as a kind of combination French *café chantant* and English music hall.[10] The current draw was the statuesque Madame Warton, or Wharton, who, it was said, had begun professional life posing for artists in life classes at the Royal Academy and who had once ridden ostensibly unclothed at the Coventry fair as a latter-day Lady Godiva, attracting many more than a single pair of Peeping Tom eyes.[11] A sometime model for that celebrated painter of nudes, the idealistic mental voluptuary William Etty, Warton was infamous from London to York for her impersonations, clothed in pink fleshings, of pseudoclassical *poses plastiques*.[12] A playbill from the period touted "Madame Warton's Unequalled Tableaux Vivans" and featured her presentation "Venus Rising from the Sea" (see fig. 1). In a room of Savile House (now the site of the Cafe du Globe), variously called Walhalla or the London Eldorado (the "Eldorado Music Hall of evil fame," as the memoirist H. G. Hibbert remembered it), Madame Warton and her attractive troupe of women dressed in fleshings had been regularly found, over a period of years, presenting tableaux and poses.[13] A foretaste of the ballets eventually to be mounted in a theatre on this site occurs in Madame Warton's "grand new tableau of Giselle & the Night Dancers."[14] Within the range of entrance fees, the one-shilling admission soon became identified as the price for the "Promenade," encouraging the patronage of the casual visitor. Evidently some effort was being expended to distinguish such upscale attractions from presentations like those described in *The Swell's Night Guide* of nude or half-clothed living waxworks on offer in Windmill Street, Piccadilly.[15] As persistent playbill and newspaper publicity indicated, half-promised risqué presentations were being carefully shrouded by orotund claims to the contrary, even as the representation of decorous classical subjects included such signal opportunities for the display of ostensible female flesh as Guido Reni's *Venus Attired by the Graces*, Rubens's *Judgment of Paris*, Canova's *Nymph*, and Raphael's *Bacchanalian Triumph*.[16] In 1848 Walhalla had been redecorated and opened as the Salle Valentino, and in 1852, in a revamping strikingly prescient of the venue built in the 1880s on its site, it became the Théâtre des Variétés or Leicester Music Hall.[17] Overall, the tone of the advertising and the changes of name reflected a nervous striving for respectability, as if some unacknowledged debility of the form required persistent denial. In the summer of 1859, as the *Peeping Tom* reporter had discovered to his evident interest, Madame Warton and her troupe were presently enhancing the cafe's questionable reputation, enticing writers for racy magazines and hundreds of other pleasure seekers, amateur or otherwise, to partake of its lurid ambiance and glimpse its recherché sights.

Eager to feed his readers' presumed curiosity, the *Peeping Tom* reviewer condescends to share his experience by providing a handy "swell's guide" for gentlemen young and old who don't yet know their way around town, especially that heterogeneous region of foreign and native raciness, Leicester Square. No other district in London, in the writer's opinion, boasts "an equal amount of aspiring fallen humanity"; here the French influence, from "internal filth" to "outward show," is everywhere on view.[18] The same freewheeling Gallic flavor characterizes the cafe itself, the reviewer promises. He sardonically ticks off the attractions comprising its motley history: a casino, a troupe of "Poses," and a variety of other inducements, including marionettes, clairvoyant ladies, wax figures, boxing tournaments, incubating machines, and dramatic readings. Going downhill at a rapid rate, as an anonymous *café chantant* it "sang itself to death." Now it is exclusively the Cafe du Globe, he continues, leading his reader up the stone and iron steps and noting that admission is free except for a modest charge of sixpence to cover "creature comfort." The present attraction at the cafe, he explains, is once again Madame Warton's troupe, whom the manager, fortunate man, has persuaded to present "a series of Tableaux Vivants, of historical and mythological subjects." (George Augustus Sala would later describe them, less ideally, as "some clumsy caricatures of good pictures and good statues, enacted on a turn-table by brazen men and women, called *Poses Plastiques.*")[19]

On entering the cafe's "magnificent salon" the first-time visitor is immediately struck by its air of "elegance and chasteness, comfort and convenience" (fig. 5). Dominating the room from all sides are "immense, gorgeous plate glass mirrors," reflecting multiple receding images, while "massive glass-drop chandeliers" flood the salon with light. Upholstered seats ring the walls; before them, marble tables, with additional rows of tables set end to end throughout, surrounded by chairs sufficient for fully a thousand loungers. Once his eyes adjust to the oppressive glare, the would-be swell can make out groups of men, and women and men, smoking and drinking.

Meanwhile, on a small stage at the rear, three women in togalike costumes have taken up what are meant to be classical poses, though somehow they miss their mark. Presumably they represent the Three Graces, a familiar classical trope, but the conjunction of women draped in classical

5. *"Café du Globe, Leicester Square."* Peeping Tom, *27 June 1859, 1.*
*By permission of the British Library.*

garments and disengaged onlookers taking their visual fill at their ease begins to produce, in the journalist's mind, a troublesome effect. As if he had never scrutinized it before, the reviewer begins to discern in this ungainly vista something beyond what a mythological subject might denote. The audience of the cafe is made up, he explains, largely of "any amount of ancient swells," whose bold gaze indicates that they are satiated with ordinary reality ("used up," as the current phrase would have it) and have come to feast their eyes on something else. Not so original and classical as cafe publicity pretended, the attitudes these women take up, posed in garments that reveal much more of their bodies than would any respectable costume for street or parlor, have been arranged, and their subjects selected, he insists, with every intention of avoiding "lewd ideas." And yet, he concludes, despite himself, that these women have thrown aside "that greatest jewel in the female casquet — modesty" and hidden "the genuine blush of nature beneath the cyprian's rouge." And it would seem to be their own fault for having done so.

The journalist's heated tone betrays his emergent discomfort over what he sees: a crowd of impotent sexagenerians gazing longingly at a group of young women who do not allow themselves to know, or are unable to acknowledge, that they serve as the objects of that gaze and, in so doing, abandon modesty for ill repute. The expert guide and his apprentice swells appear to stand transfixed in a moralized hall of mirrors, where the gazer and the gazed upon are replicated ad infinitum. Almost despite himself, the *Peeping Tom* aesthete-turned-moralist has surmised what feels like a home truth, sensed all the more powerfully for its multiple reflection: through the professional act itself of posing, of self-display, for the entertainment of uninvolved onlookers, a woman sacrifices her innocence and virtue. Notwithstanding the assumed distance of the hired poser, participation in the show effectively creates a knowingness, a calculated attractiveness on her part, captured metonymically, in the *Peeping Tom*'s pretentious, pseudopoetical language, in the verbal figure of "the cyprian's rouge" — the prostitute's paint. The result is a loss of purity that no amount of classical drapery can obscure.

An almost elegiac quality has superimposed itself on the breezy, supercilious tone of the *Peeping Tom* writer's account. A seemingly uncomplicated erotic journey to a prime pleasure ground has unexpectedly turned into an excursion into a morally ambiguous arena, resonating with disturbing implications that remain to trouble the mind.

## A VISIT TO THE EMPIRE THEATRE OF VARIETIES

Were we to take a longer perspective on the attractions offered by Leicester Square at midcentury from a vantage point near the century's end, we would find ourselves arrested by a richly suggestive coincidence. In this longer view, the tableaux vivants described in the *Peeping Tom*'s account of 1859 can be seen to anticipate the appearance some thirty-five years later, in the summer of 1894 and in a very different theatrical world, of a much larger-scale series of tableaux and spectacles, performed in an even more luxurious, mirrored, and creature-comforted theatre in the square, the magnificent Empire Theatre of Varieties, built just ten years before on the site of the now vanished Cafe du Globe. In that elongated perspective, the *Peeping Tom* journalist's sudden access of troubled conscience wryly anticipates the formulation, in that same summer of 1894, of a more unambivalent, conscientious, and principled moral judgment by another visitor, this one a woman of uncompromising standards and formidable articulateness, a woman moreover possessed of an abiding impatience with the chronic ills of the world and (as she viewed it) the deeply compromised situation of women in it. Her visit — in fact, her series of no fewer than five visits over several weeks — to the gilded venue that had become the successor of the Cafe du Globe would lead her into a notorious theatrical inner sanctum, from which she could see on the stage below what were, in her view, the indecent, provocative costumes and morally objectionable performances of ballet dancers; at the same time, from that vantage point, she would find herself in what was to her the highly offensive presence of unaccompanied, sumptuously dressed, elaborately made-up high-class prostitutes. This double-edged experience, multiplied five times over in succeeding weeks, would prove to have a far greater, much more resounding effect than that produced by the *Peeping Tom* reporter's obscure, fugitive account. For it would soon set in motion a highly publicized onslaught against the successor of the Cafe du Globe by a determined cohort of social purity activists, inspired and organized by the equally determined latter-day visitor to the Empire. Those activists would themselves find the spectacles now on view there, along with the character of the audience observing them from the perspective of the second-tier promenade, reprehensible enough to justify a concerted attempt to shut the whole enterprise down.

The story of the controversy that arose, as a result of those visits, over the shows and the patrons, and the policies and the practices, of the Empire Theatre has attracted much subsequent attention; but it has never before been told in all its fascinating and broadly signifying detail.[20] Nor has that controversy been examined, despite the remarkable place it holds in the history of modern culture, for what it has to reveal with regard to sexual and social relations between women and men and between men and men, or for the light it sheds on the ethical and moral values disputed over by persons of opposing views on the place of art and entertainment in modern society. It has also not been scrutinized for the way it helps to flesh out the pervasive effect of British imperialism on contemporary consciousness and on patterns of life and behavior in the later years of Victoria's reign. And, finally, it has not been linked with one of the most interesting phenomena in the history of the modern theatre, the simultaneous emergence in the late nineteenth century of a more sophisticated, varied, and moneyed audience and of the efforts of an insistent municipal government to control and regulate that audience's social and cultural character and even its moral behavior.

Taking here the form of an extended visit of our own to the Empire Theatre of Varieties, Leicester Square, the story begins in that summer of

1894 and extends for something over a year into the future, to a point, in October 1895, where the eventual outcome of the controversy became clear for all to see. To be sure, the roots of the controversy might be observed to go back well over a century, to restrictions imposed and precedents set by early eighteenth-century theatrical legislation; but that is a history well known in scholarly circles and not a formative influence on the controversy over the Empire license.[21] It will suit our purposes best to begin with the visits to the Empire of that singularly determined woman reformer and the emergent, ultimately stunning strategy adopted by a small but potent phalanx of social activists who also visited the Empire, saw for themselves what was there, and agreed with the earlier visitor that something had to be done. The strategy they conceived was the simple but effective one of attacking the legal basis on which the Empire, like all other theatres in London, was permitted to open its doors and carry on business: namely, by means of a license secured from and renewed annually by the London County Council, a governmental body created in 1888 by the Local Government Act, and more specifically through the intermediary of the council's licensing body, the Theatres and Music Halls Committee, established in 1889. The mandate given the Theatres and Music Halls Committee by the parent council was to oversee and regulate the activities of London theatres and music halls and to vet the dozens of applications arriving annually in the late summer and make recommendations to the council, the actual licensing authority. The very existence of the county council was one very large reason why the theatre world had changed so greatly since the days of Peeping Tom adventurers' forays into the dark urban jungle of venues in Leicester Square and the vicinity, routinely licensed by willing or preoccupied magistrates.

By the 1890s the theatrical landscape was without doubt a much altered one. The act that brought the county council into being had effectively put all London theatres and music halls on notice that a higher, more fastidious tone was going to be the thing. From the day of its empowerment the council had embraced an organized strategy of municipalization, pursued on behalf of the people of London, and one of its foremost goals was to purify and tone down music-hall performance. Under the act the council had assumed powers previously held by the justices of London and Westminster (and then, in part, by the Metropolitan Board of Works), controlling the administrative county of London and keeping a vigilant eye on all forms of entertainment except actual stage plays (which remained under the jurisdiction of the Lord Chamberlain and his Examiner of Plays). Over the six years since the council had come into being, and over the five since the Theatres Committee had swung into action, a much different, more tense and anxious atmosphere had begun to prevail, even as the predilections of London audiences east and west remained not only varied but robust and, to a significant extent, ungovernable. By the early 1890s, the beginnings of large-scale conflict were already in evidence. The visit to the Empire of that single determined investigator was catalyst enough for the tremendous uproar that would presently ensue.

### TWO PRINCIPAL ANTAGONISTS

From the very beginning of the developing controversy over the relicensing of the Empire Theatre, two figures whose stories are central to the conflict emerged in high profile: George Edwardes, theatrical entrepreneur par excellence and manager and part proprietor of the Empire and other thriving theatrical enterprises in the vicinity of Leicester Square and the Strand; and Laura Ormiston Chant, a magnetic platform orator, prominent member of the National Vigilance Association, and fearless defender of social purity — the woman whose series of visits to the Empire during the summer of 1894 were to set the fires of righteous indignation flaming in various reformist sectors throughout the land. Laura Chant and George Edwardes were, to all appearances, unlikely antagonists, largely because up until this moment they had inhabited such separate and mutually exclusive spheres. Yet, notwithstanding these discrete worlds — or, perhaps, because they were so discrete — these two personages, once they were perceived to be ranged in opposition against one another, came to define, embody, and symbolize not only the emergent issues that grounded the conflict, but also the feelings, beliefs, and values of uncounted additional persons who found themselves passionately engaged and deeply affected by it and its likely or hoped-for outcome. As tempers flared and the situation deteriorated, the antagonists took on the guise, willy-nilly, of starkly opposed characters in an intense drama neither tragic nor comic but perhaps more akin to melodrama, with its generic strife between the putatively good and allegedly evil and its more-or-less constant accompaniment by a large, cacophanous orchestra of close, noisy observers. At times the conflict might have been seen to veer perilously close to burlesque, were it not for the gravity of the issues it generated and the great deal of money at stake. Nor could anyone, in the late summer of 1894, when the controversy began to boil, have predicted with any confidence that the forces, personal, political, and ultimately social and cultural, that would marshall themselves in support, variously, of Edwardes or Mrs. Chant would reach near-epic proportions, creating a pitched battle involving numerous warriors and legions of partisan onlookers, and in the process leaving virtually no one neutral.

From the very beginning, in fact, the conflict took on a rigidly uncompromising character, despite the seeming unreadiness or disinclination of the ostensible victims (the genial Edwardes and his colleagues and sympathizers) to do battle. Spurred on by the inspiring leadership of Mrs. Chant, the small cohort of reformers who would appear one October morning at a meeting of the Theatres and Music Halls Committee was bent on denying the Empire the renewal of its license — or, in any event, determined to change in radical ways the entertainment available there and even the character of the audiences that witnessed it. For their part, Edwardes and his Empire codirectors seemed largely untroubled, from the time they got wind of it, by the threat the reformers were posing. It was mostly business as usual. On 28 July 1894, in anticipation of the annual October licensing meetings of the Theatres Committee, Edwardes had once again made what he might well have believed was an entirely routine application for the renewal of the license of what was now London's premier theatre of varieties. And he and his confreres might have been pardoned for not perceiving anything particularly ominous when, one morning in late September, Edwardes received a courtesy copy of one of a set of identical letters sent on the twenty-second of the month by a group of citizens, all of them members of the National Vigilance Association (though writing as individuals), to the chair, Richard Roberts, of the Theatres and Music Halls Committee, identifying themselves as Daniel Shilton Collin, Miss H. Hood, Mr. T. Fish, Mrs. E. Bailhache, Mr. F. R. Brook, and Mrs. Laura Ormiston Chant. In their letters they declared their intention of attending the 10 October meeting of the committee for the purpose of opposing the relicensing of the Empire Theatre of Varieties, claiming that "the place at night is the habitual resort of prostitutes in pursuit of their traffic, and that portions of the entertainment are most objectionable, obnoxious, and against the best interests and moral well being of the community at large."[22]

Yet, had Edwardes paused over the wording of the complaint, he might have felt a twinge of anxiety over the fact that the combination of charges of indecency both on the stage and in the auditorium constituted a fresh approach to familiar charges of bad morals and could perhaps flag this particular threat as somewhat more serious than usual. In any case, faced with identically worded complaints signaling a well-coordinated joint effort, Edwardes seems to have found it prudent to alert his solicitor, C. F. Gill, and Gill's colleague Arnold Statham, and to plan to take them along to the Theatres Committee hearings the next month. It may be fairly asserted that, at this early point, Edwardes and his advisors had little if any idea of what the Empire directorate was in for in the coming weeks and months.

Over the intervening two and a half weeks, Edwardes appeared to be content to go on managing what was rapidly becoming one of the most formidable theatrical empires of its time. After all, complaints about indecent performances lodged by people clearly unsympathetic were no novelty to proprietors of music halls, and objections to prostitutes in the theatre were centuries old, as was their presence itself. What was more, there was much that was ordinary, straightforward, and time-consuming about the management of multiple theatrical enterprises — but also much that drew from Edwardes the most ingenious, mark-making moves to consolidate, develop, enhance, and realize profits. The making of musical comedy was his special gift, and the making of large amounts of money from it, and from other new initiatives in ballet and variety theatre, comprised a talent amounting to genius.

The controlling presence of the Empire enterprise, "ruler of the front of the house," and one of the best examples in late Victorian life of the right man in the right place at the right time, Edwardes had fingers in a dozen pies.[23] Born George Edwards in Clee, near Cleethorpes, Lincolnshire, on 14 October 1852[24] of Roman Catholic parents (the father Irish, the mother English), the youngest of seven children, he was swiftly becoming one of the most important and original entrepreneurs of the late Victorian theatre and the foremost deviser and popularizer of musical comedy in the period.[25] Having failed the entrance examination for the army, the young Edwards was asked by a cousin to supervise a third-rate touring company of *The Lady of Lyons*; the opportunity for stage management changed his life, and he adopted a theatrical career then and there. Engaged by Richard D'Oyly Carte and rising to acting manager (a post with wide-ranging managerial duties) of the Opera Comique in 1875, he then moved on to the Savoy Theatre, new in 1881, under Carte, where he also became acting manager.[26]

Having added a second "e" to his name — an ambitious bid for distinction to accord with his rising state[27] — and, in due course, having married a former actress, Edwardes got on well enough to purchase, in 1885, a half-interest in the Gaiety Theatre, a prominent landmark in the Strand, from the ailing John Hollingshead, on whose retirement the next year Edwardes bought him out and became sole manager, developing, said a longtime associate, a formidable "capacity for understanding exactly what the public wanted."[28] What it now wanted, Edwardes was discovering, was not so much burlesque, a famous commodity at the Gaiety but a waning form, as something that began to be called musical comedy, less a definable genre at first than a mélange of lively, sprightly things musical, romantic, and comic, and featuring as always a chorus of beautiful, exquisitely costumed dancing girls in frothy skirts and petticoats who showed their ankles or kicked and showed their legs (but only once or twice) — an appealing package tied up in the sparkling ribbon of an easy-to-follow narrative, "always light, bright, and enjoyable."[29] His second effort in this direction, *Dorothy*, which opened at the Gaiety in September 1886 (and after whose title character his first-born child was named), would achieve a phenomenal run of 931 performances.[30] From an early point Edwardes had begun developing the innovative idea of the long run, keeping his pieces up for six months at a time, or more, and changing to give patrons something new at Christmas. The combination of brilliant talent, clear-sightedness, and good luck produced a series of successes, punctuated by only occasional failures; such were the vagaries and risks of theatrical entrepreneurship.

By 1886 Edwardes had prospered well enough to buy a fashionable house for his family at 6 Park Square, Regent's Park, from which he would be driven daily in his own brougham to one of his theatres or to his office in Wellington Street. Afternoons were spent at the racetrack whenever he could spare the time; weekends, at his country house, Winkfield Lodge, or at Ogbourne Maisey, where his brother Major John Edwards ran a racing stable and Edwardes had bought a manor house and three thousand acres.[31] Friends and clients lunched with him at Romano's or the Savoy Grill, where his own table awaited them.[32] By 1893 he had fallen in love and was carrying on an affair with a young actress, Miriam Clements, to whom he had given a minor role in *The Geisha Girl* and whom he had installed in a house in St. John's Wood.[33] In this same year Edwardes built a theatre named after his client, the American producer Augustin Daly, in

Cranbourne Street, Leicester Square, just steps away from the Empire, leasing it to Daly at a substantial profit but soon using it himself as a second theatre, after the Gaiety, to produce romantic operetta variants to musical comedy.[34]

Signs of success were already conspicuous when, in 1887, Edwardes headed up a syndicate that bought the Empire Theatre from Daniel de Nicols, the hugely successful proprietor of the Café Royal. Both de Nicols himself and Edwardes became shareholders in the venture, with de Nicols, who held the freehold and the buildings, retaining a controlling interest.[35] At the Empire, the Gaiety, and elsewhere Edwardes went on to mine new wealth in the rich veins of musical theatre, ballet divertissement, and even legitimate theatre, along with the chanteuses, lions comiques, gymnasts, and other staples of traditional music hall entertainment, all the while developing a singular reputation for "consummate *sang froid*."[36] Photographs and sketches of him from the time, along with caricatures generated by the licensing controversy, portray a solid, slightly overweight, well-dressed presence; consistent in showing a round-faced man with hair closely cropped in the fashion of the Nineties, clean-shaven except for a prominent moustache, they nevertheless seem undecided as to whether his eyes are simply farseeing or betray a slight anxiety over what meets his gaze (figs. 6, 7, 8). Like Hollingshead, his former colleague at the Gaiety, Edwardes had a high-pitched voice that struck "a plaintive note."[37] Though something of a hypochondriac, he was not a man to be taken lightly.[38] "His slow, drawling talk (the delight of imitators) and apparently careless manner concealed," said an obituary writer in 1915, "a very powerful will and a very shrewd mind."[39] Edwardes's professional contemporaries were not shy in acknowledging his preeminence. The musical comedy singer and actress Ada Reeve, who played the title role in Edwardes's big Gaiety hit *The Shop-Girl* in November 1894, described him on their first meeting as "tall, well-built and a trifle fat; his hair was fair, crisp and curly, his moustache was lavish, and he had the most vivid blue eyes."[40] James Jupp, for decades the stage-door keeper at the Gaiety, describing his legendary diplomacy and tact, characterized him as "essentially a sporting man."[41] A true man-about-town, as the French chanteuse Yvette Guilbert recalled, he "lived like a lord, elegant in speech and in manners."[42] Later in Edwardes's career a popular magazine reminded its readers, who needed no reminding, that Edwardes in evening dress made "the

6. *"George Edwardes, Manager of the Gaiety and Daly's Theatre."*
Prominent Men of London. *1907–9, 75.*
*National Portrait Gallery, Heinz Archive and Library.*

most gorgeous presentment of any man in London." He was, said the
admiring writer, "a very fine fellow indeed."[43]

The insider H. G. Hibbert's more discriminating account emphasized
Edwardes's "engaging manner," his "charming ingenuousness," and
"the deadly skill in persuasion" typical of his Irish countrymen. While

7. *George Edwardes. In* Dramatic Opinions and Essays with an Apology by Bernard Shaw. *Vol. 1. London: Archibald Constable, 1907. Extra-illustrated; opp. 290. Folger Shakespeare Library.*

*8. George Edwardes.* The Green Room Book, or Who's Who on the Stage.
*Ed. Bampton Hunt. London: T. Sealey Clark, 1906. 113. PP2496 hc.*
*By permission of the British Library.*

studiously averse to arguments, there was no keener man of business. Wildly extravagant, he was also ridiculously generous with both salaries and presents to actresses — a way of averting argument and neutralizing disturbance, Hibbert thought. And yet he drove hard bargains; reclining on a settee near midnight, after a hard day at the racetrack, a pipe in his mouth, he was "at his deadliest."[44] An inveterate gambler, Edwardes took great delight in horses, stocks, and the all-night card table, and in his professional life the sheer scale on which he operated resulted in setting new thresholds for profit, and for risk.[45] "His whole life, in fact, was a gamble," Reeve concluded, identifying in Edwardes a crucial amalgam of qualities: recklessness, generosity, sociability, and "a fine and convincing self-assurance."[46] No man in London, said the theatre professional's weekly vade mecum, the *Era* (trade paper of the licensed victuallers), knew the inner workings and outer life of the theatre or the mind of the paying public better than he.[47] Among the accolades showered on Edwardes on his twenty-fifth anniversary in management in 1911 was the judgment that he deserved "to rank with the great captains of industry."[48] A later, more dispassionate assessment by the scholar of popular entertainment Peter Bailey portrays Edwardes as by turns a "Svengali, martinet, snooper and sugar daddy," and "a more complex and darker figure than standard accounts allow."[49]

Aside from the sheer boldness and confident nonchalance of Edwardes's profile, what may have contributed to his being singled out as a target by reformist elements in London society in 1894 was the degree to which he stood symbolically for the twin evils, as single-minded advocates for social purity viewed them, of drink and prostitution, equally prominent in Victorian society. Given the availability of exorbitantly priced alcohol and comparably expensive women in the five-shilling promenade of the Empire, Edwardes, lounge suited and silk hatted and constantly in view, could easily have been perceived by those antagonistic to his interests as a kind of high-class publican. Seen in this light, he could be said to have imposed and maintained a rigorous but spurious respectability on a generic figure that in lower-class situations embodied "the gamut of social ills," as a later social critic has characterized the pub proprietor, taking money from the customer and bestowing inebriety in return, harboring the prostitute but blithely ignoring the problematic basis of the leisure activity thus afforded in his domain, offering opportunities largely unavailable elsewhere for the mixing of different social classes, and so profiting from the unhealthy nature, as some would have alleged, of the leveling effect thus created.[50] Although it was by no means inevitable that Edwardes and the Empire would cross swords with the various militant exemplars of antivice that partly peopled the Theatres and Music Halls Committee of the London County Council (to say nothing of such exemplars in reformist groups and society at large), the distinctive character and incomparable cachet of the Empire Theatre of Varieties must have rendered it a nearly irresistible target for hostile attention. Finally, Edwardes's affable sense of camraderie, his confident assumption of access to money and the opportunities it could purchase, and, above all, his easy air of ownership, extending even beyond the properties he held and managed, comprised a character different in almost every conceivable way from the profile, unambiguous and unmistakable for its own articulate sense of self-possession, unswayable conviction, and sharp-eyed firmness of purpose, of Edwardes's chief antagonist, Laura Ormiston Chant.

The woman who would repeatedly visit the Empire Theatre of Varieties in the summer of 1894 to judge its manifold excesses for herself and who, shortly after, would begin the formal attack on this theatre was born Laura Ormiston Dibbin, in Woolaston, near Lydney, Gloucestershire, on 9 October 1848. Her mother was Sophia Ormiston; her father, Francis William Dibbin, a civil engineer with a considerable reputation, occupied at the time in the construction of a tubular railway bridge over the River Wye at Chepstow. Laura was the fifth of nine children, and the second daughter. An intelligent, passionate, and rebellious child, as her granddaughter Marjory Lester has feelingly described her, Laura was "a great trial to her parents." "We were very strictly brought up," Mrs. Chant recalled with some bitterness, "and delinquencies were punished in the stupid, brutal way that is now dying out among intelligent people." At length her parents moved back to London, where her father, disapproving of the high-church ritual at the Kensington Parish Church, began taking his family to the Kensington Congregational Chapel. There the Reverend Doctor Stoughton's preaching made a lifelong impression on Laura. Finding her parents' harsh discipline ultimately intolerable, at age fifteen she ran away from home. Sent off to boarding school in Chester as a result, Laura had the good fortune to study art with the chaplain, Charles Kingsley, and to develop her musical talents.[51]

After leaving school, Laura went back again to her family, who by that time had moved to Bruton, Somerset. She obtained a teaching post in

Huddersfield, Yorkshire, but the preparation proved so demanding and the climate so hostile that she became ill and had to return home once more. Impatient at what seemed too aimless and genteel a life, yearning for purposeful activity, and poignantly aware of the great injustice in the world, she took the advice of the well-known nurse Dora of Walsall and in 1868 began to train for a career as a nursing missionary at Nottingham General Hospital. For this decision to embrace what was then considered a low, degrading occupation, Laura's father forbade her ever to return home again — a rejection that would have a deeply formative effect on his headstrong daughter. Having completed her probationary period, and in the meantime having given up the idea of being a missionary, she undertook a nursing career and became Sister Sophia (taking her mother's name) at London Hospital, Whitechapel, the largest hospital in Great Britain. There she remained for two and a half years, met and fell in love with her future husband, the house surgeon, Thomas Chant, M.R.C.S., and made the decision to abandon nursing in favor of the study of medicine — a courageous choice for any woman of the time, but a characteristic one for Laura Dibbin. Meanwhile, unable to continue at the London Hospital once her marriage plans became known (a house rule forbade association of male and female staff), she spent still another trying period of her life as the assistant matron of a lunatic asylum, involving her in work apparently so grim that she never mentioned it afterward. After a year there, she became a governess and companion to a mother and her family of girls. Finally, in 1877, at the age of twenty-nine (much later than usual for a woman in this period), Laura married Thomas Chant. Three daughters and a son were born of the union.[52]

By the time of her marriage Laura had apparently abandoned the prospect of a career in medicine in deference to the wide demand for her services as a public speaker. During the period of her young adulthood, when many women her age had already married and were raising a family, she had begun to pursue an alternative career, acquiring experience as a public speaker by working with philanthropic organizations. Her first public address attempted a topic no less ambitious than women in the nineteenth century, advocating the franchise for women on the same terms as men.[53] She took up advocacy in the areas of women's suffrage, temperance, social purity, and liberal politics, becoming also a lecturer on literary subjects. No matter what cause she championed, she would swiftly become its fearless partisan.

Increasingly, the cause of social purity attracted her attention and claimed her efforts, even though she never entirely abandoned her earlier interests. In the early 1880s she took part in Josephine Butler's work for social justice for women, speaking everywhere, despite the hostility of some audiences, in favor of repeal of the Contagious Diseases Acts.[54] Later she would support the passage in 1886 of the first Children's Act. Following the emergence in 1883 of the Central Vigilance Committee, she contributed to the broadening activities of the purity movement by addressing more than four hundred meetings in a twelve-month period from July 1885.[55] In 1888, as a delegate to the First International Council for Women, she made the first of a series of voyages to the United States and Canada. There she continued lecturing, preaching, and organizing in the cause of combatting what she told a St. John's, Newfoundland, reporter in 1890 were "the two great evils of the day — Intemperance and Impurity."[56] On this visit her itinerary included Montreal, Ottawa, Toronto, Boston, and then Chicago, where among her accomplishments was the establishment of a refuge for erring women.[57] Her prominence and effectiveness while in the United States are implied in her membership in the Women's Club of Chicago and her honorary membership in the New England Women's Club.[58] At a meeting of the International Council of Women in 1888, Mrs. Chant identified herself as a grandniece of Edmund Burke and pleaded in his name "on behalf of oppressed women all over the world" that they should be given the right to vote.[59]

By 1890 Mrs. Chant had a place on the executive committees of the Women's Liberal Federation of England and the National Society for Promoting Woman Suffrage, along with membership on the council of the National Vigilance Society of Great Britain and Ireland. A longtime editor of the National Vigilance Association's official organ, the *Vigilance Record*, Mrs. Chant was also the author of a collection of little sermons, *The Prodigal*, as well as of various pamphlets on temperance, poor law, politics, and purity. Before the dust had settled on her attempts, in concert with her numerous colleagues, to deny the Empire Theatre a renewal license, she would write and publish an impassioned justification of their efforts in pamphlet form, *Why We Attacked the Empire* (1895). Later she would write a novel, *Sellcut's Manager* (1899), in which she would embody an ideal only imperfectly realized in the case of the Empire controversy: in the first chapter a music hall burns down and is subsequently rebuilt and managed on more humanitarian principles. In addition, keeping her musical interests current, she composed many hymns and songs for children, collected in ten volumes under such titles as *Sea-shell Songs, Daisies and Breezes Action Songs,* and *The Wise Owl Action Songs*; perhaps her single most popular composition was "The Golden Boat," in use in schools through the 1940s.[60]

Even as her family grew, Mrs. Chant continued to carry on an extremely active life, including a second tour to America in 1890 and a third, in 1893, to attend the "Great Parliament of Religions" in Chicago. Her London house in Gower Street, an American reporter noted, was "a refuge for the destitute, and a place where broken lives and hearts get mended under the influence of love and care."[61] At her death on 16 February 1923, the *Times* obituary described her as "one of the first women of her time to make a real mark as a public speaker," praising her "sincerity and earnestness" and singling out her bravery in such actions as bringing relief to Armenian refugees in Bulgaria and taking nurses out to the Greek frontier in Crete, for which she received the Red Cross from Queen Victoria.[62]

By the time Mrs. Chant turned forty-six, on 9 October 1894, the day before the Theatres and Music Halls Committee convened to deliberate on the question of the Empire license, she had been married to Thomas Chant for about eighteen years. To judge from a photograph of the couple made in 1889 and handed down in the family for several generations, the marriage was a happy one, though perhaps tried by the strains and conflicts endemic to a public life as extraordinarily active and controversial as Mrs. Chant's (fig. 9). A photograph published in a feminist periodical in November 1894, at the height of the Empire controversy, captures the likeness of a pleasant-faced woman of uncompromising mien, confident but not stern, with clear-sighted eyes balanced behind a nose prominent enough to become, perhaps inevitably, part of the exaggerated graphic vocabulary of a series of sometimes cruel caricatures generated by her attack on the Empire (figs. 10, 38, 39).

While actively engaged in bringing up her four children, Mrs. Chant in marrying a surgeon had attained a social and economic status that had largely freed her from the drudgery and constraints of a domestic routine. Freedom of that kind was crucial to Mrs. Chant's remarkable effectiveness as advocate and reformer, for behind the phenomenal emergence in this period of assertive, determined women, active in the fields of social justice,

*9. Dr. Thomas Chant and Laura Ormiston Chant. Thomas Fall, 1889.*
*Courtesy of Marjory Lester.*

10. *Laura Ormiston Chant. Accompanying Sarah A. Torley, "The Empire Theatre. An
Interview with Mrs Ormiston Chant,"* Woman's Signal, *1 November 1894, 273–74.
Women's Library, London Metropolitan University.*

suffragism, and other causes whose day had dawned, lay a fundamentally
enabling situation regarding family life and domestic relations. Mid-
Victorian prosperity had allowed many women to escape the hard, oppressive lives led by their less fortunate contemporaries and predecessors,
exchanging that existence for the problematic luxury of doing little or

nothing. The transition from ideal wife to perfect lady was not the product of feminism; on the contrary, by and large feminism was itself the product of the emergence of a sizable class of women who possessed the economic wherewithal, the energy, and the leisure (conferred by the presence of servants, nursemaids, and governesses in their households) to rebel against a meaningless life of leisure in favor of a sometimes driven devotion to meritorious social causes.[63] The unprecedented breadth and solidity of the campaign against the Contagious Diseases Acts (1864, amended 1866 and 1869) were the result of the efforts of such middle-class women, many organized under the aegis of Josephine Butler's Ladies National Association for the Repeal of the Contagious Diseases Acts (LNA) — an organization founded in 1869 in response to the exclusion of women from the National Association (NA) formed in the same year with that goal in view. Propaganda published by the LNA invited women to transcend formidable barriers of public opinion to join ranks with their "fallen sisters," implementing a feminist politics of identification to which Mrs. Chant in her time would fully subscribe.[64]

Having risen into this more leisurely class of women, and imbued with the political and moral values of her activist peers, Mrs. Chant was at liberty to pursue her considerable gifts in both social and artistic spheres, and did so. Chief among her varied talents was her flair, amounting to genius, for public speaking. "The announcement of her presence," said the *Vigilance Record*, "is sufficient to ensure a crowded room."[65] A telling early example of Mrs. Chant's effectiveness as a platform orator may be found in a report from the annual meeting on 13 June 1883 of the Social Purity Alliance (founded by Josephine Butler in 1873), at which she gave a forceful speech on the social importance of sexual purity.[66] Her strong feelings on the subject were evidently formed partly by her nursing experience at London Hospital. In her speech she related an anecdote about a "poor outcast" woman who had come into the hospital to die. "In the silence of the night," Mrs. Chant recalled, "as I sat by her, she poured out the story of her by-gone life. There were pages of it so sad that I could scarcely bear to hear them, and one could only ask oneself, 'What must they have been to suffer?'" One night, Mrs. Chant recalled, the woman was "plying her dreadful trade" and accosted a young man whom she found to be quite different from those she customarily encountered. He said to her, "'I am so sorry to see a woman leading this life. I have a sister at home about your age. Cannot you find a better way of earning your living than this? Do go to some good Christian woman and ask her to help you get back into an honest life.'" That was not much to tell, Mrs. Chant remarked to her audience, but it needed to be thought about: "That man's kind words the only bright, pure spot to look back upon at the end of that storm-beaten life."

Later in the same speech she related the story of her rescue of a woman from an attempted seduction. She saw a young man accost and pick up a young woman, evidently a servant, in the Underground. Mrs. Chant followed them, and when they got out she did so too. "I need not tell you," she continued, "the language an indignant English mother would use on such an occasion with an ignorant child's fate trembling in the balance," but "it did its work and sent the scoundrel flying off as fast as his feet would carry him." She accompanied the girl home and persuaded her mistress to forgive her for her lateness. This is what one must do, Mrs. Chant explained, "to be brave in the cause of purity."[67]

Bravery in the cause sometimes moved Mrs. Chant to extraordinary lengths. Before the attack on the Empire she had been active in opposing indecent entertainments and prostitution in the theatres, but had not succeeded very well. Trying one target, then the other, she failed to effect any improvement in conditions. It is significant that, in singling out the Empire Theatre for attention, Mrs. Chant was concentrating on both targets at once, and she came as close to success as at any time in her public career. Throughout that career, as a crusader for social purity Mrs. Chant held to what she believed were clear and consistent principles of reform, based on a deep conviction of the desperate state of the world, shared with the audience of her speech to the Social Purity Alliance. In the theatres and music halls, she explained, "every attraction woman possesses is pressed into the side that tends to evil and sorrow."[68]

These were the experiences that had formed the views, the motives, and the goals of this unlikely, late-blooming provincial woman, leading her ultimately into the joint presence of George Edwardes and his solicitors, her National Vigilance Association colleagues, a crowd of eager, impatient onlookers and journalists, and the Theatres and Music Halls Committee of the London County Council, meeting in their chambers in Spring Gardens, in Charing Cross, on the morning of 10 October 1894 to take up the matter (among many other matters) of relicensing the Empire Theatre of Varieties.

# 1 : Mrs. Chant at the Empire

**THE EVENING OF 30 JULY 1894**

Laura Ormiston Chant was moved to visit the Empire Theatre of Varieties because of the unhappy experience there of two American male friends. As she would later explain to the members of the Theatres and Music Halls Committee, earlier in the year her friends had gone to the famous theatre of varieties in Leicester Square with the object, innocent enough, of hearing coster songs sung by Albert Chevalier, a famous exemplar of the genre. They appeared to have missed Chevalier, but what they found at the Empire was shocking in the extreme; they complained of "the character & the want of clothing in the ballet" and of being "continually accosted at night & solicited by women."[1] Having been alerted by her friends to what they considered indecent exposure on the stage and scandalous behavior, including solicitation, in the second-tier promenade, Mrs. Chant decided to investigate, but put off her visit until July, when the "living pictures," the Empire's more homely term for tableaux vivants, were causing a great stir. She may have suspected that the Empire's living pictures would be as offensive as those she had heard of at the Palace Theatre of Varieties, a short walk to the north from Leicester Square, where simulated nudity was nightly on view; her colleague W. A. Coote, the secretary of the National Vigilance Association, had seen and complained about a whole series of what he thought flagrantly unacceptable presentations involving apparently scantily clothed or fully unclothed women presented in alluring poses. Mrs. Chant's first experience at the Empire would confirm her American friends' opinions and would even move her to plan a return visit, and then another, as she and her colleagues in the NVA began to consider how they might respond to a situation they viewed as outrageous and intolerable.

No record appears to have survived of their collective intentions, but the arrival in late September of a unison chorus of letters of intent from six members of the NVA at the hearing rooms of the Theatres and Music

Halls Committee speaks well enough for itself. In fact, Mrs. Chant would end up visiting the Empire promenade no fewer than five times in the weeks leading up to the October meetings of the Theatres Committee. On each visit she was accompanied by a sister or one of her NVA colleagues. On the first three visits she wore plain dress but found that this attracted undue notice and singled her out as different. "You had better mind how you behave to-night," she remembered overhearing an attendant cautioning an outspoken woman in the promenade, "as there are strangers round." From then on she wore her favorite party dress — "such a pretty dress," she later told a reporter for the *Vigilance Record*, "the same dress I spoke in at the Women's Suffrage Festival at Boston — black lace over coloured silk, with an opera jacket and a pretty little bonnet to match." The presence of the bonnet would still have proclaimed her a stranger — "after all," Mrs. Chant admitted, "there was not much evening dress about it" — nor would her constant note taking have gone unnoticed.[2] Still, there was a limit to Mrs. Chant's ability, or inclination, to blend in with her surroundings, and she had more important things to accomplish than to try to remain invisible. Although she "did not wish to attract unnecessary notice," she "was there to take notes & make my observations," she later would explain to the members of the Theatres Committee. The very fact that she and her companion would actually have gone together to the infamous precincts of Leicester Square at night speaks of her unusual courage and determination. To have returned four additional times was the act of a woman on a crusade.

At some time shortly before 8:00 P.M. on the evening of 30 July 1894, Mrs. Chant and her friend Lady Henry Somerset, one of the vice-presidents of the National Vigilance Association, up to London from her mansion in Reigate, set out alone from the Chant residence in Gower Street, a respectable middle-class and professional neighborhood, and headed toward Leicester Square, about a mile to the south. Their destination was that "elysium of the jeunesse dorée," the Empire Theatre of Varieties.[3] Mrs. Chant had serious business to conduct, of a nature particular enough to warrant bringing along her opera glasses. There was a great deal for her and her companion to see and observe from the moment they arrived in Leicester Square (fig. 11).

Situated just at the center of the north side of the square, at the historical moment of Mrs. Chant's arrival the Empire Theatre of Varieties was enjoying an ever-mounting reputation as one of the most popular, fash-

11. *Empire Theatre, Leicester Square, 1896, from the Coventry Street Corner of the Gardens.* Round London. *London: George Newnes, 1896. James Ellis Collection.*

ionable, and luxurious establishments in London. Erected on the site of the historic Savile House, earlier the home of the Cafe du Globe and other entertainments and destroyed by fire in 1865, the Empire had been designed in 1882 in the French Renaissance style by the highly reputed London architect Thomas Verity, who had adapted the idea of a panorama to the more particularized needs of the high-end music hall.[4] Verity's design, for a theatre originally to be called the Pandora, had incorporated not just one but two promenades, though the upper space would draw the lion's share of attention and custom. Along with a richly ornate proscenium arch, capacious stage, and generous auditorium replete with upholstered stalls, the design featured two shallow tiers, the first with three rows of seats in front of a range of loges, the second providing four rows of seats overlooked by a wide promenade; above them, a gallery of seven rows ranged behind an arcade supporting an oval conical ceiling (fig. 12). Verity's idea espoused a charming "sky" effect that anticipated the atmospheric interiors of large-scale American and British cinemas of the late 1920s.[5] A combination of expansiveness and intimacy, with a heavy admixture of fantasy, was evidently the goal.

Verity's elegant, extravagant design reembodied an architectural approach to popular entertainment implemented in Leicester Square itself some years before. In 1860, the Royal Panopticon of Science and Art, on the east side of the square, underwent conversion and reopened as the Alhambra Palace Music Hall, affording a spacious auditorium, an encircling promenade, a generous proscenium arch, and a stage wide and deep enough for great troupes of dancers. Such features were reminiscent of the design adopted in Paris in these years at the Ba-ta-clan and Folies Bergère but also of that popular alternative to stage plays, the *café chantant*, which charged no admission fee but offered entertainment, mostly sung, for the price of a half-franc drink. Patrons were free to smoke, to roam about, and to converse among themselves, so long as they continued to refresh their libations.[6] The same principles obtained, in the 1880s, at the new Eden Variety Theatre in Paris and the Theater unter den Linden in Berlin, where, in both cases, typically the number of persons in attendance far exceeded the number of seats.

Similarly, at the Alhambra, in a spacious open area along the circumference of the auditorium, gentlemen and couples could sit at tables, partake of food and refreshment, and enjoy a clear view of the entertainments in progress on the stage below, including but by no means limited to spectacular ballets of a hybrid form developed out of opera and pantomime.[7] The new Alhambra, predominantly Moorish in style, rising in 1883 from the ashes of the old, which had burned the year before, featured an unusual arrangement of tiers, with a second, promenade tier affording an uninterrupted view of the stage and easy access to a contiguous lounge, replacing a former separate refreshment room.[8] There were three ballets nightly, "Pantomimic, Dramatic and Spectacular," boasting a corps de ballet of 150 and a band of sixty musicians conducted by the Alhambra music director Georges Jacobi. Operatic selections were included on the bill as well, along with a "Great Variety Show," with "Singers, Acrobats, Jugglers and Eccentricities" — "The best French, German, Italian, American and English Artistes."[9] "Its ballets were the envy of Europe," the Irish conductor

*12. Empire Theatre. The auditorium. Clp.* Illustrated London News.
*James Ellis Collection.*

and composer James Mackey ("Jimmy") Glover remembered of the Alhambra in 1913, "its beauties on the stage the envy of youthful England, and its beauties in the promenade the talk of London."[10] Earlier in its history, a less charitable observer of the Alhambra promenade and its unescorted ladies of the town had called it the "Alcedama of licenced vice, the festering spot of all London."[11]

Such was the presumably intentional competition for the newly constructed Empire, which materialized in 1884 and which vied for the same audience, though on a smaller scale. Returning to the Empire in 1899 after an interval, Max Beerbohm characterized it as "the reputed hub of all the wild gaiety in London — that Nirvana where gilded youth and painted beauty meet, to the strains of music and the twinkling of Terpsichore, in a glare of electric light."[12] Writing from the nearer distance of 1897, the singer Emily Soldene, long a favorite at the Alhambra, ecstatically described the "gorgeous, luxurious appointments" of the Alhambra, the Palace, and the Empire: "the light, the gleam, the sparkle, and the gay

*abandon* of the audience, the magnitude of the entertainment, and the ballet! — the ballet crowded with the most beautiful girls in the world,
dressed in abbreviated costumes, designed by the finest artists of Europe,
dancing to an immense band composed of splendid musicians, playing
under the batons of eminent *chefs d'orchestre*."[13] The famous French
chanteuse Yvette Guilbert, who began performing at the Empire in 1891,
remembered in a similar way the atmosphere generated by such a smart
audience, all of them, men and women alike, in evening dress. Guilbert
exclaimed over the taste, the luxury in the ballet, known throughout
Europe, the "artistic dignity in the choice of programmes," and the "quiet
elegance in production."[14]

In such favorable circumstances the Empire's second-tier promenade
soon became the dominant attraction of the house — became, in fact, "the
Cosmopolitan Club of the world."[15] Although surely she had never visited either of these great variety houses before, Mrs. Chant, who in
recent years had taken aim, severally, at indecency on stage and in the
audience, must have been at least generally aware of the racy reputation
the two great houses shared, a product only partly of the combined
attractions of ballet in various forms and music hall turns that appealed
to a strikingly heterogeneous public. She was very likely aware, also, of
the notoriety discreetly cultivated by their respective managements, a
reputation heavily dependent on the officially unacknowledged presence
of the highest class of prostitutes in the Alhambra and Empire promenades. Frequenters of Leicester Square would certainly have sensed a
special resonance in such comments as John Hollingshead's identification
of the Alhambra as "the first really great theatre of varieties in England."[16] The Empire, second in order of emergence, would quickly
exceed the elder venue in luxury and prestige, if not in size. By the time
of the attack on the Empire license in 1894, the theatre had achieved an
unparalleled, authentically international reputation. The publisher
Grant Richards described the second-tier lounge of the Empire as "like
the *terrasse* of the Café de la Paix in Paris: if you sat there often enough
you would see pass everyone you wanted to meet, all your acquain-
tances."[17] In Act 1 of *The Importance of Being Earnest*, which premiered at
the St. James's Theatre in February 1895, only a few months after the
Empire controversy erupted, Wilde's Algernon Moncrieff casts the same
knowing eye in that universally familiar direction in proposing that he
and his friend Jack Worthing "trot round to the Empire at ten."[18] In the

context provided by recent events, the St. James's audience would have understood the full implications of the reference.

How the Empire had reached the state of phenomenal success achieved by the time of Mrs. Chant's arrival in Leicester Square comprised a cautionary tale with a happy ending. As the Empire Theatre the structure had opened its doors on 17 April 1884; for three years, despite a heavy emphasis on spectacle, it failed to succeed with the various operettas, burlesques, ballets, and even promenade concerts that were tried.[19] Then, under the new joint management of the seasoned producer Augustus Harris and the brilliant young George Edwardes, manager of already thriving interests in several London music halls and theatres including the Gaiety, the Empire was redecorated and reopened as the Empire Palace of Varieties on 22 December 1887.[20] The program for that evening illustrates the combination of classical and trend-setting ballets with music hall turns that would spell success for the enterprise.[21] Harris, lessee and manager of Drury Lane, and Edwardes had joined forces with Daniel de Nicols, proprietor of the Café Royal, to form a company called the Empire Palace Ltd. with £15,000 in capital, controlled by Edwardes and colleagues Hector Tennant, Walter Dickson, and J. C. Collier as codirectors, along with the "courteous and genial" C. D. Slater, also a member of the team, as acting manager.[22] De Nicols had held a mortgage on the Empire on which he had foreclosed on 30 August 1886, proceeding to try his own hand at management.[23] Failing decisively, he quickly abandoned his solo effort but kept his stake in the Empire by forming the company with Edwardes and Harris.[24] Relinquishing the license for variety entertainment obtained from the Lord Chamberlain, the syndicate took out a music and dancing license, on whose basis the new company grew, and the house reopened on 22 December 1887 with varieties and ballets, resulting in a long series of successes. The palmy days of the Empire had begun.[25]

The Empire's success coincided with, and in fact contributed to, a swiftly developing contemporary transformation both in theatre architecture and audiences. Taking full advantage of the advent of electricity in public theatres in the early 1880s, new venues had abandoned the gaudy, tawdry music hall of times past and embraced a resplendent new standard captured in the phrase "theatre of variety," characterized, said an early history of the music hall, by "its classic exterior of marble and freestone, its lavishly-appointed auditorium and its elegant and luxurious foyers and promenades brilliantly illuminated by myriad electric lights."[26] A broader, partly aristocratic, and more sophisticated audience quickly began to respond. The plan, conceived by Edwardes and Harris (though apparently adapted from the Alhambra's similar policy), of combining music and variety acts with ballet succeeded so brilliantly that the Empire even more than its competitor became known, according to the contemporary pictorial guide *Round London,* as "one of the most fashionable variety theatres in Europe."[27] Ivor Guest, a later historian of the Empire ballet, took a sidelong glance at the Empire policy and its result in commenting that "the aim was to preserve the classical dance, and at the same time, with an eye on the music-hall public, to create a new formula with roots in contemporary entertainment."[28] A contemporary observer, especially if also an Empire stockholder, might have smiled at the idea that Edwardes and Harris's preeminent goal was to preserve the heritage of high terpsichorean art. Guest, who hardly mentions the variety acts that invariably appeared on the program with ballet, let alone acknowledging the conglomerate nature of the audiences that swelled the Empire's public spaces and especially its second-tier promenade, was projecting back into another, earlier age the more rarefied aesthetic standards and artistic agenda of his own, post-Diaghilev era. The fact was that the Empire was making significant amounts of money for its investors, no less than for Harris, Edwardes, and de Nicols, by offering a winning combination of dance, spectacle, song, and variety acts, as well as the most recent "living pictures," designed to appeal to the widest possible range of tastes and interests.

Bernard Shaw provided a succinct thumbnail sketch of Empire fare and audiences when, as music critic for the *World,* he made his way to the Empire one evening in October 1892. There, he reported, "I immediately found myself, to my great delight, up to the neck in pure classicism, siècle de Louis Quatorze. To see Cavallazzi, in the Versailles ballet, walk, stand, sit, and gesticulate, is to learn all that Vestris or Noblet could have taught you as to the technique of doing these things with dignity." Shaw's description of the full evening's entertainment, musical and otherwise, captures an accurate idea of the variety and excellence of the fare and as accurate a sense of the clientele. "Now is it not odd," he commented, "that at a music-hall to which, perhaps, half the audience have come to hear Marie Lloyd sing Twiggy-voo, boys, twiggy voo? or to see Mr Darby jump a ten-barred gate, you get real stage art."[29]

Although significant elements of the Empire audience had not yet made their appearance as the theatre began its nightly entertainment at

8:00 P.M., the world of pleasure into which Mrs. Chant and her companion were intruding was a thriving, bustling one of gilded luxury, rife with fantastic elements all designed to draw the seeker of pleasure away from humdrum reality and over the threshold of a provocative, anonymous world of sentimentalized idealism, easy morality, and extravagant make-believe. Proceeding inside the theatre, shortly before the first ballet began, Mrs. Chant and her companion found themselves in a foyer rather Renaissance-like in character — the first instance of a playful architectural eclecticism on view throughout the house. Walking straight on, through an entrance hall designed in an Indian motif, originally predominantly black and gold and highlighted in a deep, rich crimson, but more recently redecorated by the younger Verity, Frank, they would have immediately ascended the central grand staircase, "Pompeian" in treatment, to the second tier and its promenade (fig. 13). There an attendant at a separate pay box would have scrutinized two unescorted ladies of a certain age with a quizzical eye (the ladies would soon enough understand why) and then, satisfied of their character though taken aback, perhaps, by their unusually plain dress and the early hour of their arrival, would have collected two half-crowns from each. Already, from the vantage point of the top of the staircase the two women would likely have been impressed with the quasi-Persian character of the promenade's decor and the nearly ubiquitous presence of large, plate-glass mirrors set off by highly ornamented gilt frames, on which small, shaded electric lights were clustered (fig. 14). As they entered the promenade, they would have been instantly struck by its wide, semicircular expanse of open space under a low ceiling, providing a generous area for walking up and down and affording a view of the stage below, largely unimpeded except for the white columns, ornamented with blue and gold trim, present in the promenade and throughout the auditorium (fig. 15).

Significantly, Mrs. Chant and her companion knew without doubt to what part of the house they should proceed; their choice of the five-shilling promenade on the second tier spoke unambiguously of their goal that night, eschewing other parts of the house including the lesser promenade below on the first tier, at the back of the pit, a comparative bargain at one shilling. Had Mrs. Chant and her companion been aware of it, they would surely have been shocked by the character of the pit promenade, well known by Empire habitués as the haunt of homosexual men. County council records contain an unsigned letter dated 15 October 1894, a mere

*13. Empire Theatre. Staircase. Clp.* Illustrated London News. *James Ellis Collection.*

six weeks after Mrs. Chant's first visit, describing the rough ejection of a man from the shilling promenade by Robert William Ahern, the front-of-house manager. The anonymous writer paraphrased Ahern as saying that the man was "a *sodomite*," as were perhaps half the occupants of that promenade, that it was the only London venue for persons of this kind, and that

14. *Empire promenade. E. O. Sachs*, Modern Opera Houses and Theatres
*(1896–98), 2: 40.*

he "could lay his hands on 200 sods every night in the week if he liked."[30]
Despite its transgressive character, the shilling promenade would remain
invisible in Mrs. Chant and her colleagues' attack on the Empire, if indeed
they were cognizant of it at all.

Far more prominent, and more compelling of attention, was the
second-tier promenade. Here, along an "ample space" approached directly
from the "strikingly beautiful" entrance hall and vestibule by way of the
grand staircase, some three hundred persons could stand, or walk up and
down, with "an entirely uninterrupted view of the stage," according to the
Empire program for 17 April 1884 (fig. 16).[31] Both promenades, affording
a generous expanse of arc-shaped walking and lounging space at the rear
of the auditorium, had proved a decisive factor in realizing the upward of
70 percent annual return to shareholders on the face values of their
shares; by July 1894 investors were willingly paying £3 7s. 6d. in the City
for a ten-shilling share and £4 10s. for a fifteen-shilling share, a premium
of five or six times the face value.[32] Speculators in such an apparently sure

*15. Empire Theatre auditorium. E. O. Sachs,* Modern Opera Houses and Theatres *(1896–98), 2: 39.*

thing might have appreciated a certain unintentional irony in references in contemporary guidebooks to the "gilded youth" who swelled the ranks of Empire audiences.

On their arrival at this juncture, the price of admission an effective license to roam, Mrs. Chant and her companion could have taken an unobtrusive seat on an upholstered bench along the rear margin of the promenade, but in fact they walked forward toward the four curving rows of

*16. Empire Theatre Promenade. Programme. Empire Theatre November 21, 1884. Clp. Illustrated London News. James Ellis Collection.*

stalls overlooking the stage, coaxial with the arc of the promenade, much like a dress circle but more shallow; there they found a pair of unreserved seats for the initial part of the program. From this perspective they would have noticed the lowering presence of the oval ceiling of the theatre, almost like a Persian carpet, and would surely not have missed the sunlight, or central chandelier, imitative of "a large flower in coloured glass, with the stamens and pistils of the flower electric lights," as an appreciative description in an issue of the *Builder* for 1884 explained. "The general colouring is in turquoise and indigo blue, rose colour and crimson, with black and gold," the *Builder* added. If they had looked farther to left and right, Mrs. Chant and her companion might have noticed that the same treatment had been applied to the box fronts, while the three other circles besides the gallery circle were Louis Seize, consisting of various colors and gold. To the left and right of the promenade, the walls of the private boxes were covered with a "highly enriched gold leather paper."[33] The sense of unexampled luxury must have been nearly overpowering — a considerable advance, in magnificence and scale, from the appointments of even the most expensive and socially distinguished theatres of the West End, such as the Haymarket with its gilt picture-frame proscenium and gilt interior, or that smaller, exquisite gem of a theatre, the St. James's, a little farther to the west in King Street.

Already, a small number of patrons were present in the promenade, sitting at tables or perhaps strolling up and down, occasionally moving from the promenade through the double glass doors into the bar contiguous with it or to the long refreshment bars along the walls of the promenade. Attendants crisply attired in blue uniforms would have offered to bring Mrs. Chant and her companion refreshment, handing them a tastefully printed menu similar to the one inserted in an Empire program for 4 February 1889, a small folio advertising the "American Bar" and listing the "Principal American Drinks." The choices among "Short Drinks" featured a champagne cocktail for a shilling and a long list of other drinks for ninepence, including a "Corpse Reviver," a "Bosom Caresser," and an "Empire Reviver"; among the "Long Drinks," most of them priced at ninepence but some few at a shilling, were a "Gin Sling," a "Mint Julep," an "Empire Cooler," a "Stone Fence," and a "Port Wine Sangaree." Such offerings, even aside from the fabulous prices, might have comprised the first instance among many of the shocks that would punctuate Mrs. Chant's visit. It is difficult to imagine her ordering anything from such a menu, much easier to think of her settling instead for water (if available) or a lemon squash, though, at eightpence, nearly as expensive as alcohol.[34] In contrast to the Alhambra, no food of any kind was available at the Empire, as Mrs. Chant would later complain.

### BALLET AT THE EMPIRE

Mrs. Chant and Lady Somerset would seem to have arrived promptly at 8:00, in time to see in its entirety the initial item on the program, the "Up-to-Date" ballet *The Girl I Left behind Me* — a piece Mrs. Chant would anatomize before the Theatres Committee in October. Two ballets would, as always, be featured at the Empire in the course of the evening, the first beginning soon after the doors had swung wide; between these two performances would unfold a succession of variety "turns" such as might be found at one of scores of music halls across the sprawling metropolis of London and its environs, but comprising the very best of what was available. Augmenting the turns, at a key point about the middle of the evening, would have been a quick succession of tableaux vivants, styled "living pictures" in the Empire program, recently introduced as direct competition with the more daring, ostensibly nude tableaux drawing great crowds to the nearby Palace Theatre of Varieties in Cambridge Circus, at the junction of Shaftesbury Avenue and Charing Cross Road.[35] Not available anywhere except at the Empire and the Alhambra, however, were the rich costumes and extensive pageantry of the grand spectacular ballets that were their chief onstage attraction. The artwork on the Empire program itself spoke in a forthright way of the theatre's central feature: from 1889 on, the front cover depicted a dancer in a black romantic tutu (longer than the hip-hugging classical tutu and falling below the knee)[36] and black tights, delightedly dancing and playing a tambourine as bouquets fall at her feet; on the back cover, another exuberant dancer in a maroon and peach costume with a lacy underskirt and dark tights waves the requisite tambourine.[37]

The Empire had been continuing to invest heavily in elaborately choreographed and costumed ballet, notwithstanding the variety of entertainment it offered, on the assumption that the thousands of pounds spent on such spectacle would produce a piece that would run for months on end and return its investment several times over.[38] The typical presence of two ballets on a long, full program carried out a policy devised by Edwardes and Harris of paying more-or-less equal attention to conventional, traditional ballets, sometimes called operatic ballets in view of their origins,[39] which possessed a strong dramatic component (the so-called *ballet d'action*, or, as H. G. Hibbert described it, "ballet on academic lines"), and to more-or-less plotless ballets, or "ballets divertissements," on more topical subjects.[40] The more traditional sort remained, in subject matter or at least in style and theme, a product of the heritage of romantic ballet from the earlier part of the century — a heritage the Empire choreographer Katti Lanner (Katharina Josefa Lanner), the resident "Maîtresse de Ballet" since 1887,[41] knew intimately well from her Viennese training and the long, successful career she had pursued as a dancer and choreographer in Europe and America. Lanner had been brought to London in 1875 to take over the direction of the National Training School of Dancing, established the next year, which would in time become a nursery for the Empire Theatre corps de ballet.[42] Lanner's personal investment in the future of English dancers paid off handsomely a decade later when she became ballet mistress at the Empire, a post she would hold for twenty years, during which time she would produce thirty-four ballets.[43]

17. *"Madame Katti Lanner."* Sketch, *15 May 1895, 121. Yale University.*

Known as "the autocrat of the Empire stage" and described by her younger colleague, the Empire's brilliant, precocious costume and set designer C. Wilhelm (the professional name of William John Charles Pitcher), as "the high priestess of the ballet," Lanner brought to her long familiarity with traditional romantic dance a considerable talent for choreography, a highly developed sense of graceful style and expressive movement, and a keen intuition for what would appeal to popular audiences.[44] If anyone "ever had a genius for inventing ballets," declared "A. S." (probably Arthur Symons) in a review of Lanner's *On Brighton Pier*, "it is Madame Lanner" (fig. 17).[45]

Once installed at the Empire and often collaborating with Edwardes, Lanner devoted that genius partly to developing prime examples of the second variety of ballet, a fine example of which Mrs. Chant would see at the beginning of the evening, the "Up-to-Date ballet" — in basic form a "ballet divertissement," lacking a distinct story line or a coherent action.[46] Entirely unpreoccupied with dying swans or sleeping beauties, this newer form did away with "all romantic and pseudo-historical frippery," William Archer explained; its setting and costumes "were not only English, but ultramodern," and its action depicted in glaring colors "the everyday fast life of the restaurant, the race-course, and the stage itself."[47] Performed in a music-hall ambiance where topicality was the order of the day, this second form of ballet seemed in retrospect an almost inevitable development. In the instance of *The Girl I Left behind Me*, working from an invention by Edwardes himself Lanner had mounted a ballet in five tableaux, to music composed and arranged by Leopold Wenzel, the music director of the Empire, and with resplendent costumes by the prolific Wilhelm, ingeniously balanced over a broad range of complementary colors to capture an illusion of light and shadow (fig. 18).[48] Delighting audiences nightly for several months by the time of Mrs. Chant's visit, the ballet featured a dance of gypsies, a dream vision with a grand waltz, a sailors' dance, and a "Grand Fête in Burmah" with children augmenting the corps de ballet, and ending with a "Grand Galop" finale.[49] Mrs. Chant, seemingly oblivious to the impressiveness of the massed forces and colorful pageantry of the ballet, concluded that the whole arrangement "seemed to be for the express purpose of displaying the bodies of women to the utmost extent." She would reach the same conclusion about the second ballet, later in the evening.

After the first ballet ended, Mrs. Chant and her companion waited patiently, wondering, perhaps, where all the reputed Empire ladies might be, for few or none were in attendance as yet. As they bided their time, they would have had little choice but to walk up and down or to sit and watch successive turns by "Texarkansas," a "Plantation, Sand, and Jig Dancer" making his English debut; the comedienne Fanny Leslie; the club expert Morris Cronin; the comedian Dutch Daly; and the vocalist Charles Tilbury. Among the turns this night that especially drew Mrs. Chant's attention and ended up scandalizing her and her companion were the Schaffer family, a troupe of acrobats whose forces included a very little girl of perhaps ten years of age, to whose treatment by her fellow acrobats Mrs. Chant took great and angry exception. The girl stood on her head

*18. C. Wilhelm, "The Hades Scene from the Ballet of* Orfeo, *at the Empire Theatre."*
Magazine of Art *18 (1894): 13. P1931pc1. By permission of the British Library.*

with her legs outstretched; the men took her up by her heels, twisted her
around, and "kicked her about the stage," Mrs. Chant later told the Theatres Committee — treatment she considered "against decency & right
feeling & even common kindness."

### LIVING PICTURES AND IMPERIAL THEMES

After Fanny Leslie's turn, shortly before 9:30, came the Empire's celebrated "living pictures." By this time a great influx of unaccompanied
ladies into the promenade had rather suddenly occurred; it seemed little
short of intentional that the Empire management had timed the living
pictures to be shown only after the five-shilling promenade was full of the
women that gave it its reputation. In fact, everything that occurred or
existed in Edwardes's establishment seemed intentional, officially or otherwise, and carefully planned, including turning the electric auditorium
lights way down to show off the living pictures to best advantage.

Alerted perhaps by NVA colleagues or aware on her own of such developments, Mrs. Chant would have followed the introduction of tableaux at

# EMPIRE THEATRE.

## TO-NIGHT, at 9.30,

WILL BE PRODUCED

## AN ENTIRELY NEW SERIES

OF

# LIVING PICTURES

1. COURTSHIP,     Misses Gladys Deroy and Sheppard.

2. NIGHT,     Misses Hetty Hamer and Constance Collier.

3. DUET,     Mdme. Fionde and Miss Blowey.

4. A FUNNY SONG,
    Senorita Candida and Messrs. Lewington and Perkins.

5. LOVES ME! LOVES ME NOT!
    Misses Marie Studholme and Jennie Barker.

6. GOOD-NIGHT,     Miss Gladys Deroy.

7. A SUMMER SHOWER ("Une Ondée," after Alonzo Perez)
    From the *Figaro Illustré*, published by Messrs. Boussod, Valadon & Cie.
    Misses Sheppard, Ford, and Fairfax.

8. PETS,     Miss Hetty Hamer.

9. THE BILLET-DOUX,     Misses Belton and Hill.

10. SPRINGTIME,     Miss Hinde.

11. CHARITY,     Senorita Candida and Miss Gladys Deroy.

12. THE THREE GRACES,
    Misses Hetty Hamer, Constance Collier and Marie Studholme.

13. THE THREE SISTERS (England, Ireland and Scotland)

*19. Empire Theatre bill. "To–Night, at 9:30. Living Pictures," 1894.*
*Mander & Mitchenson Theatre Collection.*

the Empire with considerable interest. In an attempt to keep up with the competition at the Palace, Edwardes had added "living pictures" to the list of Empire attractions the previous February (fig. 19).[50] In emulating the extraordinarily successful practice of the Palace Theatre of Varieties in mounting posed representations of classical, mythological, and traditional subjects — so-called tableaux vivants — Edwardes had laid claim to some originality of approach by translating the traditional French term into more accessible, less pretentious English and had exploited the extensive resources of his stage, combining gaslight and limelight with electricity to illuminate this briskly paced series of still poses in a novel and attractive way. Colored electric lights, precisely aimed, illuminated the subjects inside a large gilt frame on an otherwise blacked-out stage, throwing them into sharp focus for an audience that found itself plunged into semi-darkness for the duration of these highly popular entertainments, as appropriate music accompanied the exhibitions.[51] Mrs. Chant and her companion would have paid close attention to the content and visual qualities of Edwardes's tableaux, keeping a sharp eye out for what might be considered erotic and offensive material, even as they simultaneously observed the promenade audience's behavior during the presentation. The subject matter varied between scenes of current life and life historicized and idealized with old costumes; in one example, "Courtship," "in the fresh spring time a young couple, in Directoire dresses, were shown leaning over a bridge" (fig. 20).[52] If a tableaux entitled "The Three Graces," exhibited between February and May 1894, had still been on the bill, Mrs. Chant and her companion would have been able to view three prominent actresses, Hetty Hamer, Constance Collier, and Marie Studholme, impersonating a classic theme strikingly anticipated by a tableau at the Cafe du Globe thirty-five years before (fig. 21).

To these traditional and general subjects Edwardes was adding more topical and politically oriented ones, as in the tableau "British Pluck," exhibited at the Empire on 23 April 1894 (and for many nights thereafter) and represented in a sketch in the *Daily Graphic* the next day (fig. 22).[53] The scene is a battlefield on which attacking African natives are being fought off by British soldiers; in the central grouping a fiercely determined soldier aims a pistol at a cowering African. An Empire program insert advertising the impending April show touted the grand tableau for realizing "the recent stirring episode in Masonaland," where Major Wilson and a small band showed the world "how English men can fight and die in the cause of duty."[54]

Evidently, in selecting topics of compelling national interest such as British pluck, along with other more general and innocuous subjects, Edwardes was aligning himself with a long tradition of representing the hazards and exploits of empire on the British stage. In the Napoleonic era

**"LIVING PICTURES."**

Granted a taste for such form of entertainment it must at once be conceded that the Tableaux Vivants, or "Living Pictures," which now have a place on making nineteenth-century womankind enter into competition with the women of ancient Greece, for the entertainment loses nothing by its skirl of skirts. One may not be enraptured of tableaux and yet admit that the whole thing is as well done as could be.

armament for her size, with very considerable protection for her gunners. Her two heaviest pieces are of about 7½in. calibre, and are carried on poop and forecastle, while the remainder of her cannon, six in number, each of about 5in. bore, are mounted in

*20. "Living Pictures at the Empire Theatre." Daily Graphic, 8 February 1894, 5. By permission of the British Library.*

Charles Dibdin the Younger staged naval battles using scale-model ships in the real-water environment of Sadler's Wells; colonial and imperial motifs appeared frequently on the melodramatic English stage from early in the century.[55] Almost every colonial location, it seemed, was a lawless wasteland awaiting the saving influx of civilizing British forces. The theme of rescue from enslavement and barbary persisted through plays

21. *Marie Studholme, Constance Collier, and Hetty Hamer as the Three Graces. Dated on reverse "Empire 1894 5–2." Mander & Mitchenson Theatre Collection.*

*22. "The Craze for Tableaux Vivants: 'British Pluck,' the New 'Living Picture'
Produced Last Night at the Empire." Daily Graphic, 24 April 1894, 4.
By permission of the British Library.*

about the Crimean War and the Sepoy Mutiny around midcentury to the
campaigns in the Sudan in the 1880s and 1890s. Press artists became
heroes along with the military men they depicted, and in the second half
of the century battle scenes based on exact accounts in popular journals
began to proliferate in academic painting.[56] At Drury Lane in the 1880s
and 1890s Harris pursued a successful policy of presenting autumn melodrama that emphasized heroic sentiments and patriotic themes ennobling
the brave British soldier and, as the theatre historian Michael Booth
explains, glorifying "military prowess in the service of the imperial
cause."[57] Similarly, the art historian J. W. M. Hichberger has discerned an
important shift in attitude in post-Waterloo military art, pointing to
recurrent notions of "supremacy of the white races, the particular recti-
tude of the British among European nations and the country's moral duty
to defend her authority." Precedents for the late-century caricaturing of
Africans of the sort presented in Edwardes's living picture "British Pluck"
may be found in such paintings as G. D. Giles's *Tamai* (exhibited at the

Royal Academy in 1887), in which emphatic distortion of the features of the Dervish enemy makes them appear ridiculous and so identifies by contrast the superior character of the British protagonists.[58]

Edwardes would continue to mine the vein of imperial themes. If Mrs. Chant and her companion had decided to return once more to the Empire in early 1895, they would have encountered a much larger-scale effort on Edwardes's part to associate the fast-paced world of Leicester Square, London, and England with the exploits of British Empire in a revival of the 1892 "Characteristic Ballet" *Round the Town*. "The national spirit is appealed to with immense effect in *Round the Town*," said the *Era*, "with its fine display of military forces at the conclusion."[59] More particularly, as Mrs. Chant or any visitor would discover, the ballet comprised a symbolic resume of the cultural bonds that attracted audiences back to the Empire night after night and paid them the best of compliments for being exactly who they were.

Featuring settings and costumes by the inventive Wilhelm, choreography by Lanner to a scenario devised by Lanner and Edwardes, and sprightly, characteristic music by Leopold Wenzel, who in 1889 had succeeded Hervé, the first composer of operettas for the Empire, as music director,[60] *Round the Town* appealed even in its title to the Leicester Square audience's sense of the up-to-date and the here and now. Its five scenes guided the vicarious London sightseer from early morning in Covent Garden, through Trafalgar Square and along the Thames Embankment in the course of the day, to Leicester Square at night, where the fourth scene occurs in front of the Empire Theatre itself. The first night of a new ballet is about to take place, and excitement reigns; a street piano is playing, children are dancing, and fashionable ladies walk to and fro, exchanging salutations with gentlemen in evening dress. The action then moves inside to the stage of the Empire itself, where the fifth scene, entitled "Our Empire," introduces a ballet called *The Daughters of the British Empire*, representing kingdoms, cities, and towns from England and Ireland to India and Australia and from the metropolis of London itself to Edinburgh, Glasgow, Dublin, and Belfast, then back again to Windsor and Eton.[61] The blithely punning title of the last scene encouraged the audience's identification of the beautiful dancers of the Empire Theatre with the female progeny of the myriad countries and territories that came to be clasped in the British imperial embrace in the course of a long colonization. As always, in the now well-defined genre of the *ballet divertissement*, according to the contemporary observer F. Anstey, "company after company of girls, in costumes of delicately contrasted tints, march, trip, or gallop down the boards, their burnished armor gleaming and their rich dresses scintillating in the limelight; at each fresh stroke of the stagemanager's gong they group themselves anew or perform some complicated figure, except when they fall back in a circle and leave the stage clear for the *première danseuse*."[62] At the end, the stage now full to overflowing with daughters of the Empire, the figure of Britannia, "mighty and majestic, strides to the front," the surviving scenario explains, "and, clad in a cloak made of a gorgeous Union Jack, waves her commanding and protecting trident over all." Arthur Symons, journalist, poet, and inveterate witness of Empire ballets, captured the moment: "Miss Ada Vincent, in her white and pink finery — resolute not to smile — stands, with beautiful severity, for England." All that she has done, said Anstey of the prima ballerina in her triumphal conclusion, is now "charged with a deep but mysterious significance."[63]

In fact, neither Mrs. Chant nor anyone else visiting London music halls or theatres of variety in the mid-1890s could possibly have avoided witnessing the enactment of imperial themes. The Alhambra had gotten into the act as early as March 1886, when *Grand Military Spectacle: Le Bivouac* appeared; *Our Army and Navy* followed in July 1889, and *Victoria and Merrie England* would appear on the occasion of Victoria's diamond jubilee in 1897.[64] Such patriotic displays were themselves part of a much larger trend, one that speaks unambiguously about the theatrical culture of the period. A common subject in English pantomimes of the 1880s and 1890s was the "allegorical world tour," conducted by a company of chorus girls representing armed forces, industry, and the history of nations. At Drury Lane, Augustus Harris, preeminent producer of these luxury tours, inserted one called a "Dream of Fair Women" in E. L. Blanchard's 1885 *Aladdin*; again, in Blanchard's 1886 *The Forty Thieves*, he featured a procession of Britain and her colonies.[65] At the Empire, Katti Lanner would carry on the imperial theme in future ballets, most notably *Under One Flag*, a "*divertissement d'occasion*" in the form of "a pageant of the British Empire at its height," performed in June 1897 in celebration of Victoria's jubilee and featuring a patriotic ode written by the drama critic of the *Daily Telegraph* and *Illustrated London News*, Clement Scott.[66]

Imperial symbolism of the sort to which Mrs. Chant and her companion were being subjected, on this night at the end of July 1894, had in fact been present in the cover art on the Empire program ever since the Empire became a theatre of varieties in 1887, including along with other motifs a Union Jack borne by a soldier.[67] Association of one empire with another, much larger one was inevitable and presumably intended. Had Mrs. Chant had a reason for returning to the Empire three years later, in the year of the jubilee, she would have found the cover art taking even more explicit pains to associate the Empire Theatre of Varieties with the greater empire of which Victoria was queen and empress — and would have found still more blatant images of sometimes meek, sometimes stalwart women at the forefront of imperial domain, along with an even more energetic and provocative association of them with the lovely female presences on the Empire stage and, less visibly but no less tellingly, the beautiful, alluring women in the Empire promenade.

In one eloquent instance, the program cover for 20 September 1897 is completely taken up with a representation of a helmeted Britannia, trident in hand, exhibiting the Union Jack on a shield; her face is circled by flowing blonde tresses, and the strap of her white sleeveless dress has fallen off the shoulder onto the upper arm — a tactfully erotic dishabille reminiscent of belligerent, bare-breasted women at the barricades in French revolutionary art and hinting also, perhaps, at fantasies of accessible women enjoyed by male visitors to the Empire five-shilling lounge. Appropriately, this Britannia, pressed into special service, guards the entrance to a pavilion marked "Theatre of Varieties" at the top, while just below it a curtained interior in perspective opens onto a shining sea with a rising sun at its center; in the surround, a colonnade features left and right the shields of Britain's dominions, and at the top the legend "The Empire." A lion couchant balances majestically on top of the pavilion itself, above which shines a five-pointed star. At the base of the colonnade appears a shield bearing the motto "Heaven's Light Our Guide," enclosing a star; above the colonnade, the motto of the Order of the Garter, "Honi Soit Qui Mal Y Pense," decorates a stately crown borne on a pillow.[68] The connections could not be more obvious, or more blithely, grandly pretentious.

Allowing for the customary abbreviation of ballet costume (an allowance Mrs. Chant was disinclined to make), whatever the actual subject Edwardes took constant care to keep his ballets and his tableaux vivants well within the range of inoffensiveness. In September 1894 the *Entr'Acte & Limelight* praised the Empire's living pictures as being "of a very high standard." Reviewing them when first produced, the *Entr'Acte* noted "their careful avoidance of everything that could be considered allied to grossness." Having gone back for a second look later in the month, the reviewer held to his original opinion that the tableaux were "entirely void of offence."[69] The point evidently needed to be made and reiterated; the risqué productions in this genre at the Palace would come under unofficial but determined attack in mid-October, in an action parallel to the assault on the Empire, by the National Vigilance Association, which focused attention on those subjects "in which the undraped figure plays a prominent part."[70] Edwardes's addition to his tableaux of a more explicit imperial theme may have been part of a strategy to divert attention away from any hint of the erotic, while capitalizing on the obvious advantages of subjects that would redound to the glory of his Empire along with Britain's own.

In this context, Edwardes's translation into English of the French term *tableaux vivants* may well have represented more than a bland effort at clarification. Along with its conventional meaning of a posed live representation of a still picture, the French term appears to have acquired over time some curious metaphorical value. Leo Lespès's *Les Tableaux Vivants* (1865) proves to be simply a series of fictional sketches, suggesting that by this time the term is being used figuratively to describe brief, pictorialized representations of actual life. As the century moved on, the semantic field widened even more, embracing meanings much less respectable. *Les Tableaux vivants ou mes confessions aux pieds de la duchesse,* published anonymously in Amsterdam in 1870, is a piece of stylish pornography that employs the term *tableaux vivants* figuratively to mean something like "living representations of forbidden sights and experiences." In one "tableau" that leaves nothing to the imagination, the duchess summons her chambermaid Fanny and gives her a command: "Déshabille-toi, ma petite Fanny, fit-elle d'une voix faible. Et Fanny obéit. Elle était brune et robuste, ferme comme une beauté des champs, bien que lascive comme une coquine des villes. Lorsqu'elle fit tomber sa chemise, une motte noire nous apparut recouvrant un con vermeil."[71] The taboo usage survives in a later work in the same genre, *La Maison de Verre défilé de Tableaux Vivants par E. D.,* published in Paris in 1891, in which bizarre coital positions and combinations are illustrated by hand-colored prints. A partial English translation of the 1870 *Les Tableaux vivants,* as *The Marchioness's Amourous Pastimes and Some Other Merry Tales,* privately printed in London in 1893, implies a certain English reticence about the French term. Edwardes would surely have known just how accessible such pornography was from vendors in Holywell Street, in the Strand, or street hawkers in the vicinity of Leicester Square.[72] And so it was likely Edwardes may well have had more than simple accessibility in mind in translating *tableaux vivants* into the more common English "living pictures." (The reverse may well also have been true with respect to the Palace's continued use of the French term.)

In any case, Edwardes had evidently taken care that the living pictures at the Empire would stay within the bounds of propriety. There was never in his theatre "a single picture in which there has been a nude figure," he would assert categorically in a symposium on living pictures conducted in November 1894 by the *New Review*. He had seen tableaux vivants in Berlin and thought them "somewhat indecent," and he entirely disapproved, he said, of nude figures in the living pictures and would object to his own daughters witnessing them. "Of course," Edwardes explained, "an artistic pictorial study of the female form divine is a very beautiful thing, but I consider that the impersonation of the nude upon the stage is calculated to do a deal of harm."[73] As a consequence, Mrs. Chant would declare to the Theatres and Music Halls Committee that she "did not find the living pictures" at the Empire "at all objectionable." Clarifying her remarks in a letter to the *Daily Telegraph*, she said she was "charmed and delighted" by them and could object to only three, which, significantly, were received "almost in silence" by the audience.[74] Evidently (to judge from her testimony before the Theatres Committee), Mrs. Chant's response to the Empire's living pictures was that they were far enough from unequivocal offensiveness to form at best an ambiguous target for criticism. It was what went on in the shadowy arena of the five-shilling promenade while the living pictures were in progress that she found so objectionable. And so she appears to have decided at some early point to leave the tableaux alone and focus her attention on the indecency of the costumes in the ballet and the presence and actions of prostitutes in the five-shilling lounge — a double-edged attack that would prove even more potent than she might have imagined.

### UNACCOMPANIED WOMEN IN THE EMPIRE LOUNGE

Just after nine o'clock, Mrs. Chant had been astonished — or so she would tell the Theatres Committee — to see numerous young women coming into the promenade alone, unescorted, most "very much painted" and all "more or less gaudily dressed." With very few exceptions they did not go into the unreserved stalls but, instead, walked up and down or sat on the sofas and lounges near the walls of the promenade. Others took up positions at the top of the grand staircase, watching "particularly & eagerly," Mrs. Chant observed, any men who emerged from the stalls and began walking in the promenade. In no case, she explained to the Theatres Committee, were these women accompanied by anyone "except of their own type." Mrs. Chant had suddenly discovered the great open secret of the Empire's popularity, its magnetic attraction for certain men-about-town who might have some interest, slight or substantial, in the ballets or the music hall turns for which the Empire was so well known, but who had come to the Empire that night and.paid their five-shilling entrance fee for what Mrs. Chant would conclude, euphemistically, were reasons unconnected with the performance.

Some observers maintained a certain reticence about what went on in the Empire's five-shilling promenade. In June 1893 "A.S." — very likely Arthur Symons, who had begun writing regular reviews of music hall entertainments for the *Star* in 1892[75] — contributed an impression of the ballet divertissement *Round the Town* to the *Sketch*. Having seen it repeatedly over the months since it opened in September 1892, Symons knew the piece so well that hearing the music alone could evoke a vibrant mental image of the spectacle. "It amuses me sometimes," he said, "to sit at the back of the promenade, and, undistracted by my somewhat too agreeably distracting surroundings, to follow, by the sound of the music, every movement of the ballet on the stage, which I see only in my mind's eye."[76] For all his intentional coyness about the matter, what impedes A.S.'s view as he sits at the back of the promenade amidst "too agreeably distracting surroundings" claims particular attention. Another frequent visitor to the Empire, F. Anstey, was less reticent about the distractions in the five-shilling lounge. "Smoking is universal," he remarked, "and a large proportion of the audience promenade the outer circles, or stand in groups before the long refreshment bars which are a prominent feature on every tier." Paradoxically, the Empire was a perfectly respectable place where "most of the men are in evening dress, and in the boxes are some ladies, also in evening costume, many of them belonging to what is called good society," but where at the same time "the women in the other parts of the house" — Anstey means the promenades and lounges — "are generally pretty obvious members of a class which, so long as it behaves itself with propriety in the building, it would, whatever fanatics say to the contrary, be neither desirable nor possible to exclude" (fig. 23).[77]

What Mrs. Chant was encountering at the Empire, on that evening at the end of July, was a graphic instance of an issue that had preoccupied certain sectors of English society for many a year: the question of prostitutes in public places. John Hollingshead, manager of the Gaiety Theatre until Edwardes succeeded him in 1886, took a predictable stance on the issue. "It matters little whether these 'fallen creatures,' 'social evils,' 'demireps,' 'demimondaines' — call them by what name you will — number sixty thousand, seventy thousand, or a hundred thousand," he asserted; "they have their civil rights in the country like any other citizens, and as long as they behave with superficial decorum in public they can maintain these rights in any court of law." Hollingshead spoke with the seasoned voice of managerial wisdom, whose high-pitched tones George Edwardes would soon echo exactly. "You may preach to her as much as you like," Hollingshead cautioned, "you may try to convert her to virtuous ill-paid drudgery by sermon, pamphlet, 'missions,' weak tea, and strong butter thinly spread on bread, but you must not refuse her money, or inquire too curiously how it has been earned, any more than the parish or the State does when it applies for its rates or taxes. She knows, as we all know, that she came in with the Garden of Eden, and will not go out till the Day of Judgment."[78] There was nothing to be done, in short, about the presence of prostitutes in one's establishment — and nothing that need be done, so long as they behaved with the requisite show of politesse and practiced sufficient restraint.

As Mrs. Chant was quickly discovering, decorum, however superficial, was the unwritten law of music hall land, where appearances were everything. Well before the creation of the London County Council and its Theatres and Music Halls Committee, police inspectors were keeping watchful eyes on such places as the Oxford Music Hall, where in 1878 an Inspector Crook said he had seen prostitutes, "but not disorderly prostitutes," and he insisted that the Oxford "was not the resort of prostitutes."[79] Similarly, in 1881 an inspector reporting on the clientele of Lusby's Music Hall (later the site of the reformer F. N. Charrington's unsuccessful attack on music hall immorality) said that he found no more than an average number of prostitutes there and that the audience "contained a large number of respectable women."[80] The same nice distinctions were affirmed by London County Council Inspection Subcommittee

23. *"Empire Promenade, 1892." Thomas Burke,* English Night-Life. *London: B. T. Batsford, 1941. Pl. 64, opp. 126. James Ellis Collection.*

inspectors in reports of visits to the Canterbury Music Hall in 1891. "I saw none that I should consider to be prostitutes," an inspector reported that February. In August an inspector remarked, "I saw no disorder, and I did not observe any persons whose *behaviour* would mark them as prostitutes, though doubtless among such a large audience, there were many loose characters."[81]

Mrs. Chant was in fact encountering an especially troublesome aspect of a social problem that existed in London (and beyond) on an extremely large scale, a problem intimately bound up with the issue of decorum: the ambiguity of the prostitute's character.[82] "I know very well that gay women frequent the Empire," said an editorial writer (possibly the editor, W. H. Combe) in the *Entr'Acte & Limelight,* but they always have to be very careful of how they conduct themselves; should they dare to overstep "the prescribed mark" established by "a scrupulously discreet management," they are forced to retreat and prevented from ever returning.[83] Respectability at the Empire was not only a matter of proper dress and proper behavior; it entailed the ability, as in the case of the mental gymnastics of "A.S.," to see no evil — or to appear to look the other way in its presence. Perhaps an even more complex sense of the vantage point obtained: "A.S." had effectively turned his back on the stage, but his "distracting surroundings," the prostitutes in the promenade, obtruded upon his "mind's eye" vision of the onstage performance, producing a composite "aesthetic" experience in which the forms of the ladies of the five-shilling lounge, with all the sexual attractiveness and opportunity for illicit connection that they offered, were superimposed upon the forms of the dancers. Both are rendered as objects of sensual attraction and are identified as the same, or analogous, figures, undifferentiated in quality. And each group could claim a certain veneer of respectability that only served to add a certain frisson of excitement to the prospect when they came into view — actually, or in the mind's eye.

Despite Mrs. Chant's professed astonishment at the arrival of dozens of elaborately dressed and heavily painted young women — one wonders how naïve she could have been about the typical population of the promenade and whether her astonishment was as much a self-protective rhetorical device, in the context of the Theatres Committee meeting, as an expression of actual feeling — it was clear enough, after all, what could be found there, as well as onstage. The true man-about-town was cognizant of the situation and, like any urban sophisticate, would have been acquainted with the lore of the place. In his popular social history *Roads to Ruin*, E. S. Turner quotes his own near-contemporary Percy Colson on what was on view in that notorious mirrored expanse. If one turned one's back on the stage, Colson explained, the more compelling view closer in was of "the best-class cocottes who flocked to it every evening wonderfully — and sometimes fearfully — dressed, elaborately made up, highly scented and very haughty."[84] Cyril Beaumont, who considered the ballet at the Empire "primarily a spectacle," admitted that his eyes sometimes "strayed from the stage to gaze at the *hetirae* who passed along the promenade." Costumes, some dazzling, some bizarre, "some of rare beauty," all had the same purpose of attracting attention to their wearers. "The faces of the tempters, enhanced by make up, presented a most fascinating appearance," Beaumont added, "at times seductive and occasionally sinister and mysterious like certain drawings by Aubrey Beardsley."[85] Similar descriptions by Walter James Macqueen-Pope were even less subtle, and rife with erotic fantasy. "You sat at a table or on a lounge," he recalled, "and you were brought your drink by a footman either in black or blue and gold livery." As "the golden light from the stage beat upwards in subdued glow," venturers into this effective male preserve could have "the daring and bohemian thrill," he imagined, of watching "the wicked ladies as they floated . . . noiseless on the rich carpets, overwhelmingly alluring in their known 'naughtiness,' yet rather frightening to youth as well, in an atmosphere of rich, blue cigar-smoke, frangipane, patchouli and the heady scent of champagne, whilst the sound of a wonderful orchestra from below made a fitting background."[86]

Allowing for the excesses of Macqueen-Pope's lubricious fantasies, the Empire promenade was clearly a place set apart from the rest of the auditorium, affording unique vistas along with experiences quite distinct from those obtainable elsewhere in the house. Those who lounged in the promenade were in a general sense part of the audience, but in another sense were not, comprising as they did an alternative performance of their own making — and regulated by their own unpublished book of etiquette. Were the men who congregated there to venture to make the acquaintance of one of the women they saw, they might use the formula Bernard Shaw explained was the one "by which gentlemen in the Empire Theatre promenade get over the embarrassment of addressing ladies to whom they have not been formally introduced," namely, "Where have I seen you before?"[87] In a more cynical vein, Charles Pascoe described the rather loose, anonymous quality he perceived in the Empire promenade as characteristic of London society in general. A stranger "may make his way into a good deal of London social life," Pascoe asserted, "without any credentials at all." For instance, "it requires no more than a few pieces of depreciating silver to make one's way upstairs at 'the Empire,'" where he "may see something of 'social life' with the electric light turned full-on, and no one will question his title to respectability" (fig. 24).[88]

The complexity of the spectacle close at hand and the dense significance of the social transactions conducted in the promenade could perhaps have been perceivable by an observer as sharp-eyed as Mrs. Chant, but undoubtedly there would have been things she was missing. She would surely have noticed the requisite gentlemanly costume, described by Percy Fitzgerald as a dress suit with a pink handkerchief tucked into the waistcoat and a "crush" hat, easily (and noisily) expanded, together with a "kerchief, shirt, and cigarette" for accessories. (Gentlemen who needed to change into dress suits from daytime attire or who needed some sprucing up could do so in the men's lavatory in the basement of the theatre [fig. 25]). And she would have remarked on the essential gentlemanly walk, "flashy, reckless," the hat worn at a jaunty angle so as to cultivate a "careless roguish effect." Such "gentlemen" would be observed

*24. Sketch by Fred Peggot of the Empire promenade, dated "'92."*
*Caption: "It requires no more than a few pieces of silver to make one's way*
*upstairs at the Empire." Charles Eyre Pascoe, ed., London of To-Day,*
*10th ed. (1894), 149. Westminster City Archives.*

moving in pairs, Fitzgerald explained, giving the impression of having risen from a fashionable dinner table "just to stroll into this scene of pleasure." There they were, "imparting quite an air of refinement and high manners, as they lounge carelessly by, an Inverness cape lightly thrown over, but not concealing, the festive garments below" and observing the scene "with a *blasé* and haughty indifference." Even if Mrs. Chant could have generalized on her experience and comprehended that this scene replicated itself night after night at upscale venues around the West End, she would perhaps not have realized, as Fitzgerald did, that it represented one of the more important social phenomena of the age, namely, "of worthy shopmen and bank clerks taking all this trouble, night after night, 'making up' and dressing for the part."[89] Perhaps she was beginning to grasp what it meant to circulate in the second-tier promenade at the Empire, a place in which the stage performance and audience could function as mirror images of one another, each being a show in its own right.[90]

Walter Sickert, preeminent painter of the English music hall, had captured the reflexive reality of performer and audience in several of his

*25. John Copley. Men's lavatory, Empire Theatre. Colored lithograph, 1909.*
*Performing Arts Centre, Toronto Reference Library.*

works, perhaps most strikingly in *Little Dot Hetherington at the Bedford Music Hall* (1888–89), in which nearly the entire representation of the artiste Dot Hetherington, gesturing to persons just barely visible in the gallery, is captured in the reflection of a mirror placed strategically along the wall of the Bedford auditorium; the frame of the mirror itself, below which looms a set of almost ghostly empty chairs, is the single orienting clue in Sickert's complex plan.[91] A near contemporary, W. R. Titterton, alive to the intense reciprocity of stage performance and audience response and aware of the strong sense of identification it fostered, described a performance at Gatti's in admittedly impressionistic terms: "Through the mist of tobacco smoke and the swirl of the beer and the band I seem to see and hear a girl very like the one at my side, but got up regardless, and a fellow very like me, masqued in the loot of a second-hand clothes store, celebrating joyously the extravagant happenings of our everyday life." He and his companions went to Gatti's, Titterton concludes, "not as spectators but as performers."[92]

The Empire Theatre of Varieties had emerged at the perfect moment. Its full electrification, affording a bright, intense light and creating deep shadows, selectively augmented by gaslight and limelight on stage, enhanced the striking illusionary vistas available in all parts of the house, but most lucidly in the promenades, where the walls were lined with mirrors. The multiple mirrors of the Empire five-shilling promenade could reflect an audience almost infinitely, maintaining an aura of intimacy, privacy, and exclusivity in an environment simultaneously crowded and impersonal.[93]

Neither Mrs. Chant nor anyone else in the five-shilling Empire promenade could have missed the pervasive presence of these huge mirrors embellishing the walls and producing multiple reflections — "gilded mirrors that repeat you thrice," as Theodore Wratislaw, a would-be decadent poet, described them in his verses "At the Empire."[94] To say they were provided by a management eager to convince customers "of the glamour and scale of its enterprise" is certainly true, but only begins to assess their utility.[95] In his moody poem "Prologue" Arthur Symons describes his life as "like a music-hall," where, held captive by the enchantment of the stage spectacle, with a feeling of "impotent rage" he suddenly discovers that he himself has become part of the show: "I see myself upon the stage / Dance to amuse a music-hall."[96] Max Beerbohm described the paradoxical glitter and gloom of the promenade as he and a French acquaintance departed from it, on an evening in 1899: "I noticed in the distance two young men who seemed even more gloomy than the rest; my brain, I suppose, was a trifle dulled by the whole evening, for it was not until I came quite close to them that I recognised my friend and myself in a mirror."[97]

Despite what she may have been missing — might she have been stopped momentarily, at some point, seized by her own reflection? — there was much for Mrs. Chant to see and be shocked or even scandalized by among the attractions and transactions in the promenade. Soon after the unaccompanied women had arrived, she noticed a middle-aged woman who called attention to herself because she seemed to know many of the younger women and was making it her business "to introduce gentlemen to them." One interchange drew Mrs. Chant's particular notice, and she took care to pursue it through to its conclusion:

> I was standing by a gentleman at the back of the stalls, & she came
> & tapped him on the shoulder, took him away, and I followed them.
> She introduced him to two very pretty girls, who were seated on a
> lounge, one of them very much painted & beautifully dressed, & I

noticed that he must have been a stranger to them because he raised his hat to one during the introduction, & he raised his hat, and finally shook hands with the other & sat down by her. He called for drinks, & I saw them drinking together. The middle-aged woman left them. I then by-& bye, when "God save the Queen" was being played, & we passed downstairs, saw this man and this girl go off together. I also saw an attendant call a hansom for them.

At an early point — about half past nine — after the women had arrived and begun to circulate in the promenade and the living pictures had begun, Mrs. Chant was busily recording in her notebook what she judged to be "very bad" behavior. "There was a great deal of pulling about, jostling, & touching & very unpleasant language used," she found. At one point, when a tableau of Arthur Sullivan's "The Lost Chord" was exhibited, and the orchestral music was swelling to its climax, the last words were completely drowned out "by the loud & exceedingly objectionable conversation of one very tall highly painted young woman who stood near the stalls, & to whom, if I had been there for any other purpose than I was, I should have called 'silence' at once."

### LA FROLIQUE

As the lights came up again and the evening wore on, Mrs. Chant continued to observe the transactions in the five-shilling lounge, while directing her attention also to the turns succeeding one another on the stage below and, in the climax of the evening, to the second and last ballet, entitled *La Frolique: A Ballet Burlesque in Three Tableaux*.[98] Choreographed in fulsome, spectacular detail and variety by Mme. Lanner, *La Frolique* followed the traditional generic lines of a *ballet d'action* with its coherent story line and dramatic conflict, but was for all that a work whose narrative and theme alike epitomized the Empire's prevailing ethos of licentious pleasure, carefree of consequence and broadly complimentary of its audience. "Fantastically and richly harmonious," the *Daily Graphic* had said of *La Frolique*, new in May 1894 (and still running nightly in July, with some changes of cast), praising its "return to the old and best traditions of ballet" and the "exquisite colouring and design" of the dresses (figs. 26, 27).

The story begins at a fancy-dress ball, where "La Frolique," the eponymous sobriquet of the central character, performed originally by Florence Levey but now by Miss E. Tree, is engaged in a rowdy, carefree dance, the

26. *"La Frolique' at the Empire."* Daily Graphic, *25 May 1894, 4.*
*By permission of the British Library.*

forbidden *chahut*, a sort of can-can.[99] Suddenly she is interrupted by a
stern representative of the law, Monsieur Severe — a role performed *en
travesti* (that is, cross-dressed) by the Empire's experienced and expert
premier mime, Malvina Cavallazzi ("the handsome hero of Empire ballets," as H. G. Hibbert recalled) — who sternly forbids further dancing of

27. Empire Theatre of Varieties. Program, 30 July 1894.
Harvard Theatre Collection, Houghton Library.

the kind.[100] When he leaves, "La Frolique" heedlessly resumes her "wild and effective little dance," but the defender of public morals returns and summarily leads her off to jail. Brought before the judge the next morning, "La Frolique" recognizes him as one of her ardent admirers and begs to demonstrate before the court "how wholly innocent" her performance was. She repeats her dance; it proves contagious, and everyone from judge to usher follows in her steps as the curtain descends "on a scene of wild revelry."[101]

Decidedly unsympathetic to its devil-may-care exuberance, Mrs. Chant found *La Frolique* flagrantly indecent, mounted, as in the case of *The Girl I Left behind Me*, "for the express purpose of displaying the bodies of women to the utmost extent" and making no attempt to hide what "common sense & common decency requires should be hidden." One dancer — presumably the prima ballerina — wore skirts so short that her legs were entirely exposed, and Mrs. Chant had to use her opera glasses to discover whether the dancer wore tights, so close to flesh were their color. When the dancer pirouetted, her skirts "flew right up to her head," Mrs. Chant complained, "& left the rest of the body with the waist exposed except for a very slight white gauze between the limbs." A dance sequence occurred in which a line of girls modestly dressed as "Puritan maidens" is flanked by a line of monks (also girls), who then throw off their habits and appear as cavaliers "with tights up to the waist," a sequence Mrs. Chant considered "extremely objectionable." Among them was a central dancer in flesh-colored tights and a light, gauzy dress; when she arrived at the front of the stage, it seemed as if "the body of a naked woman were simply disguised with a film of lace."

As if this were not bad enough, another dancer dressed all in black lace and black tights, positioned face-to-face with the man before whom she was dancing, gathered up her costume, stretched up her leg, and kicked him on the crown of his head. No one, Mrs. Chant thought, could question whether this was indecent or not. Mentally enlisting the rest of the audience in the cause of common decency, Mrs. Chant thought that they "took these peculiarly objectionable parts very quietly," throwing themselves much more enthusiastically into the parts of the program that were "above reproach."

At the conclusion of the second ballet, all that remained on the program were some songs performed by Charles Tilbury, to which Mrs. Chant paid little if any notice, her attention being focused on the "large-scale exodus" from the theatre as the music of the national anthem rose from the orchestra pit below. She may well have had the presence of mind to station herself somewhere near the grand staircase, from which point she would have been able to watch the remarkable parade of richly dressed, alluringly hatted, beautifully coiffed, highly painted young women as they made their way down the steps of the grand staircase and out of the Empire into the street below. Some, perhaps many, had been successful in finding "gentlemen" to escort them out, among them the clientele that Grant Richards remembered were likely to have put in an appearance: "the returned tea-planter, the soldier home on leave, the seasoned undergraduate from Oxford or Cambridge, the racing man, the voluptuary and the man who without being a sensualist still every now and then was glad of the opportunity of temptation." They would have already negotiated a bargain with an approachable lady, the usual fee,

Richards said, being "a fiver" — but not before the lady in question, with perfect sangfroid, had satisfied herself as to the qualifications "both in finance and behaviour" of the man who was attempting connection with her. Many of these ladies had "charming and artistic residences" (as Richards admittedly knew from experience), and some had maids and even butlers.[102]

At this point Mrs. Chant might well have speculated, perhaps with some feelings of anxiety and concern, where a young woman who had not succeeded in connecting with a man might go. Since she knew neither the territory nor the custom, she would not have been aware of the choices available to a still-unescorted woman as the Empire closed its doors. Often the woman would move on to the Continental in Lower Regent Street or, if she were of a somewhat lower class, to the Globe in Coventry Street, a supper restaurant. Other, less advantageous or convenient destinations were within reach as well. As for the male habitués, they could be found at the Crown in Charing Cross Road, where Selwyn Image, a member of the "intellegentzia" (and later Slade Professor of Art at Oxford, a successor of John Ruskin), discoursed in learned terms about the ballet and where Arthur Symons, inveterate denizen of and commentator on bohemian life, would also turn up at the bar "within a few minutes of the closing of the Empire and the Alhambra."[103] Residing well outside that circle of familiarity, and being female as well, Mrs. Chant might not have known that even the finish of the evening had its well-established expectations. In one instance, the Blue Posts in the lower Haymarket, Edmund Yates recalled, was an ordinary public house, but no one looked on it that way, since for so many it was "the regular place of adjournment on the closing of the theatres and the dancing-halls." There, every night at midnight, "the passage from the outside door, the large space in front of the bar, the stairs leading to the supper rooms, the upper rooms themselves, were closely packed by a dense mass of men and women."[104]

And yet what Mrs. Chant would most certainly have known, and to some extent but not entirely have understood, was the extraordinary character of her experience in the five-shilling lounge of the Empire Theatre of Varieties on the evening of 30 July (and on the succeeding four evenings of her return visits). All the more shocking for its irony, it was an experience that had much to do with the efforts of an extensive cohort of young, unaccompanied women, under the pressure of intense competition, to imitate the behavior of respectable middle-class, or perhaps even upper-class, women while yet creating sufficient ambiguity in the posture to invite a certain mildly aggressive behavior on the part of men who might become their customers.

## THE GIRL OF THE PERIOD

The trend toward such borderline licentiousness had been evident for some time, according to some observers. The old-fashioned ideal of womanhood, the "fair young English girl," a girl who could be "trusted alone if need be, because of the innate purity and dignity of her nature," was being swiftly supplanted by "the girl of the period," Eliza Lynn Linton had warned the readers of the *Saturday Review* in the 1860s in a frequently reprinted essay of that title. The new pattern was exemplified by a girl who "dyes her hair and paints her face," whose "sole idea of life is fun," whose "sole aim is unbounded luxury," and whose "dress is the chief object of such thought and intellect as she possesses," Mrs. Linton explained. Living entirely to please herself, she takes it as her main task to outdo her neighbors in "extravagance of fashion," in which nothing is too extraordinary or exaggerated for "her vitiated taste." The horrifying result is that in pursuing such excesses she imitates the *"demi-monde"* in "its frantic efforts to excite attention" and then wonders when men sometimes mistake her for her prototype. Unaware of the ambiguous image she creates, she emulates the "queens of the *demi-monde* . . . gorgeously attired and sumptuously appointed," observes them "flattered, fêted, and courted with a certain disdainful admiration," and, perceiving only the admiration, fails to reflect on what a price these women have given for such advantages and "what fearful moral penalties they pay for their sensuous pleasures." If such women must be allowed to exist, Mrs. Linton asserts, let them be the genuine thing. Let us have "the queens of St John's Wood in their unblushing honesty rather than their imitators and make-believes in Bayswater and Belgravia." For, finally, it cannot be too clearly explained to the contemporary English girl that "the net result of her present manner of life is to assimilate her as nearly as possible to a class of women whom we must not call by their proper — or improper — name."[105]

The fascinating thing about the Empire was that both types of "girls" of the period were to be found in its second-tier promenade, and distinguishing between them was a supremely difficult task because the types were so nearly embodied in the same woman, through a kind of reciprocal reflection. The opportunities available to both women and men for quasi-intimate contact with unknown but attractive persons, and the possibility meanwhile of maintaining a certain privileged or protective anonymity, combined to make up a large part of the attraction of the Empire, every bit as enticing as its spectacular onstage performances. Such opportunities were never more clearly demonstrated than at the moment when the Empire was closing for the evening and the parade of the "*hetirae*" began, in a mirror-image transition that would reconnect the fantasies of anonymous life in the Empire with the wider world of Leicester Square and beyond. As the French historian Georges Bourdon explained in his contemporary book on the English theatres, when the curtain fell on the grand finale it marked no cessation, it caused no dissonance, for the spectacle was one that occurred on both sides of the footlights. Even as the audience's gaze followed the dancers performing before their palaces of painted canvas, the performers onstage could see before them "a parterre full of low-necked dresses in a palace of genuine gold."[106] The reciprocity of the experience, then, was one of its most distinctive and compelling features, and it obtained in the Empire's five-shilling lounge just as surely as on a larger scale in the theatre overall. For a woman in the Empire promenade who was also a prostitute, sizing up a potential client while that client himself was looking her over made her simultaneously a commodity and a seller,[107] an audience member and a performer, even while she took care to stay within the bounds of apparent respectability. Refraining from overt solicitation, she could still employ a variety of subtle means to engage the "gentleman" in conversation, letting him understand that she might be available and encouraging an offer for a connection that, if agreed upon, would realize its consummation outside the theatre, carrying its fantastic premise beyond the boundaries of its origin into the world at large.

By the late summer and early autumn of 1894, during which time Mrs. Chant had found reason to visit the Empire no fewer than five separate times, she would have seen and observed enough to understand and appreciate the fuller meaning in such deceptively straightforward descriptive phrases attributed to the Empire as "the world's premier theatre of varieties." She would have continued to find the same unchecked indecency, as she judged it, in the costumes of the dancers in the long-running Empire ballets. She would have come to share an understanding of what was universally known, without having to ask, by the anonymous gentlemen who frequented the five-shilling lounge: if they wanted the adventure of transgressive encounters with women who embodied a potent fantasy of erotically charged middle-class propriety and respectability, the Empire Theatre of Varieties, and most particularly its second-tier promenade, was the place, above all others, to go. As the day of the October meeting of the Theatres and Music Halls Committee drew closer, she would also have known, without question, what she would do with her newfound knowledge.

# 2 : The Licensing Committee Meets

**THE THEATRES AND MUSIC HALLS COMMITTEE**
On Wednesday morning, 10 October 1894, the Theatres and Music Halls
Committee of the London County Council convened in its usual quarters
in Spring Gardens, Charing Cross. It had a very full agenda, consisting of
the many applications for new license or renewal of license from theatres,
music halls, and theatres of variety submitted to it in the previous weeks.
Aware of the great publicity that had surfaced concerning the challenge to
the license of the Empire Theatre of Varieties by Laura Ormiston Chant
and her colleagues in the National Vigilance Association, a large, eager
crowd of journalists, partisans on either side, and curiosity seekers were
present. Impatient though all these people were, they would have to bide
their time until the application from the Empire, number 44, came up in its
turn. Meanwhile, they could also anticipate the potentially sensational
consideration of the application from the Palace Theatre of Varieties,
where, it was well known, simulated nudity could be gazed upon nightly
during the succession of tableaux vivants.

For George Edwardes there would be no auditions, no rehearsals, no
business, routine or urgent, to be conducted this day at one or another of
his several enterprises in or near Leicester Square; nor would opportunity
free him for even part of an afternoon at the races. Like all the others present in Spring Gardens, he and his solicitors would be forced to sit quietly,
but perhaps sharing feelings of guarded confidence, while the lengthy
hearings progressed. Also present and waiting patiently was a larger, perhaps even more confident group made up of Mrs. Chant and the several
colleagues who accompanied her on this October morning, a group not
limited to the five coauthors of the letters of complaint sent the previous
month to the committee. All were members of the NVA, a zealous
reformist organization and one of the most high-profile and active of various late-Victorian social purity organizations. The NVA had been
founded in 1885 to help enforce the Criminal Law Amendment Act passed

that same year.[1] Involving itself in the censorship of alleged pornography and in other aspects of indecency in public life, the NVA had emerged in the wake of W. T. Stead's scandalous, inflammatory revelations about the white slave trade in "The Maiden Tribute of Modern Babylon," an exposé published in Stead's own *Pall Mall Gazette* in July 1885.[2] It may have been the first time Mrs. Chant had attended a meeting of the licensing committee, but, as events would show, she and her NVA colleagues had taken care to make themselves knowledgeable about the legal aspects and ramifications of the complaint they would lodge.

The Theatres Committee, one of the hardest working of London County Council committees, had its work cut out for it. The number of music halls had increased steadily over the century to a peak of popularity around 1870, after which time, as populations shifted and more stringent restrictions came into force, they declined somewhat. Still, they numbered in the dozens in the 1890s, continuing to exhibit an even more remarkable mélange of audiences (heterogeneous or not so, depending on the locale), a reassuringly predictable yet varied range of offerings, and impressive powers of attraction. Meanwhile, the traditional theatre, the number of whose venues drew equal with the combined numbers of music halls, pleasure gardens, and other sites of popular entertainment around 1890, was maintaining and even increasing its perennial appeal and becoming more genteel in the process, winning back the more polite, affluent audience that had abandoned playgoing years before.[3] Behind this phenomenon of extraordinary growth and vitality lay a regulatory body that usually remained well out of sight, but whose influence on the character of popular entertainment in London was becoming increasingly intrusive and formative. The Theatres and Music Halls Committee was slightly over five years old in the autumn of 1894, having been appointed in March 1889 and given responsibility for all matters, including safety precautions, affecting the licensing of theatres, music halls, and premises used for music and dancing.[4] Licenses were required to be renewed annually. In order for a music hall to gain the committee's recommendation for renewal of license, prior inspection and certification by the council architect's department had to occur, along with a structural inspection by the Department of the Chief Engineer.[5]

Supporting the deliberations and (usually) endorsing the decisions of the Theatres Committee was the authority of the county council itself, wielded by an elective body controlled from the beginning by the London

Progressives, councillors representing Gladstonian, New Liberal, Fabian, and trade-union interests. The radical program of social reform quickly espoused by the Progressives brought many socialists into their camp, forging a successful alliance between middle class and working class and between liberals, radicals, and socialists.[6] The council membership thus stood collectively, on balance, for municipal and social reform, combining Conservative zeal with Nonconformist, teetotal, and antiprostitution forces represented by members who in some cases also belonged to the National Vigilance Association.[7]

Only now making official acquaintance with the Theatres Committee, Mrs. Chant and her colleagues would undoubtedly have recognized some familiar faces among its members. Just as surely, they would have understood the larger context in which their complaint would be construed. Any concern with indecency on the Empire stage and immorality rife in its second-tier promenade would be regarded by the licensing authorities as falling within a broader basis for governmental oversight, namely, the necessity of regulating the consumption of alcoholic drink on public premises. Social purity groups took the view that inebriety and immorality were the two countenances of a Janus-like evil, locked in morbid embrace. Governmental authorities took a similar view, ever more prevalently as the century moved on, but in practice tended to focus on the regulation of alcohol consumption itself as an indirect way of addressing the chronic problem of social immorality. Thus preoccupied, the Theatres and Music Halls Committee, along with the county council itself, ran headlong into an inevitable contingency: like so much other legislation, the licensing and regulating of premises where intoxicating drink could be purchased illustrated the long-lived irony that whatever was to be regulated had first to be defined — and, thereby, acknowledged to exist. Back in the time of King George II, an act requiring the licensing of any house, room, garden, or other place kept for dancing, music, or other public entertainment of like kind within the cities of London and Westminster had become law.[8] Laws enacted when Britain's population was a mere six million remained the only licensing authority in force, John Hollingshead wryly observed, when by the late nineteenth century the population had reached "forty millions and more of people."[9] That authority, however, had become increasingly vigilant and efficacious as the age of Victoria advanced. Before midcentury the Theatres Act of 1843 had forced tavern owners to convert their establishments to places of regulatable entertainment or to end entertainment altogether, thus inadvertently fostering the circumstances under which music halls, with their plentiful supply of "spirituous liquors" (as legal terminology would label them), began to develop.[10] The British love of music and song had been, from the beginning, a critical element in the mix. Public houses had begun offering songs and similar entertainment, first on the premises, and soon in contiguous premises which were then swiftly brought under licensing restriction in order to regulate and control them. Since the regulation of these adjunctive premises where songs were sung (eventually by professionals who had been amateurs earlier) had the effect of licensing these entertainments, they thenceforth developed under the constant eye of the law; and the law was consequently made ever more expansive and explicit in order to accomplish its regulatory goal.

By the late years of the century, the power of granting licenses having been transferred from the justices to the newly created London County Council, the council in its turn, broadening its own brief, set regulations that required a license on every place kept open for performances of "public music, or for public music and dancing, or other public entertainment of the like kind, or for the public performance of stage plays in premises outside the jurisdiction of the Lord Chamberlain." The licenses granted annually, in October, were based on applications that had to conform to regulations regarding theatres and other places of entertainment newly approved by the council on 9 February 1892. The terms of compliance, if not actually onerous, were precise. The applicant was required to give notice of intent two months before the commencement of the licensing session by posting a notice in a prescribed form on an outer door or other conspicuous part of the premises to be licensed, and also on the outer door of the police station of the parish; copies of the notice were required to be served on prescribed authorities of the parish or district.[11]

Well acquainted with all these procedures, George Edwardes was a seasoned manager whose experience with the council and the Theatres Committee went back to their very formation. Hardly ignorant of the full range of sources of income from his gilt-edged capital investment in Leicester Square, and quite used to the accusation that it was the sale of alcohol that defined the margin there between profit and loss, Edwardes seems to have taken in stride the intermittent aggressive actions against his theatre by members of the National Vigilance Association, the Social Purity Alliance, and other such organizations, sometimes acting officially or semi-officially or, as was the case in October 1894, acting ostensibly as individuals. Nor was he unfamiliar with complaints about the character of his audience, especially that segment of it that frequented the five-shilling promenade.

Such objections had been voiced before, notably by Frederick N. Charrington, London County Council member for Mile End and an heir of the Charrington brewery family, who had become a teetotaler and a crusader for purity in public life. Charrington's proactive stance had become almost a benchmark for measuring the degree of hostility on the part of municipal authorities toward the music hall enterprise. Strikingly handsome, with the mien of a polished man of the world, Charrington had undergone a religious conversion, renounced his inheritance, and pursued a career as an inner-city missionary. In 1876, in a tent, Charrington founded the Tower Hamlets Association and in 1886 opened the five-thousand-seat Great Assembly Hall, the largest prayer hall in Europe. His primary target being drink, he conveyed the water for adult baptism in beer barrels. In 1880 he began his first efforts toward the cause of purity in the music halls, focusing on Lusby's in the East End, only a hundred yards from his mission and around the corner from the brothels in Cleveland Street. The discovery that Lusby's was frequented by prostitutes propelled Charrington on a five-year crusade. Failing to close down Lusby's by having its license revoked, he distributed leaflets at the door, was beaten, "pelted with flour and excrement," and then legally restrained from describing the entertainment there as "obscene." Foiled but undaunted, he carried the battle on to the music halls of the West End, sparing no efforts to reform the Empire, the Aquarium, and other places of entertainment to make them acceptable for ordinary men and women.[12]

The nature of Charrington's complaints was already well known when, at a licensing session of the Theatres and Music Halls Committee on 1 October 1890 at which an extensive inquiry into prostitution had occurred, Charrington had voiced his opposition to the Empire relicensing in no uncertain terms. The evidence he had gathered convinced him, he asserted, that not only was the Empire a resort of prostitutes, but also its character in that respect was particularly dangerous "to young men of the better class." Students from Oxford and Cambridge could be found there (he did not mention cadets from Sandhurst, who also made up part of the weekend audience), confronting prostitution and vice in their most attractive aspects, in the persons of women in evening dress who instead of going to the cheaper seats frequented the best parts of the house. Anticipating Mrs.

Chant's complaint, he pronounced the dresses in the ballet to be "very indecent indeed." Although the presence of prostitutes in the Empire promenade was no news to most people, William Barclay, Charrington's prime witness before the committee, had professed to be shocked by those he saw. Charrington had sent Barclay to the Empire on 1 August, where he found "a great number of prostitutes walking about in twos promenading round from one end to the other — Some were sitting down."[13]

At that point, speaking in his own defense, Edwardes had said he did not — "not knowingly" — admit prostitutes to the Empire. Indeed, he refused admission to ten or twelve a night. "If we know a woman to be a prostitute and a notorious character she is not admitted," he insisted; "of course if we do not know them we cannot help admitting them." Repeatedly asked if he admitted prostitutes, Edwardes repeatedly answered, "Not knowingly." The maintenance of decorum was evidently a vital factor in such matters. Edward Birch, inspector of C Division Police, questioned on the same subject, admitted "that women — reputed prostitutes — do go into the Empire; but to say that they are prostitutes I could not." Another member of the committee, Councillor Davies, interjected that on a Saturday night he and his party "found the place was decently conducted"; there were prostitutes there, of course (they could be identified "by their manner"), but they "behaved themselves decently." The chair of the committee then brought the hearing to a close, announcing that "the Committee are agreed to recommend relicensing to the Council."[14]

And so, despite Charrington's opposition to the relicensing of the Empire on the double grounds of indecency of stage costume and harboring of prostitutes, the license had been granted, and was granted again in each year up to 1894 with no limits or conditions placed upon it. Edwardes would thus have brought to his attendance at this year's committee sessions a confident awareness that such complaints as Charrington's had consistently come to nothing and that the Empire license had invariably been granted — notwithstanding the presence on the licensing committee of a powerful and disgruntled hostile minority. In Edwardes's experience, it would thus have seemed that the membership of the Theatres and Music Halls Committee included persons who were predictable minor irritants, but the end result was that he could do as he pleased, so long as he maintained an aura of respectability in the promenade (as elsewhere in the house) and kept to certain norms, risqué though they were in the view of some, in the costumes of his dancers and the posed figures in the living pictures.

Edwardes's experience with the committee would likewise have made him familiar with the specifics of its policies and practices of supervision over the previous several years, emphasizing safety and public well-being. He would nonetheless have been aware that, from the beginning, the Progressives had begun to subject the halls to an intense moral scrutiny bent on rooting out impropriety, doing away with the ill effects of alcohol and liberating the public at large from "the pernicious influence of lascivious and vulgar performances."[15] Sir Thomas George Fardell, MP and council member for South Paddington, an advocate of municipal respectability who had been instrumental in bringing down the old Metropolitan Board of Works, had served as Theatres Committee chair before giving way to Richard Roberts, councillor for South Islington, whose politics were less perspicuous to the ordinary observer. Committee members included representatives of all political parties, conservatives and liberals alike, on the council itself (though charges of bias were brought at least once); but some, such as G. W. E. Russell, chair of the Churchmen's Liberation League and a member of the National Vigilance Association, and such other NVA members as George Lidgett and John McDougall, Lidgett's son-in-law, member for Poplar, known in some quarters as "Muck-Dougall," later to be elevated to the august post of chair of the county council, were well known for their opposition to vice, as was the noted reformer Spencer Charrington, Frederick Charrington's brother.[16] Moreover, although no women were allowed membership on the county council for some years after its creation, certain reformist women loomed large in the background. One such person was Lidgett's sister Mary Bunting, wife of Percy Bunting, one of the most powerful Methodists in the country, treasurer of Hugh Price Hughes's West London Mission (Methodist), chair of the executive of the NVA, and editor of the *Contemporary Review*.[17] Bunting's sister, Mrs. Sheldon Amos, a leading Christian feminist active in the NVA, the British Women's Temperance Association, and other organizations of similar character, was joining Mrs. Ormiston Chant and her colleagues, on that October morning, in opposing the Empire license. The impression any knowledgeable observer present at this session would have was that the NVA had mounted a formidable battery of opposition, despite the less-than-official character of their action.

Notwithstanding the apparent ease with which the Empire had obtained renewal of its license in the early 1890s, the Theatres and Music Halls Committee, along with the county council itself, could be seen in retrospect as maintaining a certain level of nervous irritability regarding Edwardes and his colleagues' extremely profitable investment on the north side of Leicester Square. The committee would surely hold in its collective memory a proposal to the council by Captain Verney, member for Brixton, that a committee be appointed to investigate the character of those music halls whose license was coming up for renewal the following autumn. At a council meeting on 2 April 1889, Verney had insisted on vigilant regulation of theatres and music halls. The single greatest expectation of the council by the people of London was, he had said, "for some improvement in the purity of public morality." Charrington had agreed, calling it "one of the burning questions of the day."[18] Evidently the council was moving in the direction of forming some agency to carry out close scrutiny in ways inconvenient for other bodies of the council. According to a report of Verney's motion in the *Vigilance Record* (the official organ of the National Vigilance Association) for April 1889, his scheme was the practical one of establishing an entity within the council "to whom all reports, anonymous or otherwise, concerning the character of the music-halls should come, and by whom all complaints should be investigated before licensing day comes round." The existence of such a body would give notice to all concerned that the council's licenses were not granted in a perfunctory manner and that the council was "fully determined to stamp out relentlessly all places which were centres of moral contagion." The authority of the council would thus be effectively used to "eliminate the poisonous canker of gross indecency and downright obscenity" that presently makes so many public resorts impossible for decent persons to attend.[19]

The issue of effective regulation turned on the seriousness of the two chronic problems of alcohol and prostitution and their perceived systemic connection; it was under the looming shadow of this allegedly insidious link that the committee and the council were becoming increasingly vigilant in the cause of stamping out moral contagion. As the committee and Edwardes himself were aware, there had been a history of complaint about the Empire over the previous five years, complaint whose dual themes were, unsurprisingly, prostitution and alcoholic drink. Moreover, as both Edwardes and the committee knew, there were long-standing laws against the harboring of prostitutes; the real question was the extent to which those laws might be enforced. Anyone in the business of serving intoxicating drink had to be well aware of the risks, and could discover the consequences of illegal practice by going no further than the *Licensed Victuallers' Official Annual*, the "Blue Book of the Trade." In the 1895 edition one could, for example, look up the generic term "bad characters" and find that, for the guidance of licensed victuallers, such characters "may be divided into thieves and prostitutes." Regarding the latter group, section 14 of the act of 1872 is quoted as stating: "If any licensed person knowingly permits his premises to be the *habitual* resort of or place of meeting of reputed prostitutes, whether the object of their so resorting or meeting is or is not prostitution, he shall, if he allow them to remain thereon longer than is necessary for the purpose of obtaining reasonable refreshment, be liable to a penalty not exceeding £10 for the first and £20 for the second and any subsequent offence, and the conviction may be recorded on the licence."

As her testimony would make plain, Mrs. Ormiston Chant and her colleagues had identified the exact legal term in which to couch their complaint about prostitutes in the five-shilling Empire promenade, for the act specifies that it is the *habitual* nature of the offense that must be shown: "It is not an offence to serve prostitutes," the act explained, "but it is an offence to allow them to 'habitually resort' to a house, or to make it a place of meeting, or to allow them to remain longer than is necessary for the consumption of reasonable refreshment. The onus of proving that prostitutes habitually resort to a house rests upon the informer, but the onus of proving that they remained no longer than necessary rests upon the defendant."[20]

Taking a step that in retrospect seemed almost inevitable, given its proactive frame of mind and reformist instincts, at a council meeting on 8 July 1890 the Theatres and Music Halls Committee formed a subcommittee for the purpose of inspection of the music halls and theatres that came under the licensing jurisdiction of the committee. Persistent in the cause of vigilant oversight, the committee proposed hiring paid inspectors. The newly formed Inspection Subcommittee was considered important enough to be chaired by T. G. Fardell, chair of the Theatres Committee itself. Contentious political differences arose at once. When the proposal for the new subcommittee was placed before the full council, at a crucial point in the council proceedings the member for Fulham, R. A. Germaine, moved an instruction to the committee to the effect that "the duties of the inspectors recommended shall be limited to matters of structure and of public safety, and shall not include supervision of the character of the entertainment." Germaine said he took the view that it was "no part of the duty of the Council to look after the morality of London." After G. W. E. Russell, vice-chair of the Theatres Committee, dissented from Germaine's view, Germaine's motion was decisively defeated by a vote of fifty-five to twenty-nine. The original question was then put, and the committee's proposal to appoint paid inspectors — whose duties would not be limited as Germaine had sought to limit them — was approved.[21]

A new era of official watchfulness had begun, and Edwardes and his managerial colleagues east and west were effectively put on notice that a higher level of careful propriety was to be demanded. At the first meeting of the Inspection Subcommittee on 19 July 1890, a list of twenty-three inspectors was approved and rigorous, detailed guidelines were established. Inspectors were to visit only such places of entertainment as the Theatres Committee might direct. They must always pay the usual admission price and never accept a complimentary ticket or free pass. A ticket should be taken for that part of the house from which the inspector would be best able to view the interior and the seating arrangements; during intervals he should visit other parts of the building to which the public has access. He should keep to the public parts of the house and under no circumstances visit the stage or any other part of the building where the public was not admitted; nor should he represent himself as being present on behalf of the county council or the Theatres Committee, nor assume any more right to interfere (as, for example, in the case of a fire or panic) than might belong to another member of the public. Within twenty-four hours of each visit he was required to submit a report in writing. A list of questions was drafted to which inspectors would include answers in their reports. Questions concerning the physical premises, proper exits, clear gangways, and hydrants and buckets for fire fighting were followed by two that were more open-ended: *"What was the character of the performance?"* and *"Had proper means been taken by the management to secure order and decorum among the audience?"*[22]

The history of the Inspection Subcommittee spins a patent tale of continued mistrust on the part of the Theatres Committee and its consequences for the proprietors of music halls. Edward Brutton, dispatched to the Empire, reported on 15 August 1890 on his inspection two days previous of its performances and audience activity, conscientiously filling in the questions on the standardized printed form. To question 8, *"What was the character of the performance?*" he replied: "The entertainment consisted of songs serio-comic & Ballads of a superior class. The juggling was good and the two Ballets could offend no one." As if he had been asked to note the point specifically, Brutton continued: "There were no indecent gestures of any kind and the whole entertainment was of a far better description than I have seen in any other music hall." Brutton's mandate was even more clearly implied in his reply to question 10, "*State any further matters you desire to bring to the notice of the Committee*": "There was a large attendance but the Hall was not crowded. There was a great preponderance of men. In the Dress Circle and upper Circle were a good number of Prostitutes (the numbers impossible to say with any accuracy). I saw nothing in their conduct to find fault with, and as far as I could see they never addressed any man unless first spoken to. I was at the Main Entrance between 9 and 10 pm and saw several Prostitutes come in but they all paid in the same way as the general Public."[23] Evidently, the women who frequented the circle areas of the Empire had learned the lesson of discretion inadvertently prescribed by Clarence Hamlyn in his *Manual of Theatrical Law* (1891): audiences, he observed, "have to recognise certain lines of conduct which are not well defined."[24]

There was clearly some worry about preferential treatment being given to women of the town; the larger question of indecent dress or behavior on the stage and off remained an open one, to be monitored at least every year in anticipation of applications for renewal of license. The issue of unofficial free access would prove one of chronic concern to the committee, as indicated in the instructions to M. Q. Holyoake, recorded in the Theatres Committee minutes of 27 June 1894, that "these premises be again inspected to see if women gain admittance to the entertainments without paying."[25] The inspectors' priorities were clear from the start, as the committee minutes for 31 July 1890 indicate: "the Inspectors should be instructed to devote their attention chiefly to the nature of the performance, and to the character and conduct of the audience, especially the female portion thereof, rather than to the structured condition and exits of the building; and to frame their reports for the committee accordingly."[26] As subsequent events would serve to underscore, the question of the physical safety of venues of entertainment was rapidly losing priority to the question of the proper behavior of their audiences.

The decisive defeat of Germaine's hands-off proposal and the adoption of a vigorous scheme of paid inspection had together established a low threshold of county council tolerance of aberrant music hall conduct. Despite Edwardes's apparent confidence in the outcome of his application, that increased level of intolerance ought not to have gone unnoticed by him and other interested parties. Nor should the increasing prominence of the National Vigilance Association in these adversary actions have been ignored or slighted. An event of the kind that gained no little press notice occurred in October 1890, when the NVA opposed the relicensing of the Royal Aquarium on grounds that pictorial posters advertising an acrobat and a snake charmer were "indecent and horrible." Recalling the event, H. G. Hibbert explained that the offending advertisement was simply an enlargement of the gymnast's photograph "in the attire accustomed of a gymnast," but the resulting public outrage whipped up by the "Central Vigilance Society for the Suppression of Vice" (another name for the National Vigilance Association) attained the scale, Hibbert thought, of an international crisis.[27] The committee recommended relicensing but required the Aquarium management to withdraw the offending posters (which had gone out of print anyway).[28] Again, in April 1893, the NVA went before the Bench of Licensing Magistrates to oppose relicensing the St. James's Restaurant, contiguous to St. James's Hall, on the grounds of "habitual contravention of the Licensing Act . . . in the grill and coffee rooms." (Already, the NVA had evidently realized that establishing the habitual nature of the offense was essential for adversarial success.) The NVA's opposition alleged that the restaurant was "a place of resort by women of notoriously bad character." The magistrates declined to rule on grounds of a technicality — the proper remedy was a summons, they explained — and, besides, there was no evidence that prostitutes, admittedly present in the restaurant, had infringed the statute.[29]

Once again the NVA had lost a skirmish, but its point had been made and noticed. Clearly enough, its target was the kind of superficially respectable activity described in Shaw Desmond's reminiscence *London Nights of Long Ago* as going on, on a Saturday night in January, in "a cozy little pub at the back of Leicester Square": "There are some rather fierce-looking females there, with very bright but very tired eyes, yet Solomon in all his glory was not arrayed like one of these, with their feathers and 'pinkings' done at the local undertaker's and with their highly laced in waists. When they drink, they do so apologetically, lifting their veils and lowering them again quickly. For Mrs. Grundy is still strong in Piccadilly."[30]

In this atmosphere of growing intolerance of licentious behavior the Theatres and Music Halls Committee had stepped up inspections. At the meeting on 4 July 1894 the subcommittee received the report of E. H. Richardson and called for the clerk to "have the premises again inspected to see if women of the town are admitted to the premises without payment."[31] Some members of the committee were evidently not willing to accept the findings of the official inspector. Some of the more zealous members of the subcommittee, concerned about the effects of the wide availability of alcoholic beverages at the Empire, decided to refer the matter to the Theatres Committee to consider, recommending that it report to the council on whether steps could be taken, and if so what steps, "to establish the principle that in future all licenses to music halls be granted on the condition that intoxicating drinks shall not be sold or consumed in the auditorium."[32] Counsel to the committee advised against attempts at such regulation as being beyond the authority of the council to enforce. The committee nevertheless concluded that each case could be considered on its own merits, and that if notable disorder was occurring the county council could address the matter by refusing to renew the license unless the consumption of drink be excluded from the auditorium.[33]

In reaching that conclusion, the committee was functioning in a way consistent with the dominant trend of the council overall. All music halls had a common feature, the entertainment being a combination of song and show with the opportunity for purchasing and imbibing alcoholic drink. From the very beginning, the council had set itself against this blend and by degrees would bring it to an end. No sooner had the council come into existence but it prohibited the sale of drink in five cases and restricted it in five others, the immediate aim being "to prevent alcoholic drinks from being served in the auditorium."[34] By the time the Empire licensing controversy had erupted, it had become unmistakably obvious that, in the collective mind of the county council as well as its Theatres and Music Halls Committee, the consumption of alcohol was inexorably linked with licentious behavior, both in the bars and the auditoriums themselves of London music halls. Even where the link was not specifically articulated, in the minds of many members of the council and of the committee itself licentious behavior was unquestionably associated, and in a causative way, with intemperance; and the reverse was equally true. And so to take aim against the wide availability of alcohol was in effect to target the immorality of prostitution.

That association emerges almost as a matter of course in the report of Inspector Richardson, who had been dispatched once again to the Empire a scant month before Mrs. Chant made her first visit there. For three nights running, 28–30 June, he watched, as his report of 2 July 1894 indicated. On the first night he saw no women enter free; on the second, he saw eight. On Saturday, 30 June, between 9:00 and 9:15 P.M. alone he saw five women enter without paying. "I then went in to the Grand Circle & there I counted 34 women promenading round some of whom I recognized as having entered three nights in succession (consecutive)[;] upstairs in a room where there is a Bar and waiters I saw 15 women sitting at tables and drinking some along with men[.] During the time I was in there I saw nine more women enter without payment & I leave any one to judge for themselves the class of women they were, and for what purpose they attended there night after night."[35] Still another inspector, Richard Stanley, evidently sent to confirm Richardson's alarming testimony, filed a report dated 7 July; against expectation, it gave the Empire a clean bill of health. Describing the character of the performance, Stanley assured the Inspection Subcommittee that "the whole of the entertainment," including ballets, variety performances, and a series of living pictures, "was entirely free of anything of an objectionable nature." He kept a close eye on the pay boxes on the box-stall and grand-circle levels and found that money was always paid. "I also kept the promenades well under observation & did not observe any soliciting whatever," he added.[36]

One may suspect that Edwardes had gotten wind of the Inspection Committee's mounting interest in the Empire and had clamped down on what was evidently a lenient though quite unacknowledged policy of allowing certain unaccompanied women to enter the five-shilling tier without payment. Evidently, increasing pressure was being put on Edwardes's establishment by the Theatres Committee; as late as the end of September, inspection was still going on, officially or otherwise. In a report dated 1 October, hardly more than a week before the licensing committee would begin its deliberations, Peter Newbould said that neither he nor his wife, who had accompanied him, found anything in the performances to "shock the feelings . . . and nothing at all objectionable in the 'Living Pictures'. The only thing any one would be likely to object to," Newbould added, "was such as to exhibit the beautiful form of Woman."[37]

Faced by a not inconsiderable group of persons, male and female, with stern, determined expressions seated in the Theatres Committee hearing rooms that October morning, Edwardes would presumably have been glad for the presence of more sympathetic onlookers as well. Along with partisan supporters of the movement for social purity — who very likely were looking for support from an important reformist segment of the committee — there were others resolutely opposed to interference with the art or entertainment exhibited on the Empire stage, whose voices would be raised to near-deafening levels of outrage in the controversy that would break out over the recommendations of the committee on this day. From nearly the beginning of their existence, the reputation of the council and its licensing committee had evidently been sufficiently controversial to produce strong reactions from prominent members of the artistic and professional communities, as in the prominent example of Selwyn Image. "This [is] the licensing renewal season," Image, an artist, sometime Slade Professor at the University of Oxford, and member of William Butler Yeats's bohemian Rhymers' Club,[38] reminded his friend Herbert Horne in a letter dated 5 October 1889. Reviewing the activities of the licensing committee, Image accused its members of "making bigger arses of themselves over the business, than ever did even the antient magistrates." They had refused licenses to the Aquarium and the Trocadero, and McDougall was making the rounds sniffing out nastiness; Image hoped he would "suffer in hell eternally, with his nose held over a privy."[39] Image's greater concern, he explained to his brother John, was that if the purity societies have their way with music halls now, "to-morrow they will go on to attack higher forms of art." The social purity movement, observed to be gaining everywhere, was "*essentially* opposed to the first principle upon which all art is based," he believed.[40] The prominence of the council's policies and practices was reflected, in October 1893, in Gilbert and Sullivan's new comic satire *Utopia Limited*, in which are introduced two "types of England's physical / And moral cleanliness," who work hand in hand toward the goal of complete social purity.[41]

Thick-skinned and indifferent to such barbs, the Theatres and Music Halls Committee filed in from its executive chambers to begin the day's business. Of the twenty-one members of the committee, those present this day were Sir J. Hutton, General Downes, Mr. George Russell, MP, and Messrs. Dickonson, Lidgett, McDougal, Leon, Beachcroft, Yates, Doubleday, Mercer, Ponsonby, Bull, Tarling, and Torr, along with the chair, Richard Roberts. Over a third were either members of the National Vigilance Association or sympathizers with that organization.[42] They appeared to take no great notice of the large representation of the general public in attendance.[43] Called to order by the chair, they began to take up various applications for licensing. Although the vast majority presented no difficulties or problems, committee members undoubtedly realized that, before the day was out, some extraordinary events were likely to occur, and likely to consume egregious amounts of their time. Yet the fact remained that, even if the formidable orator and champion of social purity Mrs. Chant and her colleagues had not given notice of their intent to oppose renewal of the Empire license, the committee knew from experience that at least some of its members would be inclined to discuss the matter of the license with care.

### TABLEAUX VIVANTS AT THE PALACE

In proceeding with its business on this Wednesday morning, before coming to agenda item 44, the application for the Empire, the Theatres and Music Halls Committee turned to a partly parallel case, item 42. This was the application by Thomas Ernest Polden for a renewal of license for the Palace Theatre of Varieties, a short walk from the Empire in Cambridge Circus, at the junction of Shaftesbury Avenue and Charing Cross Road. One of the most beautiful venues for entertainment ever built in London, having opened as the Royal English Opera House early in 1891, Richard D'Oyly Carte's proposed home for high-toned English opera had languished after Sullivan's *Ivanhoe* closed there in July of that year. Purchased by Augustus Harris in December 1892, the theatre was transformed into a music hall, the ancient but still durable Charles Morton at its helm, and given a name more appropriate to the new enterprise.[44] The Palace attracted a glittering upscale clientele, but within a year it was the subject of some controversy surrounding alleged indecency, even nudity, in the tableaux vivants that Harris, over Morton's misgivings, had introduced.

The National Vigilance Association had been quick to inspect the new genre of "living pictures." Pronouncing it a novelty "of a very undesirable character," the *Vigilance Record* defined the form: "The pictures are represented by living persons, who pose in certain attitudes, giving an artistic turn to this ingenious method of entertaining the public." Artistic though they may have been, some of the pictures were "decidedly indecent and calculated to demoralise not only those who take part in the performance, but also those who witness it." Having denounced them in a sermon, the Reverend W. Carlile, pastor at St. Mary-at-Hill, Eastcheap, was challenged to go to see them for himself. Although he found most unobjectionable, five were "a shameful outrage and scandal to the modesty of any good woman." His view hearkened back to the attitude expressed more than three decades before by the reviewer of tableaux at the Cafe du Globe for the *Peeping Tom*: "It is impossible," the Reverend Carlile concluded, "for women, thus exhibited with the merest vestige of clothing, to retain their simplicity and modesty."[45] William Alexander Coote, the redoubtable secretary of the NVA, had a term of description more elegant, perhaps, but one not untroubled by ambiguity: he pronounced the Palace tableaux "the ideal form of indecency."[46]

The Inspection Subcommittee had been quick to respond to the arrival in London, late in 1893, of Eduard Kilanyi and his troupe, who opened their rapidly acclaimed series of tableaux vivants at the Palace in November of that year.[47] Hot on the heels of this attractive novelty, on 25 November 1893 Maltus Q. Holyoake inspected the Palace Theatre of Varieties and on 26 November submitted his report. He had been directed specifically to observe the tableaux vivants and so took a five-shilling orchestra stall. His attention, he explained, "was chiefly directed to the entertainment, in which I did not see anything deserving serious objection." The tableaux vivants were, however, "a new departure":

> Some of them are very clever representations of pictures, and several are of a classical nature, represented by, apparently semi-nude, or nearly nude women. The last one, 'Aphrodite,' was apparently quite nude, except for a scarf over the loins. I say, *apparently*, because in every case, I observed that the body, arms and bosom, were completely clothed in very delicate close fitting fleshings, which when a warm light was thrown on them, appeared like nature. The tableaux appeared as though in a frame. They were certainly very beautiful, and the audience seemed to approve of them, and applauded much. They were evidently not regarded as indecent, but as skilful and artistic living representations of well-known paintings and sculptures.[48]

In pointing to the presence of fleshings, Holyoake had called attention to an essential element of costume in use for decades. In 1846 the *Art Union* had explained, of ostensibly nude tableaux vivants, that the persons engaged in imitating works of fine art "are not nude, but wear a dress fitting the person nearly as closely as the skin itself" (fig. 28).[49] Identifying

28. *"Costume de Salammbô, porté par Mme Gorschakoff, aux Tuileries."* Pierre de Lano,
Les Bals travestis et les tableaux vivants sous le second empire. *Paris: H. Simonis
Empis, 1893. Plate betw. 50–51. 7743dd21. By permission of the British Library.*

himself as a journalist and bringing to bear both a sophisticated knowledge of his subject and an evident talent for amplification, Holyoake went on to comment on the aesthetic and moral implications of what he had seen. "Some people, however," he said, "would strongly object to such public and complete display of the female form, by living women. There is much to be said on both sides of the question. It is a matter of difficulty to fix the exact point where propriety ends, and impropriety begins."[50]

Holyoake was sent back to the Palace at various times, including 9 August 1894; in his report dated the next day he recorded looking at the Palace's fourth series of tableaux vivants and again indulged his penchant for descriptive detail. "The Moorish Bath," he said, was "the most daring of the undraped representations — the prominent figure being an apparently entirely nude woman (though encased I believe in delicate pink fleshings) with a slight transparent gauze thrown across the lower portion of the body. The figures are so still and artistically arranged that unless one is very close, it is difficult to tell that they are not merely pictures. The audience consisting largely of ladies" — presumably in the stalls; in his first report Holyoake described a vantage point from that part of the house — "seemed to see nothing objectionable in the pictures and they were vigourously applauded."[51]

And so, on the same day that the Empire license came up for renewal before the Theatres Committee, the question of the doubtful acceptability of tableaux vivants at the Palace was raised in the context of its management's application for renewal of license. The committee had received letters of objection to the Palace relicensing and faced opposition also from the National Vigilance Association, represented at the committee meeting, though again unofficially, by W. A. Coote, who by 1894 had been secretary of the NVA for nearly ten years. A carefully orchestrated double challenge to music hall entertainment was evidently under way.

Claiming he was acting merely as a private citizen, Coote explained that he had been to the Palace to view the new entertainments. Scandalized by what he had seen, Coote described its offensiveness in great detail. In "Ariadne" there was represented "a naked woman lying on the back of a lion. There were four or five wrinkles on the lower part of the body distinguishing it from an ordinary picture. The left leg was placed under the lower part of the right, to produce the wrinkles. She was lying in such a position that had it not been for the tights gross indecency would have resulted." "Naiad" constituted in his view a parallel case, in which "a naked woman" was represented. Coote hastened to qualify the term: "I believe tights were worn, but it was a matter of inference and faith rather than actual knowledge." "A thin piece of gauze was thrown slantingly across the person," he added, "but not sufficient for its purpose."[52] As for "The Polar Star," it represented "a perfectly nude female — at least," he interjected, "it appeared to me to be perfectly nude — standing on a pedestal. Her arms were extended above the head, holding an electric lamp."[53] Inadequate or not, the sash draped across the midsection was evidently a crucial factor.

Morton, manager of the Palace, known (inaccurately) as the "father of the halls" for his successful transformation of the Canterbury Arms tavern into the Canterbury Hall in 1852 and for his construction of the first purpose-built music hall, the Oxford, in the West End in 1861, was then called.[54] He acknowledged that the color of the tights worn was "flesh colour, or as near flesh colour as possible."[55] In a symposium published in the *New Review* a month after the October licensing session, Morton claimed to be unable to see indecency in some of the nude or seminude pictures at the Palace. People who come to see them, he said, look on them "from the purely pictorial point of view" and are more taken by "the ingenuity of the effects" than by "the fact that they are looking upon young women wearing little more than fleshings, with, in some cases, plaster moulds over the breasts."[56]

Morton's point of view was that of the theatrical entrepreneur, whose business it was to create a satisfying illusion of reality through the most effective technical means available. Coote's, in contrast, was that of a hostile member of the music hall audience who felt preyed upon by an illusion he knew was not real and so could not be objected to on technical grounds, and who was nevertheless convinced he was being asked to believe in that illusion as a reality — one that by its very nature was sexually teasing and arousing and therefore offensive in a public place. The celebrated dramatist A. W. Pinero enjoyed a more sophisticated understanding of the phenomenon, but his conclusion was the same. The "intrinsic attraction" of living pictures was "vivid impersonation," Pinero argued, and, therefore, when the spectator "sees a woman clad only in a garment representing the bare skin, he knows that he is looking upon a woman who is impersonating a naked woman, and to impersonate a naked woman upon the stage is obviously an indecency." Bernard Shaw, who often found himself in conflict with Pinero's ideas, took another point of view in this instance too. Having finally been drawn to the Palace in April 1895, by an address of Coote's to the Church and Stage Guild, to see the living pictures for himself, Shaw found it "only too obvious to a practised art critic's eye that what was presented as flesh was really spun silk." The illusion produced on the ordinary music hall audience was nevertheless "that of the undraped human figure, exquisitely clean, graceful, and, in striking contrast to many of the completely draped and elaborately dressed ladies who were looking at them, perfectly modest." The living pictures, he concluded, were "not only works of art: they are excellent practical sermons."[57]

Whether Shaw's defense of the Palace tableaux smacked of the disingenuous or not, it remains the case that the spectacle of the female body, presented as the object of the male gaze, had consistently, over long years, involved a measure of eroticism, together with a less well acknowledged sense of appropriation and possession of the gazed-upon object. In the historical context of the contentious hearings progressing on this October day, the dancer, no less than the pose plastique or tableau vivant, exemplifies the point. The fictional première danseuse, Clara, in John Mills's midcentury novel *D'Horsay, or The Follies of the Day,* "one of those wasp-waisted, captivating nymphs who catch hearts in abundance with their heels, and open the purse-strings of their adorers with the yawning lift of a floodgate," illustrates the fascination of the type. Mills described the view of the ballet dancer available from the "omnibus box," a double box on either side of the proscenium arch at Her Majesty's Theatre, from which she drew "innumerable glasses to a common centre, decked in flowers and a confusion of folds of gauze scarcely secreting that particular part of the leg whereon the fastening of the stocking is generally clasped, and smiling and making others smile to see her *pirouette* as the star of the *ballet.*"[58] A later fictional dancer, Selene Eden, a product of the English fin de siècle poet John Davidson's perfervid imagination, revealed the secret of how she engaged "the aching senses of the throng." Once the veiled leader of a troupe of dancing girls "nude as they dared be," she now danced solo and "unveiled." In constant whirling movement before a crowd of lustful men, she sees their eyes fixed on her "like glowing coal." Blowing them a kiss as the limelight vanishes into darkness, she dances on and on as the lights come up again, flinging her feet above her head as, "wilder, fleeter, higher bound," she is bathed in multicolored light. All the while, her face remains "pure as unsunned chastity, / Even in the whirling triple pace." That, she explains, is her "conquering mystery."[59] The erotic potential of the dancer, like that of the posing woman, was clear enough, and yet the situation with respect to the limits of propriety remained, as Davidson's poem illustrates, ultimately ambiguous, or even controversial. As inspector M. Q. Holyoake observed, "the borderline which divides the legitimate from the objectionable is not well-defined."[60]

Pressed by Councillor Beachcroft to explain why he withdrew the tableau entitled "The Moorish Bath," Morton acknowledged that he did so "partly owing to a letter from Lady Henry Somerset" protesting its indecency. The directors saw no advantage to keeping it on "if there was the smallest objection to it." Urged by Councillor Russell to give "an understanding that nude pictures shall not be produced in the future," the solicitor C. F. Gill, who along with his colleague Arnold Statham was representing the Palace management and who would also represent the Empire later that day, demurred, explaining that this might "lead to the withdrawal of some of the most beautiful pictures that ever existed." Gill asserted the willingness of the Palace management to "withdraw at any time any particular picture objected to by the Council." Declining to descend to such detail and voting seven to one against Gill's proposal, the licensing committee declared the case a cautionary one, recommending to the council "that a license for music and dancing be granted, on the undertaking that the management will exercise greater caution in the future, and on the same condition as last year, to be endorsed on the license, namely, that there shall be no promenade, and that the applicant will not allow intoxicating drinks to be sold in the auditorium."[61]

The decision provided a clear foretaste of things to come. Issues regarding the inappropriate exhibition of the female body and the effect such exposure has both on the woman who thus reveals herself and on the witnessing audience would become part of a widening circle of contextual significance as the controversy over the Empire license moved toward its boiling point.

### THE EMPIRE APPLICATION

The committee shortly turned to George Edwardes's application, dated 28 July 1894, "for a renewal of a license for music and dancing for the Empire Theatre of Varieties, 5 and 6, Leicester-square, 41, 42, 43 and 44, Lisle-street, and 6 and 7, Leicester-street."[62]

As in the case, some minutes earlier, of the Palace controversy, no sense of a mere routine proceeding could possibly have obtained. A little over two weeks previous, the committee had been given notice by a group of citizens, members of the National Vigilance Association led by the noted reformer and advocate of women's rights Laura Ormiston Chant, that they intended to oppose the relicensing of the Empire and would attend the committee session to make their case. In identical letters sent to committee chair Richard Roberts by Daniel Shilton Collin, Miss H. Hood, Mr. T. Fish, Mrs. E. Bailhache, Mr. F. R. Brook, and Mrs. Laura Ormiston Chant, they charged that "the place at night is the habitual resort of prostitutes in pursuit of their traffic, and that portions of the entertainment are most objectionable, obnoxious, and against the best interests and moral well being of the community at large."[63] (Lady Henry Somerset, a stalwart supporter of Mrs. Chant and her companion on at least one visit to the Empire, was unable to attend the licensing hearings owing to her absence in America.)

In a highly biased account of the day's proceedings, the *Pall Mall Gazette* described Mrs. Chant and her colleagues, offering a list that augmented that of the authors of the letters of complaint. Mrs. Chant, and likewise Mrs. Annie Hicks (national organizer of the British Women's Temperance Association), were well known, the *Gazette* said; Shilton Collin and Mr. Livesey were Liverpool tea merchants, while the Reverend Mr. Brooks was "a curate who parades the streets at midnight, wearing a surplice and accompanied by a choir." The last was Miss Phillips, "a lady who, although elderly, is so ignorant of life that before she recently went to the Empire she had never been to a theatre in her life, and she was shocked beyond the wildest flight of her imagination," never dreaming "that anything so desperately and Babylonishly wicked existed in the world as the Empire ballets."[64]

Mrs. Chant's letter to the committee, written on stationery bearing her home address, 49 Gower Street, W.C., was dated 25 September. As she noted in a postscript, she had done George Edwardes the courtesy of notifying him on 22 September of the group's intentions. Duly forewarned, Edwardes was present, with his counsel Messrs. Gill and Statham, of the firm of Allen and Son. Edwardes's application having been noted, deliberations began, and Mrs. Chant, evidently the designated speaker for the challengers, was allowed to testify. As the present members of the committee listened and a clerk took shorthand notes, Mrs. Chant began an extended, eloquent argument against the relicensing of the Empire.[65]

Beginning with the shocking experience of her American friends on their night at the Leicester Square theatre of varieties, she explained her reaction to her own repeated visits there over several weeks, starting with the evening of 30 July. Her purposes in attending, she said, had at first been to inspect the living pictures and to ascertain whether solicitation went on openly in the promenades, as her friends had assured her it did. Dismissing the living pictures merely as unobjectionable, she turned quickly to the two accusations she was bringing against the theatre, "namely, that the promenade is nightly used by men & women for the purposes of prostitution" and "that parts of the performance on the stage are exceedingly indecent." She explained that her plan in speaking to the committee was, first, to substantiate her agreement with each of the two points of the indictment and, second, to call corroborating witnesses. What would be involved in her presentation, she indicated, was a close description of both her first visit to the Empire and subsequent visits; though she was not explicit about it, she would, in effect, telescope those five visits into a comprehensive single description, for purposes of her argument.

Mrs. Chant acknowledged what a serious charge it was to bring against a public place of entertainment that it harbors prostitutes; by the same token, it was quite a serious matter in itself "to state that a woman is a prostitute." Yet, she assured the committee, before she had finished they would find out what "good grounds" she had for making such accusations. She and her companion, Lady Henry Somerset, at first chose unreserved seats in the five-shilling promenade stalls and found that very few people were there until after nine o'clock. Then, to her astonishment, she saw numerous young women entering, "most of them very much painted, all of them more or less gaudily dressed." None were accompanied, except perhaps by others "of their own type." Hardly a one of them entered the promenade stalls, where she and her companion had been sitting. Instead, they sat on the sofas and lounges in the promenade itself, walked up and down, or stationed themselves at the head of the grand staircase — evidently a prime vantage point — from which they eagerly watched the men who moved out of the stalls and walked in the promenade.

Something that particularly caught her eye was the presence of a woman noticeably older than these young women, who evidently knew a large number of them and was making introductions wherever she could with certain men present in the promenade. She observed one instance at close range. As she stood at the back of the stalls, the woman approached a man standing next to her, "tapped him on the shoulder," and led him away to where two attractive young women were sitting on a lounge. Mrs.

Chant followed and saw the middle-aged woman introduce him, as if a stranger, to them. He politely raised his hat to each, then shook hands with one, sat down beside her, and called for drinks; Mrs. Chant saw them drinking together, at which point the older woman moved away. Later in the evening, Mrs. Chant added, she saw the man and the young woman "go off together" and observed an Empire attendant hail a hansom for them.

Mrs. Chant's testimony about this transaction was couched in consistently understated terms. Clearly she knew what she was about, and apparently she had decided to allow straightforward description to accomplish the task of explaining the shocking fact that an older woman, perhaps a former prostitute herself, was acting as a procurer in the Empire promenade, presumably on the basis of some tacit agreement with the young women she serviced (and, not unlikely, a further tacit agreement with the Empire management that it would turn a blind eye to such goings-on). One notices a closely reigned-in tactfulness in the tone of Mrs. Chant's description, as if she sensed that an overtly judgmental account, replete with shocked accusations of illicit trading in flesh, might prove counterproductive. She had evidently determined to let the facts speak for themselves.

Continuing with her story, Mrs. Chant said she noticed that, despite its favorable vantage point on the stage, the young women in the promenade paid scant attention to the stage performance, particularly during the sequence of living pictures, when the required darkening of the theatre seemed to license all kinds of bad behavior. There was much "pulling about, jostling, & touching," she said, along with "very unpleasant language." She was tempted to interfere in the loud, rude behavior of one of the women, but restrained herself. "I was there to take notes & make my observations," she explained, "& did not wish to attract unnecessary notice." How Mrs. Chant succeeded in maintaining a low profile escapes understanding, even after she had exchanged the plain, quiet dress worn on her first three visits for something fancier and therefore, paradoxically, less eye-catching. A sharp-eyed woman with prominent facial features who had eschewed pastel colors for a black, lacy dress, wearing a bonnet instead of an elaborate flowered hat, taking notes but surely not a journalist, must have been cause for even more comment than Mrs. Chant allowed herself to notice — as in the case of one of the attendants (all on "familiar terms" with the women in the lounge) who warned an obstreperous young woman to mind her behavior in the presence of "strangers."

Certainly no one who knew her, and many who didn't, would ever have doubted Mrs. Chant's courage, but there must have been widespread surprise or even astonishment in the Theatres Committee hearing room that day when she went on to explain that she had invited several of the Empire ladies to tea in her Gower Street drawing room to talk with them about their lives. (Presumably she issued these invitations during her visits to the Empire.) She wished to lead them, she said, "to a better life," but, one and all, they insisted that the Empire promenade "is the best place where they can carry on their trade." Such was the cachet of the Empire that simply being there allowed them to get better prices from the men they met. They simply "could not do without the Empire." Mrs. Chant made as much of this point as she could; she had "talked over this matter with them as to what this life is leading," she explained, "& their testimony, absolutely frankly & candidly given, is that they go to the Empire night after night because they can meet with gentlemen & make better bargains."

Having described the prostitution active in the Empire promenade, Mrs. Chant now turned her attention to the second of the two indictments, the indecency of stage performance. Evidently, despite owning a pair of opera glasses, Mrs. Chant had little or no experience of ballet and was unprepared for the traditional brevity of dancers' costumes. The two ballets she saw on her first visit, as well as on subsequent occasions, both appeared to her to be designed expressly for the fullest possible display of women's bodies. No attempt is made to hide what "common sense & common decency" would require to be hidden, she protested. She had to use her glasses to determine whether a dancer's legs were uncovered or encased in tights, so closely did they match the color of flesh. This dancer wore only a very short skirt, and as she whirled in pirouette it flew up and left the rest of her body entirely exposed except for "a very slight white gauze" between her legs. Mrs. Chant was particularly shocked by a sequence in which a double corps de ballet, all female, represented Puritan maidens, "modestly & prettily dressed," and, opposite them, monks, who at first extend their hands in blessing but then suddenly throw their robes aside, revealing themselves cross-dressed as cavaliers, "with tights up to the waist" and little additional clothing. When it was the turn of the prima ballerina to dance and she came downstage in her "light, gauzy" dress, the lighting was such that she appeared like "a naked woman . . . disguised with a film of lace." No less shocking were the actions of a dancer all in black, in silk tights and lace dress, who "gathers up all her clothing in the face of the man before whom she is dancing, & stretches up her leg, & kicks him upon the crown of his head." No one, no matter what their tastes might be, could conceivably fail to condemn such actions as indecent, Mrs. Chant asserted.

Going on to complain of the rough treatment of a little girl, perhaps ten years of age, by a troupe of acrobats, treatment that violated her sense of "decency & right feeling & even common kindness," Mrs. Chant sensed a need to keep her audience on track. Wary of introducing too much detail into her testimony, she began to move to a conclusion by underscoring the gravity of the matter at hand. Directly addressing the "gentlemen" of the committee and identifying herself as speaking in the name of "the women of England," she said she felt the greatest confidence in approaching them. Even if they were unable "to feel as keenly" about these things as she might desire, she was asking them to do what they have been "watched" and seen to do before: "to purify our public amusements from those elements which we hold to be quite unnecessary, & which we see bring so much shame & ruin in their train." She did not appear before them "as one who objects to dances or objects to theatres," she explained. She loved these things and wanted others to be able to see them too "without having the baser passions roused" and without lowering the present standard of decency, so hardly acquired. One cannot expect that standard to be held to by the "poor girls" in the ballet who have little choice but to be "shamelessly exposed." Rather, in "a civilized community" it must come from those who rise to oppose the low standard exhibited both on and off the stage of the Empire — from those who have only a single object in view in mounting that opposition and are constantly working to affirm a higher standard of public entertainment. The amusements of the great city of London must be such "that young men can go to them without being entrapped and seduced by these sad poor women"; they must be such that young women can go with lovers and brothers without having to feel what she herself felt that night, when the woman in black kicked the crown of the male dancer's head. A pair of French visitors had been standing behind her and her sister, as the ballet progressed, she remembered. When the moment of the kick occurred, one of them murmured that it was just too much — "C'est trop fort," he had exclaimed — and left the theatre.

In this moment of her testimony Mrs. Chant had touched and revealed the deepest level of her feelings. It was not merely outrage, strong though that was, over what she found to be the pervasive prurient atmosphere at the Empire, both in the dancing on stage and in the activities predominating in the five-shilling promenade. She had suddenly discovered — perhaps in the very act of narration — that she was profoundly embarrassed, not simply on her own account but on behalf of all the women of England, to have found herself in the intensified presence of so much that ran completely contrary to all she believed in and all she stood for. If there was a substratum of anger over this discovery, as very likely there was, Mrs. Chant kept that response well in check. The most remarkable quality of her entire testimony, along with its fierce articulateness, was its measured restraint, even as she narrated the extraordinary story of her successive visits to the Empire and described in eloquent detail what she saw, what transpired there, and what her reactions were to it all.

And so, in these last moments of her testimony, Mrs. Chant continued to keep her head and remain calm. These were the reasons she appeared before the committee this day, she said, and she hoped her witnesses would corroborate the two essential points at issue, namely, "that the promenade is made nightly a common resort for women who are leading the life of prostitutes, not only once or twice, but every night, & that some of the performances on the stage are indecent & objectionable."

Her first visit to the Empire had evidently proved to be momentous for Mrs. Chant, moving her to repeat it several times and then to rally her colleagues, in the service of social purity, to come before the committee that day in order to oppose the relicensing of the Empire Theatre of Varieties. Proceeding now with the second part of her attack, she called a series of witnesses, including Mrs. Annie Hicks, the national organizer for the British Women's Temperance Association (to which Mrs. Chant herself belonged). The magnitude of public interest already generated by the 10 October hearings is reflected in accounts of the proceedings, published the next day or soon after, by the *Daily Telegraph*, the *Times*, the *Era*, and the *Music Hall and Theatre Review*, among other journals.[66]

Responding to Mrs. Chant's questions, Mrs. Hicks explained that she had visited the Empire one evening and had "heard a man talking to a woman, and in reply to something she said, he replied, 'Oh, you are not very young,' and after some further conversation she heard the woman say, 'I can find you a nice little one.' After still further conversation," Mrs. Hicks continued, "they went out together." Mrs. Hicks said she had no doubt from the things they said and the signs they gave that they left "to fulfill the intentions of the conversation." She went on to describe a "young girl of about sixteen years of age" and "rather beautiful," who came in "dressed in a silk dress, with white lace." Her manner led Mrs. Hicks to believe the girl was unaccustomed to the Empire promenade and "was under the protection of other women."

Charles F. Gill, Edwardes's solicitor, a celebrated criminal defense and divorce lawyer,[67] well known to the Theatres Committee, now rose to conduct a cross-examination. Gill's "steady style," based on detailed mastery of the case, had made him a formidable presence, as did his one mannerism, a habit of taking off his glasses to emphasize whatever emotion — "surprise, doubt, indignation, encouragement, or incredulity" — he wished to express.[68] Despite Gill's sterling reputation, by the end of the day on which he defended the Empire Theatre his client George Edwardes would have cause for disappointment in his choice of representation. Gill asked Mrs. Hicks, "Do you object to women going to places of entertainment alone?" "No," she replied, "I think that women ought to be able to go into any assembly alone." "Exactly on the same footing as men? — Quite so." "And not interfered with," Gill persisted, "so long as they conduct themselves with propriety?" "Yes," was the answer. Mrs. Sheldon Amos, wife of the formidable author of *A Comparative Survey of Laws in Force for the Prohibition, Regulation, and Licensing of Vice in England and Other Countries*, published as early as 1877, was called and gave corroborative testimony.[69] Convinced that the Empire promenade was the nightly scene of solicitation, she described it as "the worst place she knew in civilised countries in the matter of prostitutes." The dancing on stage, she thought, was "designed to excite impure thought and passion," and during the presentation of the living pictures, when the theatre was darkened, "the behaviour was worse than before." Interrogating Mrs. Amos, Gill discovered that she had visited the Empire no less recently than the previous Thursday and Friday, when, she insisted, she heard "two or three bargains in progress between men and women." The next witness, Daniel Shilton Collin, identified as a tea merchant in London and Liverpool, said he had attended the Empire almost twenty times in the previous three months; on one visit he had "counted well-nigh 180 women of objectionable character." The Empire was, he thought, "notoriously a show place for that kind of thing." Proceeding to interrogate each of the witnesses, who corroborated her own testimony in whole or in part, and who were then cross-examined by Gill, Mrs. Chant rested her case.

Gill then began to cross-examine Mrs. Chant herself. Mrs. Chant stated that she had visited the Empire five times in all. Gill pursued the point, extracting the information that, on each occasion, she went with some second person — the first time, with Lady Henry Somerset. On the first three occasions she dressed "quietly" and was watched very carefully, Mrs. Chant explained. The fourth and fifth times she dressed "gaily," wearing "her prettiest evening dress" so as to obtain information "more easily."[70]

Gill went on to sum up the case for the Empire. Well-meaning though they were, Gill said, the witnesses were "persons of the most violent and extreme views," presumptuous in taking care of other people's morality and dictating the kind of entertainment that should be offered to the public. Several gentlemen possessed of considerable capital and enterprise had spent lavishly to mount on the stage of the Empire "the best performance that money could possibly produce," resulting in a theatre filled to capacity. Consequently, "any reflection upon the entertainment was equally a reflection upon the spectators." Immoral persons were entitled to be in the promenade, he asserted; as long as they "conducted themselves with propriety," they were "not to be intefered with." The Empire management "took every possible precaution" in the interests of "proper management," Gill added, and he urged the committee not to be led astray by the "extremely improbable stories" they had been told.[71]

One of the notable elements of a mostly unremarkable speech was Gill's insistence that the lavish expense itself of capital on stage performances constituted an argument for relicensing; presumably it was unfair for investors, especially persons of great means, to be deprived of a return in kind. More to the point and more effective, perhaps, was Gill's suggestion that an indictment of the moral quality of stage performance was by implication an indictment of the morals of the audience as well — a view with which many reformers themselves might have been inclined to agree. As subsequent clashes of opinion on the subject would show, this argument of Gill's was a sword that cut both ways.

Gill then called George Edwardes and proceeded to examine him, in what was a sequence evidently well prepared beforehand but somehow unable to engage with the depths of feeling and conviction displayed by the forces opposed to relicensing. In reply to questions, Edwardes emphasized the extensive steps taken by the Empire management to ensure the security of the house. A staff almost one hundred strong, headed by a retired police inspector and several sergeants, was responsible for the good conduct of the audience. "Practically everybody is inspected before being allowed to enter," Edwardes assured the committee, "and nobody goes in without paying for admission" (an assertion disputed by Theatres and Music Halls subcommittee inspectors, and whose truthfulness Edwardes surely knew was highly questionable — but, then, he was not under oath). Edwardes was not, of course, disposed to deny the presence of prostitutes in the promenade, but he went to some lengths to make sure of their decorous behavior. "A sergeant and detective are in the promenade seeing that the women there behave themselves properly," he said. "If anything like marked accosting is observed," he explained, "first the woman is cautioned, and for a second offence she is taken out of the house." The same was the case with men, and indeed it frequently happened that women were prevented from entering in the first place.[72]

The circle of testimony, challenge, and response was coming full, as the two persons whom many viewed as principal antagonists were now granted an opportunity to face one another. Unlike Edwardes, Mrs. Chant had not retained a paid intermediary but had conducted her own opposition — a tactic that held, among other advantages including that of immediacy, the chance to confront the one man who more than any other, in her view and that of her associates, stood behind the systematic exploitation of women, both onstage and off, in the Empire Theatre, and the sad and dire consequences such exploitation produced for them and for contemporary society.

Questioning Edwardes, Mrs. Chant pursued the issue of the alleged indecency of the costumes of the ballet. She asked him "whether you see anything objectionable in the ballet, and, if not, whether you would like to see your wife's body exposed as the bodies of the people were in the ballet." Edwardes responded, perhaps somewhat testily, that his wife was not a dancer (she was in fact a former actress, Julia Gwynne), but he insisted that in any case "there was absolutely nothing in the dresses that was indecent."[73] They did of course reveal "the form of the figure," but the dancers all wore "tights and trunks." "Nothing," he added, "could be seen but the legs, which could not be considered to be indecent."[74] (Edwardes's change of tone might have derived in part from discomfort over being reminded of a liaison with another actress, Miriam Clements, just around this time.)

Did Mrs. Chant begin to lose her composure at this point? Or, as was more likely, did committee chair Roberts, detecting a heated exchange in the offing, and perhaps chafing over the advancing hour, summarily call the proceedings to a halt? In any case, for some reason the record of the confrontation between Edwardes and Mrs. Chant is much briefer than might have been expected, producing a sense of anticlimax. Nor was any record kept of the extensive time consumed by deliberations over the Empire relicensing. All the same, a fair idea of it can be inferred from the amount of surviving documentation: all told, the hearing over the Empire license left in the public record a residue of testimony and cross-examination totaling 141 pages, including the clerk's subsequent transcription of shorthand notes.

### THE COMMITTEE'S DECISION

During the course of deliberations Gill had challenged the councillor and Theatres Committee member James F. Torr on grounds that he was also a member of the council of the National Vigilance Association, additionally identifying Mrs. Sheldon Amos and Mrs. Chant herself as members of the NVA. Both Torr and Mrs. Chant denied that the complaints against the Empire had been lodged officially by the association. Gill suggested that it was "a matter of good taste" that Torr refrain from participating in the deliberations of the committee. Surprisingly, Torr acquiesced.[75] A greater imponderable was the curiously distanced posture of the NVA with respect to the attack on the Empire. In its ninth annual report, published in 1894, the NVA listed its General Council; the names comprised an effective who's who of the social purity movement in Britain: Mrs. Sheldon Amos, Percy W. Bunting (chair), Mrs. Bunting, Mrs. Ormiston Chant, T. Fish, Ellice Hopkins, Rev. Hugh Price Hughes, W. T. Stead (controversial editor of the *Pall Mall Gazette*), and James F. Torr. Lady Henry Somerset and Josephine Butler were two of its seven vice-presidents. William Alexander Coote served as secretary. The full title of the organization was "The National Vigilance Association and Central Vigilance Society for the Repression of Criminal Vice and Public Immorality." In the tenth report of the association, published in 1895, Torr's name is gone, a tacit indication of his resignation under pressure. The report is full of summaries of the NVA's activities, the opposition to the Palace license by W. A. Coote being a prominent feature, but no information is provided on the opposition to the Empire. Evidently, as Mrs. Chant took every opportunity to explain, there was no official connection between the attack against the Empire and the NVA. The absence of

Coote's name from the list of those who wrote to the Theatres and Music Halls Committee to oppose the Empire license is indicative in itself of that dissociation. Why the NVA chose to remain at more than arm's length from what would become one of the most successful, large-scale attacks on alleged public immorality in the mid-1890s remains unclear (especially in view of the great credit the NVA would later take for it), unless it was to avert a charge of packing the Theatres and Music Halls Committee in its favor. The embarrassment induced in J. F. Torr over his simultaneous membership in the Theatres Committee and the NVA may have been a telling point.

The committee now retired to consider its decision, in what immediately became a highly charged atmosphere. As a full sessions house audience waited impatiently, and with speculation rife in the air, the committee's deliberations went on and on, lasting a full three-quarters of an hour. A motion that the Empire license not be granted was defeated by almost the narrowest of possible margins, six to five. A second motion, "[t]hat it be recommended to the Council that a licence for music and dancing be granted on condition, to be endorsed on the licence[,] that the promenades be abolished and the spaces now occupied by them be disposed of to the satisfaction of the Council," was carried six to two. (Evidently some members of the committee were abstaining on some of the questions.) Still another motion, "[t]hat the following condition be added that no intoxicating drinks be sold in the auditorium," also succeeded, though by the much narrower margin of five to four. Although banning alcohol from the halls entirely would have been illegal, in 1894 the council ruled that no new licences would be granted that permitted the serving of alcohol. Meanwhile, a kind of grandfather clause prevented the council from refusing a license solely on grounds of alcohol consumption if the hall had been in existence before it came under the council's jurisdiction.[76] All the same, within these historical limitations the committee and the council could, and did, exercise broad powers. William Saunders, council member for Walworth, was evidently right on the mark when he wrote, in his 1892 history of the first county council: "It would be as safe for a man to put his hand in a hornets' nest as to take part in a Music Halls Committee."[77]

Finally, at 6:30 P.M. Richard Roberts came forward and announced the outcome. "The decision of the Committee," he said, "with regard to the case of the Empire is, that they will recommend the renewal of the license on the condition that the promenades be abolished and the space now occupied by them disposed to the satisfaction of the Council and that no intoxicating drinks be sold in the auditorium."[78] This recommendation would be forwarded to the council for official decision during its meeting later in the month.

In announcing these results Roberts explained that James Torr had felt a conflict of interest, stemming from his simultaneous membership on the committee and on the council of the National Vigilance Association, preventing him from taking part in the committee's deliberations. Torr asked Roberts to say that, in order to avoid any imputation of partiality, he would immediately resign from the NVA.[79] Given his connection with the NVA and his declared objection to the form-fitting costumes of ballet dancers, had Torr participated in the decision he would very likely have sided with the five committee members who voted to deny the Empire its license. Although Torr's vote would not have changed any of the decisions made in camera by the committee, a six-six tie, which would have defeated by the barest possible margin the motion to deny the license, would have indicated even more forcefully the persuasiveness of the testimony given by Mrs. Chant and her colleagues and would have sent an even clearer message to the county council along with the committee's recommendation.

If any sense of disappointment that the committee did not actually deny the Empire its license overshadowed the outcome of the proceedings in some quarters, no trace of it surfaced. As an excited audience dispersed and journalists raced to file reports for the morning papers, Mrs. Chant and her colleagues departed, the sweet taste of triumph on their tongues, leaving George Edwardes and his solicitors to confer on what measures might be taken to defer or stave off what now could be seen as a rising tidal wave of adversity. And yet, no matter how grave they privately felt the situation to be, they would have been hard pressed to imagine, let alone to admit, how threatening and longlasting their difficulties would soon become.

# 3 : Repercussions

## THE EMPIRE STRIKES BACK

On Thursday, 11 October, the day after the Theatres and Music Halls Committee had recommended relicensing the Empire Theatre of Varieties, but with restrictions he must have viewed as completely intolerable, George Edwardes gave notice to the London County Council of his intention to appeal the decision.[1] Meanwhile, news of the committee's recommendation was spreading with predictable rapidity. On the very day of the hearing the *Daily Telegraph*, which along with the *Pall Mall Gazette* would offer the most extensive coverage of the controversy, engaged in a preemptive strike by publishing a leading article that identified the Empire promenade as the locus of the problem and explained the futility of attempting to suppress what went on in its expanses.

Adopting a tone of arch bemusement and condescension, the editorial writer began by crediting Mrs. Chant and her colleagues for "the courage, the virtue, the strict personal propriety" they evinced in the face of the barrage of reproaches they must expect for their manifest ignorance of the world. The Empire promenade is understood to be a part of the theatre where, for an entrance fee of five shillings, "visitors of both sexes may lounge during the performance and partake of refreshments." The simple truth is that people cannot be forced to sit still throughout an entertainment; if attempts are made to prevent them from congregating for refreshment and conversation with friends, disorderly gatherings instead of orderly ones will be the result. Surely, even these "well-meaning ladies and their friends" cannot deceive themselves so much as to believe they can "suppress public thirst by forbidding wine and beer in a music-hall, rebuke the sense of beauty and grace by lengthening skirts, or eradicate the ancient and universal social evil of nations by persecuting and driving those who minister to it into seclusion and despair." The most useless thing in the world, the writer continued, is to imagine that an evil can be gotten rid of "by thrusting it out of sight." The London streets at night are a sufficient indication of that uselessness, and the actions of Mrs. Chant and her colleagues will only serve to intensify such "disgraceful sights" by pretending they don't exist, thus denying the unfortunate women they drive into shameless behavior the "possibility of a little modesty, a little refuge, a little pity." In the opinion of the *Telegraph*, the Empire promenades represented just the kind of concession that "prudent virtue" finds necessary to keep vice "well in order." If such "tyrannical puritanism" is allowed to have its way, either gaiety will be driven out of public life and incurable evils forced to fester under the surface, or else "general opinion" will break out of all restrictions and create a state of things much worse than anything we now can see.[2]

To whatever extent he might have agreed with the sentiments of the *Telegraph* writer, Edwardes would have been hard pressed to find the necessary time to respond to and counter the severe restrictions on the Empire license recommended by the Theatres Committee. His usual full routine of multitheatre, multitroupe management, full and varied, included auditions, attendance at rehearsals, reading of plays for the Gaiety — and, beginning in 1893, for Daly's — interviewing actors, actresses, singers, and variety artistes, arranging contracts for performers, managing the schedules and details of provincial tours, and dealing with a constant high volume of mail while fending off or accommodating a nearly endless stream of persons who wanted his good offices or needed a loan.[3] This same month of October his production of a new comic opera, *His Excellency*, by W. S. Gilbert, with music by F. Osmond Carr, would open at the Lyric on the twenty-seventh, and in late November his musical comedy *The Shop Girl*, destined for a run of 546 performances, would premiere at the Gaiety, to be followed the day after Christmas by the holiday entertainment *Hansel and Gretel*, at Daly's.[4] Notwithstanding all these obligations, there was much to be pondered and much to be done to try to save his theatre in the days leading up to the special licensing session of the county council on 26 October, when the fate of the Empire would be decided. An intensely practical and clear-sighted man, for all his biases, Edwardes faced up to the dire situation in which he found himself and roundly took up the challenge.

Despite the scanty records of his management of the Empire and his other enterprises, and despite the irregular cash flow occasioned by investments in shows that had not yet opened, it appears likely that Edwardes would have put other almost equally urgent matters aside long enough to mount, with the help of managerial colleagues and solicitors (who would soon rush to his support in print), a concerted counterattack. On the evening of Friday, 12 October, he took the expedient of giving a formal fortnight's notice to the employees of the Empire. At the same time he began a publicity campaign designed to win any undecided persons to the Empire's side. In an interview given on Saturday night, 13 October, Edwardes assured the readers of the *Telegraph* that, should the recommendation of the licensing committee to close the promenade and prohibit the sale of intoxicating liquors in the auditorium be endorsed by the council, the result would be "absolute ruin," and the theatre would have to close its doors. To be sure, Edwardes's threat to close the Empire in the face of alleged certain ruin had an element of truth in it. The financial base of the establishment had not changed significantly, if at all, since 1892, when the Empire's balance sheet, published in the *Manchester Guardian*, showed box-office receipts of £95,900, costs of £97,000, and receipts from the sale of drink totaling £21,787, thus indicating that more than 18 percent of the Empire's total income was related to drink and that sales of that commodity spelled the difference between profit and loss. Edwardes's claim the year before in the *Manchester Examiner and Times* that it was the gate money and not drink from which his profits derived consequently ignored, or even attempted to suppress, the true facts of the situation.[5]

The Empire theatre staff understood the situation perfectly well and was maintaining cordial relations with the management, Edwardes noted to his interviewer. He added that, to be candid, he was unprepared for the sweeping changes called for by the committee; since the theatre had first opened, there had not been "one single entry made on the books either of the County Council or the police which reflected discreditably on the management of the place." If, however, the council were to endorse the actions of its licensing committee, the closing of the theatre would be a "moral certainty."[6]

Keeping up the pressure, in a long letter to the *Telegraph* published two days later Edwardes explained the reasons for his decision to warn his employees of impending disaster. Given the prospect that the full council might second the committee's recommendation, he said he felt it only his duty to give his employees official notice. Leaping to his own defense, he then went on to declare that for the seven years of the Empire's existence under the present management there had been nothing against it. With respect to the police and the council both, management had "a clean sheet." Serious money had been laid out in order to comply with all the committee's and council's requirements, "structural and otherwise." The reward for such good behavior was that, while the council itself still had nothing contrary to say to the Empire, "the evidence of some ladies of extreme views" had had the consequence of removing privileges the council had granted without reservation. He hoped the council would not be so easily influenced as to cede control of public entertainments to "the new woman." If it did, he could candidly predict the resulting dissolution of "one of the most powerful companies ever brought together," along with "certainly the most successful theatrical venture of our times." Were that to happen, it would be a clear indication that certain "gentlemen in authority" had been easily led astray "by a few female orators."[7]

Edwardes's attempt to denigrate and trivialize his opponents, while simultaneously crediting them with power sufficient to lead away certain gentlemen temporarily in authority — that is, elected by their constituencies through a democratic process to a term on the council — had the somewhat ironic effect of revealing the surprising weakness in his and his colleagues' stance vis-à-vis the concerted forces of municipal government. And the anxious, irritable tone of the letter suggested how much aware he may have felt of weakness of that sort. Solicitor Gill's argument, orchestrated through a combination of general statement, interrogation of witnesses, and summary, had amounted largely to the verbal equivalent of inviting a gentleman about to enter the Empire lounge, a man of the world impeccably attired in evening dress, crush hat tucked under his arm, to explain why he was entitled to all the benefits of the status quo, with an implicit apology for having to ask him to explain himself in the first place. It seemed likely that Edwardes could not see beyond the bulwarks of privilege that he believed shored up the entrance to the Empire and its promenade as surely as did its gates and doorman. The Empire strategy was fallible because it did not — could not — account for attitudes and opinions, represented so prominently on the Theatres and Music Halls Committee (to say nothing of the larger membership of the council itself), that either scorned such entitlements or even considered them morally offensive. Edwardes could do no better, it seemed, as his letters and interviews in the press made clear. Yet his puzzlement that a previously unblemished record did not constitute a persuasive argument for continuance of unreserved privilege seems not a little disingenuous. At the same time, his snide comment to the press, to the effect that the committee could at least achieve consistency in its rulings by letting the "new woman" control the licensing of all public places, may have reflected no little fear that a repressive puritanical takeover was no longer a complete impossibility. While there was no suggestion that Edwardes had lost his nerve, it was almost embarrassingly clear that he had lost his composure and was somewhat the worse for the lack of a clear head.

## THE THREAT OF CLOSURE

The Empire had only begun to fight. As agitation, happy or unhappy, over the licensing committee's recommendations began to surface in the pages of journals of almost every stamp, on Wednesday, 17 October, the *Telegraph* printed an elaborately self-defensive statement issued by the directors of the Empire Theatre explaining in near-excruciating detail the significance of the menace posed by the conditional relicensing of the theatre and, once again, threatening the imminent closing of the Empire. The Empire license was granted by the magistrates in 1887, and it has been renewed by the council every year "without comment or opposition," the statement began. Moreover, the previous chair of the Theatres Committee had stated that the committee had no intention of interfering "with existing licenses" or the original conditions on which they were granted. The Empire had expended some £8,000 to upgrade the entrance to a theatre that has always been completely free from "*double entendre* or vulgarity." Much money has been spent on the stage itself and in the auditorium in order to comply with the council's requirements; in fact, the Empire has rushed "most cheerfully" to respond to every council suggestion. Just this week a new ballet has been produced, entailing "a very large outlay." No mark against the theatre can be discovered in the books of either the council or the police. Moreover, if any artiste sings even one verse of a song not previously vetted by the management, instant cancellation of contract ensues. Empire employees currently number "six hundred and forty-seven," and in addition there are dependents numbering "about 3,000 souls," predominantly of the poorer classes. If the recommendations of the committee are approved by the council, "the Empire will be compelled to close its doors." (A cartoon in *Punch* would soon show a placard placed against the door of the Empire claiming "3000 Employees will be Thrown out of Work if This Theatre is Closed by the LCC.")[8] Bad enough that three thousand persons will be "deprived of their daily bread" with winter coming on; worse, closure will entail some £200,000 of lost capital to shareholders, along with a great sum to the owner of the freehold.[9] A historical point of real importance had also to be mentioned: the theatre was constructed on the basis of plans approved by the present council's predecessors; hence, because of the particularities of "entrances, exits, and structural difficulties," it would prove "absolutely impossible" to comply with the committee's recommendations.[10]

In addition to predicting the financial ruin of the enterprise, the directors had fallen back on an argument regarding the intrinsic purposes and constraints that followed from the architectural design of a variety theatre itself. That design, approved by the authorities before the county council came into existence — specifically, of a promenade where large numbers of persons could walk up and down while enjoying an unobstructed view of the stage — made it, in the view of the Empire directorate, virtually impossible to implement the committee's recommendations regarding physical alterations. Already a significant factor, the issue of the primacy of the physical space of the promenade would loom ever larger as October gave way to November and event succeeded event.

The seemingly specialized space on the second tier of the Empire devoted, by virtue of its very design, to the opportunity to promenade while retaining an unimpeded view of the performance evidently had much in common with other places of public resort where women of doubtful, or all too patent, reputation could freely congregate. At the same time the Empire promenade had lately acquired an unusually intense symbolic significance. While to some it represented a licentiousness intolerable in a public place, to others it signified the very epitome of personal liberty and freedom of association. It was critical, then, that in threatening the imminent closing of the Empire if the recommendation of the Theatres and Music Halls Committee were endorsed by the London County Council, Edwardes and the Empire Theatre directors attribute the alleged necessity of closing to the matter of purpose-built space being lost, and not solely to financial concerns.

Also on 17 October Selwyn Image, who as an associate of the activist liberal clergyman Stewart Headlam had interested himself in liberal causes, including the advancement of ballet, published a letter in the *Pall Mall Gazette* on the same theme but set in a broader context. Closing the promenade at the Empire will undoubtedly prevent "a particular assemblage of women," Image acknowledged, but if such action involves closing the theatre, a vast number of respectable people will be deprived of their entertainment and "immediate disaster and consequent moral danger" will be visited upon "hundreds of well-behaved, hard-working men and women" employed backstage and in the front of the house. Image also took up a point he said was widely acknowledged in private but seldom in public — the belief, as he viewed it, that "this form of vice is so deep-seated as practically to be ineradicable," given the conditions under which human nature presently exists. The "root of *this* evil," he explained, "lies in the innate and permanent sexual attraction man has towards woman, and woman towards man."

The less pitying, more sharp-eyed political view of a "Candid Playgoer," writing in *To-Day* on 20 October, was that for the last five years the Empire had paid a dividend of 75 percent, with the result that shareholders had gotten their original capital back in dividends more than three times over. What is bad for the Empire is good for the Alhambra, the writer asserted, since the Alhambra is now the only music hall with a lounge licensed for the sale of alcoholic beverages. The author of a letter to the editor of the *Financial News* likewise cautioned against pity for the plight of Edwardes, who was claiming that he must close his theatre, in view of the annual receipt by shareholders of dividends of between 70 and 80 percent (on the face value of shares) and the current value of their shares as more than three times their original cost.[11] (Earlier in October the Empire directors had declared another interim dividend of two shillings and sixpence on fifteen-shilling shares and one shilling and eightpence on ten-shilling shares.)[12] The writer also offered a glimpse into the network of capital investment reflected in the Empire's astonishing success, pointing out that Daniel de Nicols, founder and proprietor of the Café Royal — one of the most fashionable haunts of persons of leisure in London — was the largest shareholder in the Empire company. (The writer perhaps did not know that de Nicols was the freeholder as well.) The popular playwright Jerome K. Jerome took a similar stance, noting the same facts about the munificent dividends and asking whether it was impossible for an establishment as prosperous as the Empire to be maintained "at a reasonable profit" under the same conditions that affect the Palace, which has no lounge. He could hardly believe it, Jerome said, "and for the Empire as the Empire I have not much pity."[13]

### PLANS FOR ALTERATION

While reactions to the committee recommendations proliferated in the press, the pulpit, and almost everywhere else, the Superintending Architect's

Department of the council, Theatres and Music Halls Branch, was busy preparing a report on possible alterations in the Empire auditorium consistent with the committee's recommendation. Dated 22 October and accompanied by sketches, the report summarized the results of a survey of the building "for the purpose of ascertaining what additional seating could be provided and the alterations it would be necessary to make so as to best give effect to the recommendations of the Committee." The report focuses on the two promenades on the first and second circles, each of them eighteen feet wide. On the first circle 104 extra seats could be added to the present capacity of 130 (not including the private boxes), leaving a six-foot gangway at the rear; floor-to-ceiling height at the top row of seats would, however, be only seven feet. On the second circle, where present seating accommodated 129 persons, 89 extra seats could be installed, leaving a nine-foot gangway at the back. A total of 193 additional seats could thus be placed at the rear of the two circles by invading the space currently occupied by the two promenades.[14]

The report went on to consider the implications of the present seating and the proposed alterations. The seating capacity of the building presently stood at 1,330, and "the average number of persons said to be admitted nightly is 1,800; this gives an average of 470 persons for which there are no seats to view the performance." It could be concluded therefore that this was the average number of persons using the promenades in the course of the evening. (Many of these, however, were casual visitors who did not remain for the entire night's performances, a fact that did not enter into the committee's deliberations.) A marginal calculation in pencil showed the net result of adding the proposed 193 seats: a reduction of the 470 persons to 277.[15]

Thus the proposal for alteration of the spaces at the Empire, in answer to the committee's recommendation that the promenades be abolished. The second recommendation of the committee, calling for prohibition of the sale of intoxicating liquors in the auditorium, would have no less broad an impact, the report continued, for it "will involve the removal of two refreshment bars in the stalls, one in the pit, one on the 1st circle, & three on the 2nd circle." In addition there would need to be made "an enclosure to the pit saloon and to a refreshment bar on the first circle."[16]

Requiring structural alterations had the inconvenient effect of raising questions about the technical knowledge of council members. In the deliberations of the 1892 select committee of Parliament on theatres and places of entertainment, the experienced theatre architect Walter Lawrence Emden had cast aspersions on the ability of the county council to adjudicate the need for structural alterations in theatres in a responsible way. "If they had the knowledge," Emden had said, "they would know which [requirements] were important and which were not; not having the knowledge, the consequence is that the poor owner has to suffer by having forced upon him the requisitions, whether they are useful or beneficial or not."[17] Interrogated by the select committee on the same point, William Bailey, until recently the manager of the Alhambra and former longtime manager of the Metropolitan Music Hall in Edgeware Road, said he disapproved of the council's having the authority to enforce structural alterations. At the Metropolitan, "Certain men came one week and ordered a thing, and three weeks after another set of individuals called, and they had the thing entirely changed again, and put us to a great deal of expense. I have no faith in the London County Council," he concluded.[18]

Taking the same view, a writer in the *Builder* later pointed out the fallacy of requiring a building constructed along the lines of certain requirements "to be cut about and adopted for entirely different purposes." The original owners had required an "ample promenade room," not "a maximum number of seats." As in other countries, income from the enterprise was not predicated on "actual seating accommodation"; hence, only the entire reconstruction of the auditorium would allow for expenses of performance to be fully covered by the sale of seats. "Part of the essence of a 'Variety' entertainment," the writer explained, "is a certain freedom of restraint" regarding seating; room for promenading was "a recognised necessity."[19]

The availability of alcohol in the "promenade-room," as well as the doubtful character of many who consumed it there, went unmentioned in the *Builder*'s protestations. In fact, what the writer euphemistically described as "a certain freedom of restraint as to seat" was proving to be the paramount objection of those who condemned the loose behavior on view nightly in the mirrored expanses of the Empire promenades. Aside from any more practical considerations, the proposed construction of dozens of new seats in the current promenade spaces had a symbolic value greatly at variance with any mere need to accommodate a larger number of spectators of the ballets and music hall turns on view on the stage below. Such values were not to be discovered explicitly stated in the opinions advanced and debates waged over the issues surrounding the Empire relicensing, but in a longer perspective they loomed large all the same.

Meanwhile, within just two or three days after the Theatre Committee's decision, the *Daily Telegraph* had received such a deluge of letters pro and con that it began a series entitled "Prudes on the Prowl" (the phrase is sometimes credited to Clement Scott, play reviewer for the *Telegraph* and the *Illustrated London News*), comprising voluminous excerpts or even entire communications. Notwithstanding the *Telegraph*'s predictably adverse editorial stance toward Mrs. Chant and her fellow reformers — a stance reflected in numerous cartoons appearing in other publications more or less simultaneously (fig. 29) — the *Telegraph* went out of its way to present a broad, wide-ranging selection of representative views for or against the recommendation.

A predictable theme was what one writer described as the "tyranny of the Pharisee." Offering a vivid picture of loose morals and indecency in various public places such as the Argyll Rooms in the London of forty years before, the writer pointed out that he had been able to escort his wife, a woman "as pure, as refined, as earnest where her own sex is concerned, as any female platform preacher," from their box at the Empire through the "obnoxious semi-circle" of the promenade to her carriage, "and not one objectionable expression soiled her ears, not one instance of indecorum attracted her attention." Such is the progress that London has made away from degradation, a progress threatened by the "platform prigs" whose "pestilential policy" may reduce the city to a last state worse than the first.[20]

Correspondents took up a broad and various range of subjects, some becoming ever more inventive in their crafting of pseudonymous signatures. "A Publican and Sinner," turning the onus of proof back on the social purity crusaders, wondered how many members of the Theatres and Music Halls Committee were themselves members of vigilance and purity societies, and how much of the personal property of one of the female agitators was derived from houses where drink is sold and vice is housed. F. A. Baldwin's opinion was that if music halls are to be shut down, railway stations, public thoroughfares, certain public buildings, and places of worship should be shut down too, since all are "promenaded" by the women under attack. "Sympathica" cited the sad story of an "unfortunate" who wrote to the reformers for help but was effectively rebuffed; better to try to help such persons, said this writer, than to close down or restrict the enjoyments of the people. Clear the streets first, said

OUR EMPIRE IN DANGER.

ST. GEORGE AND THE DRAGONS.

29. *"Our Empire in Danger. St. George and the Dragons."*
Entr'Acte & Limelight, *20 October 1894, 8. Harvard Theatre Collection,*
*Houghton Library.*

"Afghanistan," and only then the music halls, where one finds "the minimum of impropriety and the maximum of refinement." "A Living Picture" maintained that the fanatical reformers "insult our sense of pride and manhood." A plea on behalf of dancers who will lose their employment if the Empire shuts down came from "An Old Empire Dancer," who feared that such "girls" would become like the "180 women of doubtful character" whom Daniel Shilton Collin claimed to have counted in one evening in the Empire five-shilling promenade. "Anti-Humbug" pointed out that one can find women of the class objected to in two of the largest churches in the metropolis. C. M. Manning observed that the two American gentlemen of Mrs. Chant's acquaintance who were shocked by sights at the Empire were "not at all like any American gentleman I have met in my travels." Speaking on the side of the opposition, a self-styled "Puritan" reported her visit to the Empire with a young friend to see *On the Pier*," and she agreed with Lady Henry Somerset and Mrs. Chant that the ballet raises "impure thoughts in the minds of the young"; while at the Empire she counted over twelve ladies "without gloves on" and, moreover, saw "indecent attire" in some two dozen men and boys.[21]

Other writers to the *Telegraph* brought more penetrating and sometimes cynical insights to bear. "A.B." questioned the politics of the Theatres and Music Halls Committee's instantaneous decision in favor of the reformers. "Who were the wire-pullers of the opposition?" he asked. "Anglo-Indian" suggested that the committee, not the Puritans, be blamed for the current state of affairs, and that voters who objected should throw them out at the next election and install "a sensible set of men who know the world and human nature." Speaking for the opposition, "X.Y.Z." took the view that Edwardes had "entirely given himself away." If the Empire must be closed because the promenade is eliminated and drink in the auditorium is disallowed, then these clearly are the sources of the "extravagant dividends" paid by the Empire to shareholders, and so it is only common sense to close the Empire and similar places. "H.N.P.," writing from an undisclosed address in Gower Street, added in a similar vein that the Empire should not have a promenade if the county council denies one to the Palace; such a decision should apply evenly to both houses.[22]

These writers displayed a predictable range of sophistication and thoughtfulness, or their lack, from the most naïve and superficial, as in Austin Fryers's insistence that "theatres are for playgoers, not for prurient prudes," to the unconventionally pragmatic, as in the case of "Clericus," a clergyman who argued against actions that would force prostitution out onto the streets, calling for a more practical solution — which he did not specify — instead. In his experience, he said, women who have accosted him and then apologized when he identified himself as a clergyman have asked to be helped to a better life. He has written to homes and societies on behalf of these women, but has found "the rules so stringent, the work so hard, and the real sympathy so slight that it took all the heart out of me." "A Loather of Humbug" insisted that those who find any impropriety in the beautiful tableaux vivants or the "splendidly dressed" ballets only display a "hopeless and ignorant fanaticism."[23]

George G. Gray, LL.D. and Justice of the Peace, one of many who sided with the principle of decorum above all, brought his personal experience to bear on the issue. Since prostitution "cannot be extirpated," he argued, the only thing that can be attempted is "to ensure order and decorum, and to remove temptation as far as practicable from the ordinary paths of the general public." He has spent many an evening in the Empire and has never been interfered with, but walking down Regent Street he has been accosted, "and sometimes clutched, by woman after woman." Thus, the "only ultimate effect" of closing down the Empire will be to depreciate its value in temporary favor "of some other place to which the class may migrate." Echoing George Gray's judgment about the propriety of the Empire lounge, "Honi Soit" reported that he had taken his wife there and walked in the promenade; there was no attempt at accosting, nor anything in language or gesture to offend "the most fastidious." He did not speculate what his experience might have been had his wife not been on his arm, whereas "C. V. H." said he had been accosted fifteen times in one evening "at the spot in question."[24] The ostensible decorum maintained by the Empire was evidently a much valued commodity. Theodore Wratislaw, poet and friend of Oscar Wilde, wrote to the *Pall Mall Gazette* to second Arthur Symons's view of the decorousness of the Empire promenade. He knew the Empire was "a paradise of order and propriety" in comparison with other London music halls, he said, and "little fault" is to be found in the conduct of the place. In fact, he insisted, "a fairly innocent *ingenue* might pass through the promenade and performance of any music-hall," including the five-shilling Empire promenade, "without eating of the fruit of the tree of knowledge."[25]

A "West-Ender" offered a thoughtful discussion of the relation between ethical principles and the practical realities issuing from the council's threatened actions. The council should not be "a monstrous, melancholy, and narrow-minded tyranny," he argued; indeed, reformers must be perfect specimens of virtue themselves or they cannot legitimately condemn others less pure. The fact is that European cities deal with the problem of prostitution by toleration; those "hapless members of society" are treated as human beings, allowed to enjoy the right of orderly people who congregate "for pleasure or refreshment under due control," so long as they cause no scandal. The history of the closing of such notorious places as the Holborn Casino and the Argyll Rooms shows that such expedients serve only to drive prostitutes out into the streets.

And so a great range of opinion of varying degrees of cogency was gaining wide circulation, thanks to the editorial efforts of the *Telegraph*, which, however, also took care to publish the occasional long letter full of intelligent, trenchant criticism. Persons unfamiliar with the sordid, grim realities of street prostitution and, in particular, the night hells of Leicester Square need to be taught the baleful consequences of shutting down places like the Empire, said "M.F." in a densely detailed communication to the *Telegraph* on 16 October, laying out an extraordinarily telling analysis of the situation. The former Holborn Casino and Argyll Rooms were at least under the control of the police, who could "enter and interfere" as frequently as they judged to be necessary, dealing with evil in a way that kept it out of the public eye. But these places were shut down and then succeeded by "night clubs," charitably called "dancing clubs," which do not open until 12:30 A.M., admitting the "frail freight" free of charge as a way of luring men in and, by exacting an admission charge from them, avoiding the scrutiny of the law. The scenes there can hardly be described:

> Within a radius of one hundred yards of the Empire Theatre at the present moment there exist at least a dozen of these night hells, where some of the members say good evening with an oath and good morning with a champagne bottle. . . . Here you can dance with the best and the finest of the demi-monde to the strains of a more or less efficient orchestra, with vitriolised drink supplied to you at fabulous prices, while the master of the ceremonies will come up to you with suggestions not to be repeated. Here, if you are in that way inclined, you can have a music-hall song-and-dance turn supplied to you between the waltzes, if you are of a "variety" loving turn of mind, and from here you can be taken home to some of the souteneur

robbing dens of Soho if you are not careful, and I need not say what is in store for you if you are not in the company of "One who knows." It is from a place of this description that you can be lured where you will soon find that all your money can be stolen from you in a few hours. . . . It was at one of these places, kept by a man who has "done time" twice, that I saw a poor fast woman felled to the ground with a blow from the fist of a pugilist. It was at one of those places that I, with my own eyes, saw another poor creature well soaked in drink persuaded to divest herself of every vestige of her clothing and dance to an applauding crowd of shameless cardsharpers and well-dressed rogues and vagabonds. It is at these dens that the licensing laws are openly defied, that the lowest form of human scum is allowed to gather under the legalising aegis of a club and the purity policy of the goody-goody Council.

"Are we, then, to be driven to this?" M.F. asks. It must be remembered that such places "do flourish" and will continue to do so more and more as the county council goes on closing up or restricting "legitimate amusement." The reformers are mistaken in thinking that vice can be eradicated "by putting it beyond the bounds of civil compassion and recognition," the writer insists, and the council would be exceeding its powers and rights through such an attempt. Elucidating a clear principle underlying the matters under discussion, the writer concludes that, if the council succeeds, people will have lost "that individual freedom of action which is the one and only root of real morality."[26]

### IMPERIUM ET LIBERTAS

As the wheels of appelate justice began to turn and Edwardes readied himself for what now promised to be the ordeal of the council's meeting, had he taken the time to follow the correspondence in the *Telegraph* he might have derived some small comfort, at least, from the tenor of many of the letters. A dominant theme in the missives written over the days after the committee's decision and collected under the rubric "Prudes on the Prowl" was that of individual freedom, a theme whose clear and resonant term of preference was "liberty." "Another Englishman" wrote to condemn attempts to shut down the Empire as "tyranny of the worst, lowest, and vilest description," amounting to "a vicious intolerance of personal liberty."[27] On 13 October the *Saturday Review* joined the fray in a strongly worded article castigating the originators of the onslaught on the Empire and the freedom of association it offered. Focusing on the intense period of a few days when tableaux vivants at the Palace and the Empire and the music-and-dancing license at St. James's Hall were taken up by the Theatres and Music Halls Committee, the *Saturday Review* leaped to the defense of freedom in a piece entitled "Pharisaism and Music-Halls." The "floodgates of social purity" had been opened at that very moment, the author of the article tartly observed, "and a torrent of nastiness, sufficient to corrupt the youth of England for generations to come, was poured forth." The critics of these entertainments had given their true motives away. In opposing the tableaux at the Palace, W. A. Coote had described them "with a minuteness and vividness of colouring worthy of Boccaccio." Then the Empire was attacked by Mrs. Chant and six other persons officially unconnected with the National Vigilance Association but "animated by all its fiery zeal." In the view of the writer, the principal charge against the living pictures at the Empire was the lowering of the level of audience behavior simultaneously with the lowering of the lights. The upshot of the efforts of these determined zealots was that the license was recommended for renewal subject to "ruinous and mischievous conditions." The tyrannical imposition of these persons' standards upon "the tastes and amusements of their neighbors" was bad enough, said the writer, but the pruriency exhibited and fostered by their procedures "is worse," and likely to cause "more harm to the public than the evils against which they expend so much virtuous indignation."[28]

Readers were also encouraged to think in this direction by a leading article in the 15 October issue of the *Telegraph*, which noted that the recent efforts of "Purists" have had at least the one salutary result of prompting people to reflect on certain principles, the broadest of which was "the right appertaining to individual liberty." A public venue where decorum is maintained, the argument ran, confers on its clients the opportunity to congregate without restriction. Betraying an "absence of critical judgment," these prudes cannot be content with the fact that the Empire promenade is not "a scene of disorder"; unsatisfied with appearances, they pry beneath the surface "to reveal every kind of festering sore." Granted, the Empire staff has an "astonishing" ability to identify and refuse admission to such criminal elements as procurers and the women they have forced into profligacy and even thievery. But if the county council abolishes the promenade and forbids the serving of alcohol in the auditorium, the results will be that moderate drinkers will be driven to the other bars and tempted to drink excessively, and that women who now "conduct themselves with propriety" in the Empire promenade will be forced onto the streets. And thus Leicester Square, Cranbourne Street, Coventry Street, and the Haymarket "will once more become a howling wilderness of brazen-faced soliciting women and male profligates of every grade." Before long, we may begin to hear of police raids on "illicit dens of vice" that will rival "the depravity of the old night-houses of the West-end." In retrospect, the existence of such places as the Argyll Rooms, Vauxhall Gardens, and Cremorne Gardens, now all closed, is defensible as a positive good; police supervision was efficient there, with the result that "respectable persons of both sexes" could attend "without running the risk of being personally molested" or witnessing anything unseemly.[29]

The *Telegraph* thus brought to the fore an argument crucial to the thinking of many observers: that a necessary link exists between the free enjoyment of personal liberty and the efficient maintenance of decorous propriety in public places. Again and again, in letters to the *Telegraph*, the *Pall Mall Gazette*, and other journals, writers insisting on the importance of keeping good order and respectability in public places could be understood to be arguing, if only implicitly, for such a condition as a necessary one in which personal liberty may flourish. In one instance, "A Man About Town" argued that the "social evil," however ineradicable, can be "kept away from our immediate notice" — and should be, considering the potential harm done to a "rising generation of girls" by making them see prostitutes on Regent Street and elsewhere who have been forced into the open by the closing of "certain resorts."[30] Implied in the argument is the alleged infringement of young women's liberty to appear in public without being made to confront the unseemliness of illicit sexual activity. In the same issue of the *Telegraph* a writer cloaking himself in the verbal guise "Freedom" hoped that the threat by "a lot of unsexed 'New' women and prurient old men" would wake up sleepy Londoners to the need for an "Anti-Vigilance Society," taking as its motto the Englishman's "Imperium et Libertas" — sovereignty and freedom from restraint. In the swiftly rising heat of the controversy, the idea of liberty as an English birthright was surfacing almost everywhere. Richard Spearman, of the Authors' Club, took the view that the deepest concern of citizens was with "attacks on their personal liberty."[31] At a meeting at Phasey's Assembly Rooms in Lambeth Palace Road, Deputy Sheriff Beard accused the "purity party" of doing much mischief by their "crusade against an unfortunate class of women" who had the right to go to any place of entertainment "so long as they conducted themselves properly."[32]

Another writer who held a bleak view of what may happen to women who pass their prime as prostitutes, becoming "the filthy and dishonoured victims" of male lust, argued against the committee's decision. The danger, wrote an "Englishman," was that if we restrain ourselves and keep silent, we will be helping to ruin the work of half a century "in refining and purifying" the people's amusements and will "turn the dread current of poisonous vice into our own domestic channels." Restraint will only augment "the nameless horrors of abandoned sexuality" and drive to despair "the poor, hunted, men-ruined outcasts of the city" who now are doing all they can to keep their behavior decorous, in order to "preserve the last rag and vestige of their lost and stolen shame."[33]

The author's rhetoric is complex; he may appear to argue in favor of the restrictions likely to be placed on the Empire license by the county council, but he also seems to hold that any effort to purify the halls would be only counterproductive, effectively sending the women out of the Empire and back to the streets.[34] Central to the argument, however, is a view shared by many writers and frequenters of the Empire who remained untroubled by the alleged sad fate of prostitutes. Like them, like the theatrical manager and historian John Hollingshead, the social commentator F. Anstey, and presumably George Edwardes himself, the writer places a premium on respectability, on the maintenance at all costs of decorous behavior in public. The writer's logic is uneasy, but it is nonetheless clear that in his opinion decorous behavior is the only means left to these women for the preservation of decency. Such behavior can only be exhibited in a locale that places the highest value on decorum, however unspeakable the realities that lie beneath it. While some writers focused exclusively on the question of liberty and others entirely on decorum, the link between the two values was quite clear: the preservation of decorum in public places was the sine qua non for the enjoyment of an Englishman's time-honored entitlement to liberty.

As the debate over the twin desiderata of liberty and decorum became increasingly intense, another leading article in the *Telegraph* made a particular point of objecting to the obsessive prying beneath the surface of respectability that, in its view, characterized the efforts of the "Prudes." The national self-image, recently praised for its virtuousness by no less a personage than the U.S. ambassador, was no longer to be seen through rose-colored glasses, said the author of the piece; in its place had come a morbid national "self-examination." "Ferociously virtuous ladies" have been promenading, looking in vain by "the light of their own purity to discover an honest woman." But the eye brings what it wants to see; because they mistake "their own pruriency for the impurity of others," they thus perceive "rampant immorality." They are therefore to be condemned as "the slaves alike of diseased imaginations." Blind, narrow fanatics, possessed only of a "most dangerous half-knowledge of the world," they exaggerate evils that have only been dreamt of and so are led to reach "passionately unjust conclusions."[35] Such rhetoric was now generating much more heat than light, merely confirming already fiercely held opinions.

All the same, not all writers agreed that the closing of the Empire promenade constituted an intolerable infringement on personal liberty. "An Officer," citing John Stuart Mill's classic treatise *On Liberty*, pointed out that the test of the validity of placing limits on liberty was to ask if such action would "prevent harm to others." Mill had evaluated that test in great detail in his widely read and broadly influential 1859 treatise "Civil, or Social Liberty," in which he had asserted "one very simple principle," that "the only purpose for which power can be rightfully exercised over any member of a civilized community, against his will, is to prevent harm to others." That person's own good, whether physical or moral, does not constitute "a sufficient warrant" for interference, Mill argues, for "over himself, over his own body and mind, the individual is sovereign."[36] Taking as his text a phrase from Tocqueville, "the tyranny of the majority," Mill explains the great danger to which individuals are subjected by such threats from the society in which they live. Society, he explains, may practice a tyranny greater than other sorts of political oppression — greater, because, leaving fewer avenues for escape, it makes its way more deeply into the particulars of life, finally "enslaving the soul itself." It is therefore not enough to protect against the tyranny exercised by the magistrate; protection is needed also against "the tyranny of the prevailing opinion and feeling" and against society's tendency to impose "its own ideas and practices as rules of conduct" on dissenters. The interference of general opinion with "individual independence" must be limited; discovering and maintaining that limit is just as indispensable to civilized society as protecting it against despotism.[37] In an irony Mill might not have fully savored, the "majority" of moral and social reformers championed by Mrs. Chant and her colleagues seemed in fact a decided minority, staunchly opposed to the views of a majority who valued what they called "liberty" above all other goods.

Finally, on the twentieth of the month, in a leading article wearily marking the closing of the voluminous correspondence relating to "prudes on the prowl," the *Telegraph* identified the great preponderance of opinion to have fallen on the side of "liberty and common-sense as against the intolerable pharisaism of a few ill-advised prudes." If certain persons are disorderly, said the writer, let them be ejected. Otherwise, what entitlement is there "to order an inquisition into their antecedents and their habits"? No such inquiry could be conducted without interfering seriously with "the very principles and safeguards of individual freedom." The point it all comes down to, said the exasperated writer, is the fundamental "principle of individual liberty."[38]

On the same day, commenting from his vantage point as theatre reviewer of the *Illustrated London News*, Clement Scott set in perspective what he viewed as the fundamental issue. Inveighing against an "extremist party" that "looks upon all pleasures, and the theatre in particular, as a mortal sin," he charged the London County Council with the task of having to decide if "our legitimate pleasures and relaxations" are to be handed over to that party or to "men of broader, more manly, and more English views," possessed of "more toleration, more knowledge of the world, and, as I presume, far more common-sense." Betraying a tone of anxious worry, Scott called upon the full council to reverse the recommendation of the licensing committee.[39] Echoing his recommendation, on the twenty-sixth of the month — the very day the council was meeting to determine the fate of the Empire — the *Telegraph* observed in a kind of anticipatory summary that the one thing everyone was concerned about was "the necessity for good order, decorum, and respectability," adding the caveat that it was "an extremely unwise thing to peer in any prudish or inquisitive manner beneath the surface."[40] By this point, the presumed connection between liberty and the appearance of order and decorum had been reaffirmed twenty times over.

Still another aspect of the controversy, one seemingly unconnected with the question of decorum, ended up being linked with it. A major irritant to writers concerned with the infringement of personal liberty was the lack of sworn testimony in committee and council meetings. Neither the Theatres and Music Halls Committee nor its parent council had the authority to require witnesses to swear upon oath to the truth of their assertions. Interviewed along with other council members by a representative of Dalziel's agency, the architect Walter Emden stated his view that the real reason why the Vigilance Association did not go before the magistrates to achieve its objectives was that, there, its members would have to give sworn testimony; before the Theatres and Music Halls Committee they can, Emden said, make irresponsible statements and the other side cannot produce refutation under oath.[41] In its leader closing off correspondence on the "prudes on the prowl," the *Telegraph* had deplored an inquiry conducted "under conditions which would not convict a servant-girl of misbehavior." Evidence given before the committee was "wholly factitious and prejudiced," the lead insisted, amounting to testimony "absolutely unsupported by oath."[42] The *Music Hall and Theatre Review* complained even less temperately that the licensing of prominent places of amusement had never been intended to require defense "against the unsworn babblings of neurotic females."[43]

Indisputably, decorum in public places had become a highly charged issue, and no mere desire for orderly, peaceful assembly lay behind the widespread insistence on maintaining it at any cost. The *Telegraph* editors seemed nearly hysterical on the subject by the time their latest leading article appeared, and there were many others as well who panicked at the thought of the horrors to be found beneath the facade of propriety, were it not kept up with iron determination. And so the perceived necessity for decorum and its link with the general principle of liberty, along with the related principle of freedom of association, proved to be among the most important issues arising in the aftermath of the Theatres and Music Halls Committee's recommendation to the council.

At the same time, the alleged failure of wisdom (in the opinion of the *Telegraph*) demonstrated in persistent prying beneath the surface of society took on its most serious and profound implications in the central case of the tolerated, and sometimes welcomed, presence of strange-faced, unaccompanied women in the Empire five-shilling lounge. Their mostly decorous and yet ambiguous common identity as women with whom temporary connection might be made, for a price, would eventually overshadow every other issue that emerged in the early course of the Empire licensing controversy — except, of course, the issue of the renewal of the license itself.

Not surprisingly, Mrs. Chant came closer than most to describing at least some of the symbolic freight with which the attack on the Empire was so heavily encumbered. During the same period of days after the momentous 10 October meeting of the Theatres and Music Halls Committee, Mrs. Chant had swiftly become a famous or, in many circles, notorious public figure, the subject of much commentary and vilification. With mounting enthusiasm for the fray, she rose to the occasion. Interviewed at home by a *Pall Mall Gazette* reporter, who asked what the ultimate aim was of the "Purity Crusaders" — a term she evidently did not dispute — Mrs. Chant pointed to the need for a complete reform of the entertainment on view in the music halls and, beyond that, for the abolition of prostitution. Challenged on her imputation of indecency to the dancers themselves, she responded that she knew the girls onstage were "mainly . . . good," but custom had blinded them to the fact that "the absence of clothing" offended "their own self-respect." "They do not realize," she explained, "that they are exhibited well-nigh undressed for the men in the lounge, men so used up that they could not be attracted by a less sensational form of spectacle." As for the prostitutes in the promenade, they were welcome to attend for amusement, "but not to carry on their trade." Even if they did no more than raise an eyebrow or use "an impudent look?" the reporter asked. Not even that should be tolerated "in a music-hall," she answered. Then where is prostitution to be relegated? "Our ultimate aim is the entire abolition of this terrible trade," Mrs. Chant replied. Pressed for some visible indications of the improvement she believed had occurred in the situation, she at first could cite only her own appearance before the Theatres and Music Halls Committee and the "gentlemanly bearing" of George Edwardes in her cross-examination of him. In former days such an action would have subjected a woman to "ribald laughter and indecent suggestions" being hurled at her.[44]

The rescue work she and her compatriots have been doing is another proof of progress, Mrs. Chant added. She had brought a prostitute from the Empire lounge to her house, "a girl earning her £20 and £30 a week from the lounge habitués." Seeing Mrs. Chant's collection of shells, she admired and played with them, and "for an hour that girl was as simple and pure in her thoughts . . . as a child." In that space of time she forgot all about the Empire "and all about everything impure." Such are the signs of "the ultimate success of our crusade," Mrs. Chant insisted.[45]

Reacting to the *Pall Mall Gazette* interview with Mrs. Chant, Bernard Shaw addressed the economic context of prostitution and specifically Mrs. Chant's description of a woman from the Empire lounge earning £20 or £30 a week. He argued that such a statement "is calculated to make more prostitutes in a week than the 'Living Pictures' will in ten years" because it suggests that resorting to the Empire promenade will produce an annual income of £1,000 — "exactly what every procuress assures the girls whom she is tempting into prostitution." If he had invited an Empire prostitute to his house, he would forgive her for representing her annual income as between £1,000 and £1,500; "but I should not believe her." The county council sets a "moral minimum" wage of twenty-four shillings weekly for men and only eighteen for women. Yet a mere third of that will buy "an incredible quantity of daily drudgery" from "vigorous young girls," who to earn it must sacrifice beauty, youth, health, and self-respect much more completely than must any woman, no matter how licentious, who can command a thousand a year. What marriage means to such girls is living with a man "legally licensed to abuse them" as no man dare abuse an Empire prostitute. No woman would tolerate such a life if her alternative was to earn a thousand a year "under the much decenter and healthier conditions, both moral and material," that an income like that would secure. Shaw therefore appealed to Mrs. Chant to let her readers know "how much an ordinary young woman can earn as a prostitute; how often she earns it; how much she has to pay out of it for lodgings, clothes, and the services of some man to protect her from violent and drunken visitors; what her relations with the police are; what the effect on her health is of the life she has to lead, in short, how far her life is worth living in point of comfort, quite apart from conscientious scruples."[46]

Shaw's insistence on the reality of women's earnings was well taken; had he cared to pursue the point in the direction of Empire dancers, the analogy would have held true. In comparison with the alleged earnings of Empire prostitutes, even by the end of the century no dancer at the Empire or Alhambra earned anything approaching such sums, except for principals, who brought in between five guineas and twenty pounds per week. Dancers in the front row of the corps earned 30s to 35s; those in the second row, 12s 6d to 18s.[47] It was unlikely that Mrs. Chant would have known such details about the realities of dancers' lives; more likely that she would have understood something of the complex reputation mainly tending toward the unsavory, under which such young women labored. In any case, her censorious comments on the skimpiness of clothing worn by the dancers in the Empire ballet undoubtedly constituted a knowing protest against the eroticization of the female body that occurred in the act of making it a public spectacle.

Charles Booth's commentary on the profession of ballet girl in this period, in his compendious *Life and Labour of the People in London*, discussed the question of reputation from a professional vantage point. The best dancers on the stage of the Empire, the Alhambra, and comparable theatres were foreigners, Booth explained, from the dancing schools of Milan and elsewhere. European training was traditionally more rigorous and successful, making for stiff competition for English girls who aspired to a dancer's career. Those skillful and fortunate enough to make their way into the corps de ballet at the big houses had fairly regular employment all year, while others, when not working, lived with their parents, worked as dressmakers or needlewomen, or might "have recourse to less reputable modes of obtaining a livelihood." And yet, Booth thought, ballet girls leaving the theatre appeared to resemble any other group of women "leaving a respectable place of business."[48] W. S. Gilbert wrote in defense of the "humbler ballet girl" that she is "often a very good girl, working hard with her fingers all day, and equally hard with her toes all night."[49]

Testimony from an expert source endorsed the view. In the November 1889 issue of the *Church Reformer* there appeared a paper read the month before by a prominent professional dancer, Julie Seale, at the October meeting of the Church and Stage Guild. Having begun her stage career at age six as a child chosen for the Drury Lane pantomime, after five years of experience she persuaded her mother to enroll her in Katti Lanner's ballet school, where over the course of five more years she learned "dancing, and all kinds of work for the stage." She then left to pursue a career in the ballet. "Handsome and clever" and an "admirable mime,"[50] Seale became a principal dancer at the Alhambra in 1890, a post she held for a decade and more.[51] In her talk Seale enumerated the well-known difficulties encountered by dancers at home and on tour: sporadic work, untrustworthy managers, long rehearsals followed by long performances, incessant making of the rounds of agents and auditions, the fatigue of travel. As for the "perils" and "temptations" of stage life, a certain danger to life and limb was encountered in trapdoors, moving scenery, and the like, she observed, but "practically there is no such thing as temptation *in* the theatre." Such temptations as there are, she explained, "lie outside: the same for the ballet, as for dressmakers and factory girls, or any women who have to earn their living in the world." Regrettably, another sort of danger was encountered at the stage door, the danger of wrongful impersonation of the ballet dancer by those who would exploit the dancer's false reputation for glamourous licentiousness. There are many such women in London, Seale pointed out, and enthusiastic reformers, well-intentioned but revealing "a lamentable ignorance of the theatre, and of the world they are dealing with," hear those women's tales, are deceived by them, and then "recklessly insult our profession."[52]

Notwithstanding any such aura of ostensible respectability, to the popular mind the profession of ballet dancer had long been irrevocably tainted. A writer in the *Town* in 1837, commenting on the situation of the opera dancer, complained that English girls, outclassed by their foreign competitors and hired merely as supernumeraries or "figurantes," were effectively members of "an academy for whoredom," since the Italian Opera backstage was "a perfect seraglio for the use of the wealthy licentious."[53] In 1862 the diarist Arthur Munby was approached by a "shabby-genteel" fellow who said he was a "theatrical agent" and asked Munby if he wanted "any ballet girls or poses plastiques." The man said he could supply him with girls "for ballet or poses or artists models" on "an hour's notice."[54] Despite defenses of the dancer's person and calling, the popular bias against the respectability of the ballet girl almost inevitably surfaced in the pornography of the period, as in *Intrigues and Confessions of a Ballet Girl: Disclosing Startling & Voluptuous Scenes Before & Behind the Curtain, Enacted by Well-known Personages in the Theatrical, Military, Medical & Other Professions; With Kisses at Vauxhall, Greenwich, &c., &c., and a Full Disclosure of the Secret & Amatory Doings in the Dressing Room, Under & Upon the Stage, in the Light & in the Dark, By One Who Had Her Share*, published around 1868 — a work with sufficient visibility to be cited in the *Index of Forbidden Books* compiled by a Victorian student of erotica.[55]

In their section "The Prostitute Class Generally," Henry Mayhew and Bracebridge Hemyng summed up the general understanding of the ballet dancer's character — "Ballet-girls have a bad reputation, which is in most cases well deserved" — but, unlike most other observers, they linked it to pressing economic realities. Dancers' remuneration is very poor, from nine to eighteen shillings per week, they claimed, and out of these scant funds "they have to find shoes and petticoats, silk stockings, etc., etc., so that the pay is hardly adequate to their expenditure, and quite insufficient to fit them out and find them in food and lodging." Was it any wonder, then, given this state of things, that "ballet-girls should be compelled to seek a livelihood by resorting to prostitution?"[56] Mayhew and Hemyng oversimplify the range of earnings of the women in the corps de ballet; those in the middle rows made fifteen to thirty shillings a week, those in the back rows ten to fifteen shillings, and those in the front row more; all the same, Hibbert's comment that rank-and-file dancers were "shamefully ill paid" held true.[57]

Certainly it was true that the realities of life for the average dancer at the Opera or elsewhere, early and late in the century, were usually far different from the romantic or licentious image rife in popular fantasy. Frederick Strange, managing director of the Alhambra, assured the members of the 1866 parliamentary select committee on theatrical licenses and regulations that "ballet girls are thought to be very much worse than they are." Many of them, he believed, were "highly educated and respectable, good girls" and some in the Alhambra ballet were "very highly educated women." All the same, should they want tea or coffee in their unheated dressing rooms, they could not afford to send a dresser to the canteen for it; "the girls have not much money to spend," he admitted.[58] During the height of the Empire controversy a dancer who identified herself as "A Ballet Girl From Necessity" explained what her life was really like. During the day she made waistcoats for six or eight shillings a week; at night she danced at the Empire, earning additional money that supported an invalid mother and a little brother. Without her combined income, she explained, they would be in the workhouse. Such realities enforced a different sort of economic perspective: her daytime work piled up "riches for others on what will not keep body and soul together." Meanwhile, the Vigilance Society had a long list of "wealthy and noble patrons," many of whom "have become rich by a system of underpay which has contributed so largely to what they pretend to suppress."[59] Arthur Symons captured the ballet dancer's straitened circumstances more poetically in "Décor de Théâtre," verses published in 1895 in his collection *London Nights.* Describing the life of the Empire corps de ballet behind the scenes, he portrays the "little painted angels" making their way down a backstage staircase toward the stage: "The shining creatures of the air / Troop sadly, shivering with cold," while the gaslight blown by drafts "shoots a thin / Sharp finger over cheeks and nose / Rouged to the colour of the rose."[60] Radical as were her views of the necessity for purity in social life, reports of Mrs. Chant's analyses of the broad situation do not support any perception on her part of the economic inequities inherent in urban life that could drive into prostitution young women attempting but unable to earn their living by honest means. Such inequities were nonetheless widespread, as Shaw and other sociologically inclined observers were ready to explain, and close to the surface.

Unruffled by Shavian analysis or other rhetorical adversity, over the days following her testimony before the Theatres and Music Halls Committee Mrs. Chant energetically exploited the momentum created by her appearance before that body, pursuing an active schedule of talks and lectures in which she sought to publicize and reaffirm her views and those of her colleagues on the question of the Empire license. Characteristically, she often distinguished her own beliefs from those of others, as in the case of a Sunday-school anniversary sermon preached at the Offord Road Congregational Chapel in Barnsbury, where she asserted that well-meaning men and women like the Puritans were mistaken in thinking that "amusement in itself was a bad thing"; such opinions play into the hands of "profligates and libertines." There was an "amusement-loving side of life," she argued, as well as a worshiping side, and there ought to be no "broad Atlantic of bigotry and misunderstanding" between them.[61] As late as January 1895 she was still driving home that point of distinction, identifying herself, in a speech before the West Bristol Gospel Temperance Society, as "the last person to feel anything except the extreme importance of multiplying the amusement of the people," but at the same time declaring herself determined to "free the theatres from drink and white slaves as the U.S. had freed the negroes."[62]

Adopting a more militant tone in a major speech at Leamington on 15 October, Mrs. Chant observed how "tremendous" it was "to attack the most fashionable and the richest music hall in London." The Vigilance Association took the view, she explained, that "impurity in rich men's halls should be recognised as much as in poor men's." A leading article in the *Telegraph* had acknowledged the existence of the shameful traffic in the Empire promenade and expressed fear of the state of the streets if the Empire were to be shut down. But what is done in the case of a fire is to "put it out and drive it out of sight and existence altogether." That was what the NVA intended to do. Their purpose was not to close down the music halls, she maintained, but to take them "out of the hands of a band of libertines and roués" and convert them into places "to which men and their families could go for enjoyment."[63]

Speaking at a temperance meeting in Chelmsford, Mrs. Chant took as her theme the sadness and waste of virtuous young women being lost. She admitted that when she appeared before the county council's licensing committee she had no idea such a storm would erupt throughout the country over the issues raised there. The sorrow and misery of the streets were bad enough, she said, but "some of their fairest girls going to ruin" in places of amusement was "nothing less than dastardly." The Empire pays a 75 percent dividend — and yet it must close if the promenade is abolished? All that wealth and power can do is being aimed at the council to reject the licensing committee's recommendation. But the question remained, why cleanse the poor man's hall and leave "the den of the rich untouched?" As for the recurrent criticism that closing the Empire would turn women out onto the streets, the crusaders would much prefer to deal with them "when they were cold and miserable in the open air than when they were painted and successful in the promenade." The intention was "to get at their fallen sisters, and at the men at the back of them too."[64]

Speaking once again, at Presbyterian Hall, Church-end, Finchley, the day before the special meeting of the council scheduled for 26 October, Mrs. Chant responded to the sympathetic support of the meeting by pointing out that the crusaders had "let their light into the darkest holes of London." A comic side of things had emerged in the way she was depicted by writers and cartoonists in the newspapers, but the issues were deeply serious. It would be a deplorable blow, she acknowledged, if the council failed to endorse the recommendation of the licensing committee. For twenty-seven years they had been trying to get the women off the streets; now, if all went well, they were "going to stop the manufacture of them." In any case, Mrs. Chant concluded, they had already pushed away "the rose bushes that covered a seething pit of infamy."[65]

Perhaps sensing that, despite her efforts, her views had not been made sufficiently clear or had become distorted, Mrs. Chant restated her case, as reported in the *Daily Telegraph*. All she wanted was to get rid of the "unclean features" that prevent decent people "from attending and enjoy-ing the performances." She had seen the entertainments at the Palace The-atre of Varieties and was "charmed and delighted"; as for the living pictures there, she could object to only three, which, significantly, were received "almost in silence" by the audience. "Do I object to ballet?" she went on to ask rhetorically. Nothing was further from her mind. Nor did she object to "tights, as such." She knew that vigorous dancing should not be "impeded by clinging petticoats about your ankles, or even about the knees." She felt capable of designing a costume that would confer freedom "and yet clothe the limbs" — though she was not "one of those who think it a shame to have legs."[66]

The question of the propriety and utility of the dancer's costume was coming in for a larger share of attention, in the midst of the controversy. At the 10 October hearings, Edwardes had explained in a matter-of-fact way that the dress of the première danseuse was the same all over Europe, the skirt being uniformly sixty-two inches long, and the trunks are "invariably covered with tulle"; and "finally there are the tights."[67] In a pamphlet entitled *The Art of Dancing: On a Question of Dress*, published in 1891, Selwyn Image had taken up the central question of "the artistic propriety" of the dress traditionally worn by "a *Première Danseuse* in the Ballet." It has been the same for generations, he explained, because it suits "the graceful posing of body and limbs in a rhythmically progressive movement." It takes pains and skill to learn to perform the movements of ballet, he pointed out, and we must learn to appreciate what is comprised in the details of the real art — for example, "this or that niceity in the turn of a neck, a wrist, an elbow, a knee, an ancle" — in short, the steps and their combinations that "go to make up the Dance." It is therefore an important question what kind of dress the première danseuse must wear "to do justice to her art." Any dress that conceals or obstructs the limbs or calls attention away from them goes completely against the purpose of "displaying the human body" in ways that the "distinctive qualities of Ballet Dancing" depend on. This, therefore, is the dress that has come down to us traditionally: "the low, tight bodice; the short, diaphanous skirt standing out well from the hips" (fig. 30). Its primary object is not its own beauty but the greatest possible "free movement of the limbs and body." In addition, its artistic value is to give "a charming effect of colour" and to induce in the viewer the sense or suggestion "of a delicate vapour hovering round her, as if she came to us amid a diaphanous, tinted, cloud."[68]

Image's language, idealizing the functional yet feminine dress of the ballet dancer, echoed earlier and contemporary ideas about the spiritual qualities of artistic dance. Just two years before, in 1889, Stewart Headlam, founder in 1879 of the Church and Stage Guild to support dancers and other performers in their calling and to combat unreasonable prejudice against the stage, published a lecture entitled *The Function of the Stage* that encapsulated his views on the subject. For Headlam, dance was an

30. C. Wilhelm, "Designs for the Costumes of Premières Danseuses." Magazine of Art *18*
(*1894*), *16*. PP1931pc1. By permission of the British Library.

idealized, symbol-making activity essentially pure in itself and conferring,
like other arts of performance, an intrinsic social utility. Ballet and spectacle ministered no less than tragedy and comedy to "the well-being of
humanity," he argued, for dancers were preeminently actors, expressing
an inner reality in apprehensible terms.[69] Consequently their clothing was
an integral part of their art. Moreover, the dancer herself represents an
interesting notion of expressive form. Headlam quotes a poem by Thomas
Gordon Hake, "The Dancing Girl," which describes how the dancer
throws all her being into her art. Like a nymph leaping out of the waves,
"from her soul's fount she springs": "Draped in her gossamer, where'er she
goes / A pliant fold her inmost grace repeats."[70] The couplet offers a striking image, anticipating an almost Yeatsian aesthetic wholeness and inten-
sity achieved by the dancer in self-expressive, self-definitive movements.
And yet, for all its succinctness, the passage simultaneously idealizes, spiritualizes, and seemingly desexualizes the dancer's activity in ways consistent with Headlam's own platonic approach to the dancer's art. Evidently,
unlike Mrs. Chant's, Headlam's professed interests lay elsewhere than in
the fleshly qualities of the woman as dancer.

Set in the context of the current licensing controversy, Image's and
Headlam's efforts to argue for the primary existence of the première
danseuse on a spiritual plane could be taken by social purity reformers
merely as attempts to deflect charges of indecency by pretending that
such issues do not pertain to art. Such efforts miss what Mrs. Chant

viewed as the essential problem with such entertainment, as she explained in a telegram printed by the *Telegraph* on 18 October, namely, "the motive at the back of it all, and the obvious suggestiveness, which makes the thing evil." To this insight she added a rhetorical turn that was already a staple of feminist critiques of a patriarchal society: "The whole question would be solved if men, and not women, were at stake. Men would refuse to exhibit their bodies nightly in this way."[71]

### DAUGHTERS OF ENGLAND

Meanwhile, as Mrs. Chant exploited her perceived advantage to the fullest, reactions to reports of her testimony and views laid their own claim to attention. "A Parent of Daughters," citing evidence from Mrs. Chant's account of her visit to the Empire promenade, wrote to the council in nearly hysterical outrage over the scene described. The pretty girl of sixteen positioned in the promenade to attract arriving men's attention, "glancing at men and then turning her head and casting frightened looks at some women under whose influence she was acting," presents "a terrible picture to contemplate and makes the blood of parents boil with indignation." The child could be taken to "a Bawdy house" and "perhaps infected with disease" and then, having been paid, might have to return the money to the procuress and then repeat the process all over again. The prospect was appalling: "how often this might happen who is to say."[72]

Behind such heated rhetoric lay assumptions about the proper place of women in society that grounded a wide range of more specific attitudes. In her early Victorian book of wholesome advice to the daughters of England on their social and domestic duties, Sarah Stickney Ellis had cautioned them not only to accept and be content with the inevitable fact of their inferiority to men, but also to found the ethical basis of their behavior and actions in society on that very principle. Having seriously reflected on "her position in society as a woman," and having examined her own nature, the young woman of the "middle ranks of society" should have discovered "a capability of feeling, a quickness of perception, and a facility of adaptation" beyond what her male counterpart possessed and that consequently "fit her for a distinct and separate sphere." Such determined self-reflection was vital for the maintenance of virtue, Mrs. Ellis insisted, for it was "appalling to contemplate the extent of ruin and of wretchedness to which woman may be carried by the force of her own impetuous and unregulated feelings."[73]

Concern for the virtue of the daughters of England on the part of moralists like Ellis or less visible writers of letters to editors took a variety of forms, but perhaps none so radical as that expressed by the author of *The History of European Morals*. In the tenth edition (1892) of his book W. E. H. Lecky repeated his heterodox assertion that the prostitute is "ultimately the most efficient guardian of virtue." "But for her," Lecky's argument ran, "the unchallenged purity of countless happy homes would be polluted, and not a few who, in the pride of their untempted chastity, think of her with an indignant shudder would have known the agony of remorse and despair."[74] Peter Gay suggests that Lecky may have gotten the idea of polluted women as a necessary evil, safeguarding the virtue of the unpolluted, from Dr. Alexandre Parent-Duchâtelet's *De la Prostitution dans la ville de Paris* (1836), in which he claimed that a man reluctant for fear of disease to consort with prostitutes "will instead pervert your daughters and your servants" and ultimately "bring misfortune . . . to all of society."[75] More likely, Lecky got the notion from W. R. Greg's widely read and influential review of Parent-Duchâtelet and other works, published unsigned in the *Westminster Review* in June 1850, addressing "the darkest, the knottiest, and the saddest" of all social problems, and ultimately advocating state regulation of prostitution as the only feasible remedy for the otherwise horrific situation that would obtain.[76]

Greg had presented what may well have been the most conscientious analysis to date of marriage and sexuality in contemporary society. Although he quotes extensively from Parent-Duchâtelet, dubbed by the *Quarterly Review* the "Newton of Harlotry" for his endless production of statistics,[77] Greg brought his own, more sympathetic insights to bear on the distressing plight of the English prostitute, whose more respectable and deliberate sisters sell themselves in marriage at the rate of ten to one, he asserted, compared to those unfortunates who fall victim to seducers out of generous but misplaced impulses to part with what they hold most dear.[78] Sexual desires are awakened at an unnaturally early age, Greg argues, by the poor regulation of nearly all educational establishments, where vicious ideas circulate freely and where licentious language and coarse, vulgar habits prevail. If sexual desire were gratified immediately on its arousal, the reverence for the female sex that leads to chivalrous behavior and eventually to love would never be awakened. For the fact is that all the "delicate and chivalric" feelings that still characterize men's sentiments toward women can be traced to *"repressed,* and therefore hallowed and elevated passion." There is no greater safeguard against "sensuality and low intrigue" for a young man than "an early, virtuous, and passionate attachment," he observed. Presumably, Greg meant to identify a time in early adulthood when the achievement of full powers of procreation naturally and wholesomely coincides with the opening of opportunity for happy marriage. Unfortunately, wide observation of contemporary society yields abundant instances of how far men fall from the standard of right thinking about sexual matters. How can men behave this way, Greg asks repeatedly, and square their behavior with their consciences? And yet, he acknowledges, given the present constitution of society, "illicit intercourse will and must prevail to a very considerable extent; and from this, prostitution, we fear, must inevitably flow."[79]

Greg remained apparently unaffected by Parent's own deep anxiety about what happens to women who somehow survive and move up out of the ranks of the public prostitute into less reprehensible callings. "They *come back into Society*," Parent explained, "they surround us," they "gain access to our homes."[80] The readmission of the prostitute into respectable society has its own dire consequences, many readers of Parent might have inferred, leading to a situation that forms an insidious corollary to Lecky's ostensibly outrageous contention. Perhaps Greg's conviction that a prostitute's fall is certain and swift prevented him from reading Parent clearly on this point. In any case, anticipating various objections to his developing argument for state regulation, Greg pointed out that no degree of individual liberty can exist at the expense of the common good; that, presently, married men frequent unregulated brothels and thereby introduce syphilis into their families, victimizing virtuous women and innocent children; and that the "tacit sanction" allegedly given to vice by acknowledging its presence is of little account alongside that "overt act of public mischief," the propagation of syphilis. Prostitution per se, however sinful, is "one of those vices, like bad temper, hatred, malice, and covetousness," that is not part of the government's duty to repress or punish, Greg observes; but a crime against society clearly falls within its province to prevent.[81]

After a near half century of arguments pro and con over the issue of state regulation of prostitution, readers of Lecky's tenth edition would have sensed a familiar ring to his argument in favor of official toleration. A measure of the wide currency of the idea occurs in Oscar Wilde's *Lady Windermere's Fan*, produced at the St. James's Theatre only two years before the Empire licensing controversy arose. Wilde turns it to witty account in Act 2, where he makes Lady Plymdale remark cynically that women of questionable reputation "are most useful. They form the basis of other people's marriages."[82] Two years earlier, in 1890, Grant Allen had underscored the idea in condemning the current "system" as "really a joint system of marriage and prostitution in which the second element is a necessary corollary and safeguard of the first."[83] From this it was an easy further step, one taken by another novelist, Sarah Grand, in 1898, to assert that men consider marriage "but a superior kind of prostitution."[84]

In his comprehensive essay "The Double Standard," Keith Thomas cites Lecky's analysis as the classic statement of the view that "a class of fallen women was needed to keep the rest of the world pure."[85] The historians J. A. Banks and Olive Banks read Lecky as defending the double standard on grounds of social expediency, and the existence of the prostitute on grounds of necessity, "the result of a conflict between the organization of society and man's sexual appetites."[86] It may be that Lecky had a more critical intention in mind. His somewhat convoluted argument may be taken to mean that married men resort to prostitutes to relieve the urgings of nature, where otherwise they would be committing adultery with other men's wives and daughters; consorting with prostitutes therefore effectively contributes to maintaining the happy home, pure and unsullied (as it were). The fact was, Lecky's argument, however outrageous and perhaps even ironic in its intent, offered troubling insight into current relations between men and women, married or otherwise, and presented a particular challenge to feminists. In a speech in Chicago given on her American tour of 1888 Mrs. Chant, missing any possible irony in Lecky's observation, had angrily attacked his ostensible view "that outcast women are necessary for the well-being of the community." "I want to ask him," she said, "if outcast men are necessary for the well-being of humanity, because, if [outcast] women are, men are."[87] The point of Mrs. Chant's riposte tends to elude scrutiny even more than does Lecky's trenchant assertion; perhaps her true intent is to erect an ironic standard of equality between women and men as a way of attacking the double standard and Lecky's apparent endorsement of it. Finally, Lecky's view, as generally understood, could not be effectively countered, even by so determined an adversary as Mrs. Chant, given society's current structure. As Thomas has so clearly explained, there were too many instances to the contrary to back up Lecky's perverse but persuasive contention.

## PROSTITUTES SPEAK OUT

Among the most interesting and occasionally poignant correspondence printed by the *Daily Telegraph* and other journals during the height of the controversy were letters from or on behalf of prostitutes themselves. In a communication whose rhetoric is extreme enough to suggest the hand of some other, pseudonymous writer with an axe to grind, "A Fallen Woman" confessed herself to be guilt ridden but hoped for sympathy rather than pity. Reformers are "iron-masked women," she complained, who set themselves far above other women, as if living in a different world, shutting their eyes to the fact that such unhappy creatures as she were also once virtuous, though now their plight is terrible, their gaiety short-lived, and their punishment "swift and sure."[88] In a similar vein, "A Soiled Dove" wrote in mournful tones of her life on the London streets. The career of a fallen woman is not one of pleasure, as so many seem to believe, she pointed out. "Have they known what it is to be starving, ill, and disheartened?" We know it, and "have to hawk our bodies about the streets, Mother Hawk abusing and ill-using us in every way" and claiming "rent" from us to spend in "show and pleasure."[89]

Surprisingly, "A Woman Who Has Not Yet Been Spoken To" spoke up on behalf of the endangered reputation of the modern-day gentleman. "An Englishman" had suggested that a lady could hardly walk in Regent Street or Piccadilly at certain times of the day or evening without being spoken to by a man. It is unfair to give men away entirely on this account, the writer protested. She was "moderately young" and considered attractive, even "handsome." She could say honestly that over the six years of her life in London, often going about alone, she has "never been spoken to in the street." If this happens to a girl or a woman, it is her own fault. "Men may be bad," she said, "but there are still some gentlemen left."[90]

"Not a Puritan" brought a more realistic and temperate viewpoint to the matter, in a letter that calls in question conventional wisdom about the sorry lot of the woman who has fallen. She had been a prostitute for a while, "through unhappy circumstances." During that time she met more kindhearted and worthy women than since her life has been "raised to a higher standard." She knows no fewer than six women in the same position who have since married, as she has, and they have become "most excellent wives in every sense of the word." Her own husband is a "thoroughly good fellow" whom she would not deceive, though she is not free from temptation. Most such women were left while young to provide for themselves; the alternative was domestic service, often tyrannized over by "perfect paragons of virtue." A partial solution to the problem might be found, she thought, in granting additional powers to magistrates to punish male seducers more heavily; a few shillings a week from the offending man does not serve to reinstate the woman in her previous position. So, often, the case is one of an "amiable weakness" on the part of the woman and "downright brutality" in the man, with the result that one party can "go on his way rejoicing" while the other is forever liable to be called "unkind names."[91]

Still another, distinctly different understanding of the situation appeared in a letter from "A Londoner," who had gone to the Empire second-tier promenade and spoken with one of the women he found there, setting down her replies to his questions in almost precisely her own language (or so he claimed). The most remarkable fact about the interview was that this woman made no apology for her life or her morals; almost as remarkable was her ability to see systemic connections among the various aspects and venues of prostitution. "What I do I do openly," she maintained. Mrs. Chant's presumptions were ignorant and unjustified. A gentleman had asked her whether if the door were open she would adopt a better life. She didn't want that, she had replied. Her life pleased and suited her; "I am very happy in it, and all the girls of my acquaintance are the same." "You don't want a helping hand?" asked the "Londoner" — he had always thought women were driven to this life. "I don't want to be reclaimed, and I won't be driven," she insisted. Where would she go if the Empire were shut down? To the Alhambra, the Palace, the Pavillion, she answered; "we can give them all a turn." What if Mrs. Chant and her colleagues could close them up too? She was not to be confused with women of Piccadilly, the woman retorted, and was superior to a "woman of society" who carries on in country houses: "But because I don't happen to wear a wedding-ring, and don't see the morality of selling my body and soul to a man I don't even care for, for life, in return for high position, wealth, and all the rest of it, am I to be down-trodden into the mire, and compelled to face an early death by prowling about Piccadilly until the small hours?" Why should she be treated as an outcast and branded a "fallen woman"? Her calling was "as necessary to the world as any other profession," she insisted, and she didn't want to be made "good" against her will; she wanted only to be let alone. If the London County Council wants to "reform us off the face of the earth," she added, they must "deal with the clubs and all that goes on in them." They should have dealt with them first, she added, and also "with the still more infamous resorts which exist for no other purpose than debauching young and innocent girls." Vigilance societies may deal with them, but then how will they prevent "the abuse of the West-end shops," whose tearooms and other refreshment places are innocently used by mothers and daughters who don't realize "assignations are being made under their noses." Even fashionable churches are "marts of vice"; St. Paul's is a common place of assignation for "City men and courtesans." The fact of the matter is that the women of the Empire promenade are very pretty and attractive, the woman concluded, and Mrs. Chant and the rest are really "spies" who out of prurient curiosity would love to know "what the men really say to us."[92]

## LETTERS TO THE COMMITTEE AND THE COUNCIL

In the same brief period during which the controversy was raging, the Theatres and Music Halls Committee along with the county council itself received numerous letters of protest, from the Theatrical and Music Hall Operatives Union, the Theatrical Choristers' Association, and many other groups.[93]

The letter from the Operatives Union, dated 15 October 1894, came as a result of a meeting held the previous day to discuss the grave situation union members saw themselves facing. Charles Thoroughgood, presiding officer, explained that conditions imposed by the licensing committee "would have the effect of closing the Empire Theatre." A member of the Empire staff cited the statistical realities of the fate that loomed so large: in addition to wives, 322 children depended on the labors of some 140 unionized stage employees. George Edwardes, who attended the Operatives Union meeting, made it clear that the enforcement of the committee recommendation to close off the promenades and prohibit the sale of intoxicating drink in the auditorium spelled "absolute ruin to the establishment and would compel them to close its doors." Adding to the gloomy statistics, Edwardes said he had given a formal fortnight's notice the previous night to some 670 employees, "upon whose labours fully 3,000 mouths depended for their daily bread." If the fortnight's notice takes effect, Thoroughgood explained, along with the 140 members of the union, more than six hundred members of the working staff and ballet would be driven out of employment. There were too many workers in the music hall business already, he added; unemployment would rise even more. The predictable sense of the meeting was then articulated in Thoroughgood's motion: "That this meeting deplores the decision of the Licensing Committee of the London County Council to impose upon the management of the Empire Theatre conditions which render it impossible to keep the theatre open, and thus throw a large number of people out of employment." The motion passed unanimously.[94]

In anticipation of the council meeting on 26 October, the Theatrical and Music Hall Operatives Union held another mass meeting on Sunday, 21 October, to consider the position of Empire employees. The executive of the union had met that morning and had recommended "vigorous action" against "the persecution to which a large number of their members were being subjected." The union was determined to prevent the adoption by the council of the licensing committee's recommendations, condemned by George Shipton, the secretary of the London Trades Council, as "a wanton piece of meddlesome cruelty."[95]

Meanwhile, the previous week, at a meeting on Sunday, 14 October, the ratepayers of Newington had unanimously adopted a resolution proposed by the officers of their association against the action of the licensing committee and conveyed it to the council members for West Newington, Messrs. Bott and Hopkins. Bott agreed to oppose the licensing committee's recommendation; Hopkins went even further. Hopkins had visited the Empire several times and found the performances not only "harmless" but "distinctly elevating." No doubt immoral women were present, but they did not make themselves objectionable. Expelling "these unfortunate women" from such places will only accentuate social problems, he insisted, and make the streets even more "disagreeable" for virtuous women than now.[96] A report of a meeting, on the same evening, of the London Cabdrivers Trade Union cited the view of its president that every effort should be made to support George Edwardes in keeping those persons so interested in the morals of the community from ruining not only public places of amusement but the cab industry itself.[97]

Other writers took up the strategy of addressing letters directly to the chair of the London County Council, Sir John Hutton, who had been reelected to his post the previous March.[98] A house porter at the Empire, Thomas Mitchell, petitioned him not to vote to confirm the Theatres Committee's restriction on the Empire license; Mitchell's letter was endorsed by forty-three "sympathising friends."[99] Similar letters, both sent on 22 October, opposing the recommended restrictions on the license came from the United Shop Assistants Union, from members of the "Grand Order of Water Rats, comprised of Members of the Music Hall Profession," and from members of the Orchestral Association, representing fifty-five out of the total of sixty professional musicians engaged in the Empire orchestra. The Cane and Bamboo Workers protested in similar terms, sending in their resolution: "That the Union while deploring the existence of prostitution and vice, protest against the ridiculous and Puritanical attitude of the Licensing Committee of the LCC believing that the cause of this vice lies deeper than that Committee seem to comprehend and can only be extinguished by the removal of that cause and not by throwing more women out of work to starvation or the streets."[100]

In contrast, members of the clergy and other religious and quasi-religious groups were inclined, not unexpectedly, toward support of the committee's recommendation. James G. King, secretary of the Royal Rescue Lodge No. 306, Independent Order of Good Templars, located at St. Alpheges Mission Hall, Hyde Vale, Greenwich, wrote to the council chair and members on behalf of the Templars membership to express "our high appreciation of the efforts of your Licensing Committee to improve the character of the places of Public Entertainment by the insertion of restrictions in the Licenses granted to these places, preventing the sale of Intoxicating Drinks in the Auditorium, and the closing of the Promenades which conclusive evidence has proved are used by persons of immoral character for purposes of solicitation etc."[101] Also on 22 October the United Methodist Free Church conveyed its request to the council to confirm the licensing restrictions.

Other, more liberal-tending organizations responded in tones of outrage and took issue directly with the stand adopted by Mrs. Chant and her colleagues. In a letter signed by its president and secretary, the London Patriotic Club wrote to the council to forward two resolutions taken in its committee meeting of 18 October: first, "[t]hat the People have a right to be amused in the manner which best suits them, and that they are the proper arbitrators of the same"; and, second, "[t]hat there has been no complaint from the Public against the exhibitions shown at the Empire Theatre" — in effect, a challenge to Mrs. Chant's claim that she spoke for the women of England. They therefore asked the council to disregard the licensing committee's recommendations and "the action of a narrow minded and bigoted faction" against the Empire's "well conducted plan of amusement."[102]

A longer letter to the council chair came from E. S. Gunn, who at first styled himself "An Observer" and then, casting aside his cloak of pseudonymity, signed his name. Gunn identified what was in his view the inevitable and fateful connection between the bars in the Empire and the prostitutes who frequented them, and offered a suggestion to solve the problem. His idea was to establish "a separate refreshment room for ladies," effectively segregating them from the males who otherwise would be marked out as the prey of "women who get their living at the expense of the health and morality of the public." Such women, in constant need of new customers, frequent the bars so as to make the acquaintance of a likely person. "If they can get their victims to stand drinks, so much the better," since, the further this strategy goes, "the less the chance of ultimate escape." Places like the Empire become "mere markets of vice" in the same way that the Exchange offers a meeting place for merchants, frequented by them simply because they are "more likely to find a customer there." If the council countermands the recommendation of its committee, Gunn added, "it will give a sort of official recognition or tolerance to the whole affair."[103]

Among the welter of correspondence received by the council on the eve of its meeting, a few letters attained a certain level of eloquence. The chair of the Wesleyan East End Mission, Peter Thompson, threw a bitter perspective on the prospects of young women who fall victim to the glamour of the Empire promenade. Those who have looked into the subject are aware how "short-lived" are "the pleasures of sin" for these women, he pointed out. The pretty girl of the Empire is soon "forced on to the streets as her only possible promenade." Larger money can buy "the youth and bloom of girlhood," and so "the ever fresh and clean supply must be lured and captured," only at length to be relegated to the streets, where they become "the hopeless, homeless, houseless hags of Whitechapel." Thompson went on to paint in truer colors such places as the mission he himself operated. Claiming to shelter unhappy women, he explained, they are really "the nurseries of the vicious, pouring the filthy and dishonoured victims of lust and wine upon the whole community." The extraordinary scene witnessed a short time ago, in which Edwardes called his employees onto the stage of the Empire and gave them notice, must be viewed either as a "hollow farce" or as "a striking testimony to the case against" the Empire: it was either a mere show, or else a confession that 75 percent in stockholder dividends "depends solely not on the excellence and interest of the entertainment but upon the promenade with women and wine."[104]

## CRUSADERS AND OTHERS

As the days before the county council meeting on 26 October grew short, some organizations in lieu of writing directly to the council took formal resolutions for or against the actions of the licensing committee. The ratepayers of Walworth, convening on 18 October under the auspices of the Ratepayers' Protection Association, recorded a unanimous formal protest against the actions of the licensing committee with regard to the Empire and other places of public entertainment, calling upon council representatives Marsland and Saunders to vote against the committee's recommendation and urging the council, if truly interested in the "elevation of public morals," to search out and abolish "the numerous sweating dens of London."[105] On the same evening, the annual meeting of the "Crusaders" in the Great Assembly Hall, Mile End Road, unanimously carried a resolution expressing approval that the licensing committee had seen its way clear, on the basis of "the most substantial evidence," to impose restrictions on certain music halls "in the interest of morality and temperance" and urging the council to reject any influence by "the rich interested persons."[106] The meeting was chaired by the well-known teetotaler Frederick N. Charrington, member both of the county council and of the Theatres and Music Halls Committee itself. As an activist in the cause of social purity Charrington was evidently untroubled by any suggestion of conflict of interest of the sort that had surfaced against his co-committee member J. F. Torr.

Perhaps the largest assembly gathered to react to the licensing committee's recommendations was one that crowded into the six-hundred-seat auditorium and onto the stage of the Prince of Wales's Theatre, in Charlotte Street, St. Pancras, not a long walk north from Leicester Square and Oxford Street, on the night of Sunday, 21 October, where representatives of the Theatrical and Music Hall Operatives, the Amalgamated Society of Painters, the Theatrical Choristers' Association, the Empire ballet dancers, the Empire scene shifters, the London Trades Council, the Amalgamated Society of Railway Servants, and the cab drivers spoke out in united voices against the terrible prospect of restriction. Hundreds of eager would-be participants were unable to obtain admission. As the meeting got under way, it was asserted that ten thousand working people would be affected directly or indirectly by the licensing committee's proposals. The secretary of the Theatrical Choristers' Association spoke "in praise of the ballet girl" and mentioned W. S. Gilbert's sympathetic endorsement of the present meeting. Edward Garrity, on behalf of the Amalgamated Railway Servants Association, suggested that if Mrs. Chant's object was to expose what was already frankly in the open she could go to St. Paul's on a Sunday night, to Westminster Abbey in the daytime, and to the National Gallery for a change. Referring to the licensing committee's recommendation of structural alterations at the Empire, Garrity asked rhetorically what would be the result if "the defenders of the Empire were to demand a structural change in the construction" of St. Paul's?[107]

Garrity was followed by a Miss Sheppard, who spoke on behalf of "the ballet girls of the Empire," having been one herself for the previous six years, by virtue of which employment she had been able to make the last years of her widowed mother more comfortable. Dancers' lives are as pure, she contended, and "their calling as honourable" as Mrs. Chant's. Gus Mitchell, speaking for the scene shifters, indignantly disputed Mrs. Chant's assertion that scanty clothing excites passions. "I am a man," Mitchell asserted, "and my passions have never been excited. And there are a hundred and forty scene shifters at the Empire, and their passions have never been excited."[108]

Bringing the meeting to a close, the chairman, Charles Thoroughgood, president of the Theatrical and Music Hall Operatives Union, called for the answer to a simple question: "Do you want the Empire closed?" As with one voice, the house shouted out its profound rejection of the very idea.[109]

And so, as October progressed, London was positively alive with meetings, adversarial and otherwise, and swarming with correspondents. The Reverend Stewart Headlam, in the vanguard of defenders of the art of the dance, presided at an overflow gathering at the Savoy Theatre protesting the licensing committee's recommendation. Russell Hall, Euston, was the scene of a meeting of cab drivers and other trade unionists, who viewed the actions proposed by the licensing committee as "disastrous to the cab industry and other trades." The Peckham and Dulwich Radical Club and other clubs in south London joined in common cause with music hall artistes and others meeting in the Lambeth Palace Road. All passed resolutions condemning the recommendation of the Theatres and Music Halls

Committee.[110] The Grand Order of Water Rats — all of them members of the music hall profession — passed a strongly worded resolution against actions that would deprive many of their membership of their living, a resolution signed by such prominent artistes as Dan Leno and Little Tich. Adopting a cautionary tone, Queen's Counsel Candy, speaking at a luncheon at the Brewers' Exhibition, warned against the mistaken assumption that the licensing committee enjoyed the exercise of judicial functions; there was, he said, no remedy against their decisions. Even the Church could not remain neutral under the circumstances; W. Evans Hurndall, in the pulpit of Westminster Chapel in Buckingham Gate, put to his congregation a resolution expressing the "intense desire" that the council "be firm and resolute in repressing incentives to immorality" in public places. The faithful "rose to signify cordial assent."[111]

### THE EVE OF THE COUNCIL MEETING
By various means at her disposal, Mrs. Chant had contrived to ride the crest of an enormous wave of reaction, taking care to articulate and promulgate her views and those of her colleagues and adding substance, force, and clarity to the already superabundant response to the licensing committee's proposals. In closing its correspondence on "prudes on the prowl" on 20 October, the *Daily Telegraph* marveled at the vast interest in the issue, "of almost unparalleled bulk and volume" throughout the country, expressed in letters to the editor; only one-tenth of the correspondence received could be published.[112] In the course of a mere two weeks, the recommendation of the Theatres and Music Halls Committee had produced a near-seismic shock of public outcry, in newspaper accounts, correspondence, and meetings, together with endorsements and protests from many quarters. The recommendation had also, less predictably but ominously, produced concrete plans for the alteration of spaces in the Empire Theatre of Varieties some days in advance of the county council's decision as to whether any such plans were to be implemented.

The drawing up in advance of plans for alteration, occurring immediately after the licensing committee meeting and seemingly in anticipation of the council's endorsement of the committee's recommendation, would perhaps appear presumptuous. The Theatres Committee may have been feeling an access of power; at any rate, it must have sensed some greatly increased momentum in its favor. Strictly speaking, it was by no means a foregone conclusion that the council would blithely second what its licensing committee, deeply divided and under evident duress, had recommended. For those who knew about them, the plans for alterations would nonetheless have taken on a definite tone, alternatively foreboding or anticipatory, depending on one's politics and point of view.

And so, by the eve of the London County Council's special session, after a fortnight during which the issues surrounding the question of the Empire license had been aired and fought over in almost every conceivable mode, format, and venue, emotion was rising so high, and rhetoric running to such extremes, that in the opinion of many observers the outcome remained considerably far from certain.

# 4 : The Council's Decision & Its Aftermath

## THE LONDON COUNTY COUNCIL MEETS

Preparatory to its scheduled meeting on Friday, 26 October, at Spring Gardens for purposes of licensing, the London County Council met in special session three days earlier, with Sir John Hutton in the chair. Eight petitions were presented urging the council not to adopt the recommendation of its Theatres and Music Halls Committee, acting as the licensing committee, with respect to the renewal of the license of the Empire Theatre of Varieties. In addition, a memorial appeared from the Committee of the Women's Local Government Society "expressing satisfaction at the recommendations of the Licensing Committee with respect to the Empire Theatre of Varieties . . . and urging the Council to adopt them."[1]

Three days later, on 26 October, the council reconvened, Sir John Hutton once again in the chair, "sitting as the Licensing Authority in respect of music, dancing, and theatre licenses."[2] The intense feeling on either side of the question of the Empire license must have been almost palpable, as a cartoon in the *Entr'Acte & Limelight* depicting the council chair at a crossroads, faced with a choice of "crankism" or "common sense," plainly indicated (fig. 31). In her pamphlet history of the Empire controversy, *Why We Attacked the Empire*, published the next year, Mrs. Chant drew a vivid picture of the great crowds, the closely packed mass of gentlemen of the press in the reporters' gallery, the large contingent of Empire friends and supporters in the visitors' gallery, and persons more nearly concerned on the floor of the chamber itself: men of the law, well-known philanthropic workers, and witnesses opposing the license. At the center of attention were four barristers, in white wigs and black gowns, holding briefs for the Empire; "against them," Mrs. Chant wrote, "arrayed in a bonnet instead of a wig and a gown of a different kind, a woman, armed with undeniable facts."[3] Seated nearby were George Edwardes and members of the Empire directorate, having sensed the occasion of a command performance. Before the council lay a total of fifty-seven petitions supporting or opposing the

IN DOUBT!

*THE CHAIRMAN OF THE LONDON COUNTY COUNCIL:* — "WHICH ROAD HAD I BETTER TAKE?"

*31. "Which road had I better take?"*
Entr'Acte & Limelight, *27 October 1894, 9. Harvard Theatre Collection,*
*Houghton Library.*

recommendation of the licensing committee with respect to the application for license of the Empire Theatre. Included were fifteen petitions "asking the Council not to confirm the recommendations of its Licensing Committee to abolish promenades and bars in places of amusement."[4]

Under evident pressure from both sides, the council proceeded with its considerable business, dealing with some 245 applications for license from theatres and music halls north and south of the Thames, a few being new applications but most of them renewals.[5] Visitors to the gallery, the press, and other interested spectators were obliged to wait patiently until the council turned to cases in which renewals of license had been opposed before the Theatres and Music Halls Committee and had been granted subject to conditions.[6] The first such case was the application for the Empire, under consideration as item 220. The report and recommendation of the Theatres and Music Halls Committee, citing C. F. Gill, the Empire's solicitor, in support of the original application and Laura Ormiston Chant and several other persons in opposition, was read out, together with the committee's ponderous rationale: "It seemed to us that the promenades were only used to a limited extent by persons wishing to see the performance, and the evidence satisfied us that the promenades were used for purposes such as the Council could not properly recognise by its license." The recommendation therefore was "[t]hat a license for music and dancing be granted, upon the following conditions, to be endorsed on the license — (a) That the promenades be abolished, and the spaces now occupied by them be disposed of to the satisfaction of the Council, (b) That no intoxicating drinks be sold in the auditorium."[7]

Mrs. Chant's pamphlet included an appendix containing extracts from speeches made before the county council that day, as reported in various newspapers and journals. It forms a useful complement to the detailed report of the proceedings printed in the *Daily Telegraph* the next day. Appearing on behalf of the Empire, Queen's Counsel Murphy introduced his colleagues, Mr. Poland, Q.C., Mr. Gill, and Mr. Elliott, and then at once launched his defense. Proposing to call no new witnesses, Counselor Murphy accepted the evidence from the committee as given and moved directly to the substance of the question. The issues raised are not small but large, he pointed out, and may bear importantly on subsequent cases. He represented an institution licensed continually since 1887 and enjoying privileges still in existence. Until 21 September, when seven identical petitions were sent to the council, no "private individual" nor "any public body" had offered objections, while thousands "as anxious that virtue and propriety should prevail as the petitioners" have been visitors to the Empire. Can it be that the small, insignificant minority now objecting "are the only real champions of virtue in the metropolis?" he asked. The council should rightly infer that, if things were not going well, attention was not paid to keep good order, and the "proper conduct of visitors" was not secured, "we should have heard of this matter long before now." London vigilance societies are made up of "people with eyes open and ears open," and yet for years the situation has remained the same and no complaint has been heard against the Empire management. In such circumstances "nothing less than a very grave indictment" ought to be permitted to interfere with the status of the house as it existed when first allowed a license.[8]

Counselor Murphy proceeded to lay two propositions before the council. First, before canceling the license of an institution maintained as well as this one you have to have "a strong and overwhelming case." That is true, not only because the owners of such an establishment "are entitled to protection from you," but also because you must not interfere "unduly" with invested capital and the honest employment of hundreds of persons. There are some seven hundred employed at the Empire, drawing wages approximating £70,000 or £80,000 a year. The nature of the case, Counselor Murphy argued, must be apprehended in that context. Is it an overwhelming one, he asked, or, though honestly made and believed in by the witnesses, "still of such a trumpery character" that, properly analyzed, "it is impossible to accept it?"[9]

The second proposition addressed the complainants themselves. Who were these ladies? Their character would be idle to conceal, nor would he utter a word of depreciation of them, Counselor Murphy said. But they are ladies "extreme in their views" and "intolerant of the views of others" — making them the "most dangerous" of all classes of witnesses. They went to the Empire "expecting and intending to see soliciting" in the promenade. Naturally, they saw it. And who is Mrs. Chant? A person of considerable ability, used to public speaking and mixing with "fallen women" in hopes of "reclaiming them." She is entitled to her opinions on these subjects, but she is intolerant of all other opinions. When she first visited the Empire in plain dress and found the visit "productive of no result," she "put on her very best evening dress" (laughter erupted, and Counselor Murphy interrupted himself to insist he had no intention of drawing "a vulgar laugh"; his comment was greeted by cheers). She went to the Empire, he continued, in a dress certain to elicit an advance from any "rude and wicked man," and succeeded. He then turned to what he characterized as "a lamentable case," illustrative of the extent to which prejudice can induce bias, the case of Miss Phillips. She went to the Empire with her companion, Mrs. Bailhache, and told the committee she believed that there was "no respectable honest woman" in the promenade that night other than herself. Can she possibly be considered an expert, or does her testimony merely illustrate the dangers of acting on evidence of that kind? What experience does she have? She attended the Crystal Palace once, and a temperance meeting at Exeter Hall, "and yet she is to be taken as a judge of the character of the pieces and the length of the dresses." Counselor Murphy then summed up his point: "This is the case on which you have interfered with this theatre, risked the employment of all these people, and sown discouragement among managers who are try-ing to do their duty. This is the strong, overwhelming case on which you are going to act — the judgments of these ladies, the inferences they drew as to the character of the people they saw, the motives that took them there, and what they were doing."

The counselor now moved to his conclusion. Suppose it were true, he proposed, that "half a dozen or a dozen women" went to the Empire to ply "their disgusting trade." Is that any more than a drop in the ocean? Do you intend, simply because the management cannot exclude every person who nods, or winks, or looks — that is what this behavior all comes down to — to act as you are now recommended to act? How do you put a stop to this sort of thing? "Where does solicitation of this character not exist?" he inquired. Is there a theatre or any public place where it does not happen? You are in the business of licensing amusement throughout the city. Do you really believe "no man ogles a woman, or no woman eyes a man," in any of these places? He urged the council, gentlemen all, to "avoid cant." What good will accrue if you shut the Empire down? Will it reduce the number of "loose women"? Appointments not made in the Empire prom-enade can be made in some other place. "You cannot make people religious or moral by Act of Parliament or by stringent restrictions," he insisted. "Religion and education are the forces on which you must depend."[10]

Queen's Counsel Murphy had made his case for the Empire on the basis of two essential points: that, since prostitution is inevitable, its presence in a properly conducted establishment should not be considered grounds for driving innocent people out of employment or depriving capital of its legitimate returns; and that those who opposed the license are a small and insignificant minority whose voice can hardly be said to represent the people and their interests, and whose evidence, moreover, is flagrantly biased, extreme, and untrustworthy. (As for Counselor Murphy's suggestion that Mrs. Chant, arrayed in her finery, had been approached by a gentleman, no evidence either from her testimony or from any other quarter supported the allegation.)

Mrs. Chant now rose to conduct the opposition to the license. She began by claiming her rights as a citizen and insisting that the council should consider no citizen insignificant. The closing of the Empire is merely temporary, she pointed out, and cannot impose more than a brief holiday on persons who are presently very well paid. If seven hundred people are permanently deprived of employment, it will be the doing of the Empire management, not the licensing committee. The Empire should be allowed to go on making its enormous dividends, "but under the restrictions of decency proposed by the Licensing Committee." Such large dividends suggest that the Empire could afford to pay its employees board wages while structural alterations are going on.[11]

Warming to her subject, Mrs. Chant summarized the evidence presented to the Theatres and Music Halls Committee, asserting that the fact of the matter was "that the promenades at the Empire are open markets for vice." The predictably hostile *Daily Telegraph* has asked, she continued, whether we propose to empty the "moral dustbin of London" by clearing the streets of fallen women and thereby clearing the promenades at the Empire. The argument is mistaken, she explained: "the poor souls fall at such places as the Empire, and then parade the streets afterwards." The saddest part of the controversy, Mrs. Chant observed, was that she and her colleagues should be accused of "cruelty to our fallen sisters." Her house has always been open as a refuge, and those whom she has rescued wish her and her colleagues well in their attempts "to purge the haunts of vice and make them better than they are." She and her colleagues want to see more entertainment in London, not less — "more gaiety and more amusement, more acting, and more music and dancing." The entire theatrical profession should thank her and her colleagues for an action that may free the stage from the accusation of contributing to the "moral dustbin." Already, London is better than it used to be, Mrs. Chant pointed out; there is no longer the amount of girl prostitution one used to see.[12]

Turning from the question of vice and prostitution, Mrs. Chant took up the issue of the people, their rights and their needs. As for the argument that the workingmen of London object to interference in their amusements, workingmen will acknowledge that the Empire is no resort of theirs, and they at least want places of amusement to which they can safely take their wives and daughters. The council's verdict today will be a tremendous one for "the advancing democracy of England," for the council must not differentiate between the poor man's and the rich man's music hall; the same treatment must be accorded to both. No one should have to look at what is obviously offensive, she argued. She referred, not to the living pictures, which are beyond reproach and indeed "open up possibilities as to the future which are delightful to think of," but rather to "the want of clothing of the girls in the ballet." If those girls say they do not want more clothes than what they wear, it is a fault of their upbringing, perhaps, and they need help from others.[13]

The arguments of those opposed to the unrestricted licensing of the Empire were thus focused, Mrs. Chant observed, on both the indecency of the entertainment onstage and the immorality that occurred in the promenades; people had the right to be protected from both sources of evil. George Edwardes really gave his case away, she asserted, the very night after the licensing committee made its recommendation, for he called his employees together and told them they would be thrown out of employment because of the committee's insistence on structural alteration of the promenades. Saying that was tantamount to an admission that "if the promenades were done away with and the sale of drink stopped in the auditorium, ruin would fall upon the Empire." He admitted that receipts at the door barely covered the theatre's expenses. One is forced to conclude that taking away the market for vice and drink will prevent the directors paying shareholders the enormous dividends they now receive. But the young men and women of London should be able to meet "for social happiness" without fear of confronting libertines and keepers of questionable houses. "To-day," Mrs. Chant concluded, "is the signing of the Magna Charta for public amusement. It is the greatest event of the time, and stern justice must be done."[14]

Returning to her first point, the question of the representative voice, on which she had been challenged by Queen's Counsel Murphy, "I pray you not to lead us into temptation," she pleaded; the truth is that "the young men and women of England are speaking through us." Sweep away the foul spots where temptation exists, she urged the council, and make London happier and England better, "free from the horrid slavery so many poor women are bound to." As she sat down, there were cheers, which were promptly suppressed.[15]

Evidently there was to be no opportunity for George Edwardes to make a statement or to be examined by friendly or hostile counsel. Pressed hard by the sheer volume of business on its agenda, the county council now moved into active deliberations. The licensing committee's recommendations having been taken up as a motion, a series of amendments was proposed. Alderman Routledge moved the unconditional licensing of the Empire, citing the anomalous nature of the restrictions in view of the lack of such at the Alhambra, a mere one hundred yards away. "The question of prostitution has, I think, been made far too much of," he observed. "Bad men and women" do exist, "but so long as they behave themselves properly they have a perfect right to frequent any place they like." Routledge characterized the evidence presented to the Theatres and Music Halls Committee as biased and the committee itself as unrepresentative of the feelings of the council as a whole. The committee is in fact "packed," he charged, in the interests of one segment of the council. Routledge named Messrs. McDougall, Lidgett, Leon, Beachcroft, and Torr as members of the committee who from the start in 1889 had formed a "solid phalanx" doing its best "to ruin the industry of the music-halls of London." McDougall himself, Routledge added, has in his character of total abstainer exercised such influence as to prevent the opening of any new music hall where drink could be sold. Those with "particular views" on the committee have no right to take advantage of their position there and impose their opinions on the whole of London. Their virtuousness, Routledge concluded, is "no reason why we should have no more cakes and ale."[16]

Another councillor, Colonel Rotton, addressed both of Mrs. Chant's two targets, the promenade and the stage itself; undeterred by her eloquence, he saw things differently, he said. He feared that to shut down "a place of this sort" would conduce to "the immorality already so rampant in the streets of London." He had been told that the proposed restrictions on the license would have the effect of abolishing the ballet and putting "400 as pretty women as could be found in London" out of work. What would happen, he asked, if women in those numbers were deprived of employment? He himself, and ladies of his acquaintance, including a relative, had been to the Empire and had seen nothing "to which a modest and pure-minded person could take the slightest objection." This, in his view, was testimony as strong as that given before the licensing committee. It was monstrous, he concluded, to make an example of the Empire, "one of the best-conducted places of amusement in London."[17]

Alderman Beachcroft offered another viewpoint on the evidence presented. George Edwardes had asserted that a list of known women of questionable character was kept at the door of the Empire and had said he would be glad to know what more could be done to stop these people. The answer, Beachcroft pointed out, was obvious: provide seats for the 470 persons who, according to good evidence, were roaming the promenade. To argue that alterations would result in driving these women from the promenade into the streets, he said, is like arguing that housebreaking ought not to be stopped because if it were it would lead to an increase in pickpocketing in the streets (a statement that elicited some laughter, promptly suppressed). At any rate, the council had no control over the streets, and moreover it was sitting only as a quasi-judicial body, with no way to gauge the value of evidence. It nevertheless had to act, giving "the best and most honest judgment" it could, influenced neither by fears of throwing Empire workers or Leicester Square cabmen out of employment nor by the biased "libertines of the *Daily Telegraph*."[18]

John Burns, a colorful, energetic Fabian socialist and an articulate spokesman for the Progressive spirit, who had been elected to the first London County Council in 1888 as the Labour representative for Battersea and who was also a Labour MP for that district, offered pointed insight into the economic aspects of the issue.[19] The truth of the matter was, Burns asserted, that the Empire has mismanaged its business. In 1889, doing what the council required it to do, it paid a dividend of 84 percent. It has gradually declined to 66 percent, "just in proportion as you have allowed that condition of things to prevail which has brought about the present crisis." We cannot be told we are ruining property, Burns argued, when, in the City the other day, a ten-shilling share in the Empire was going for seventy shillings. Arguments in favor of protecting the Empire dividends are really no more than "a commercial rig" designed to induce the county council to breach its duty to citizens. The fact is, he added, that the alterations required of the Empire by the licensing committee could be accomplished in one night with a hundred carpenters.[20]

Burns, who had a reputation for tolerance of others' opinions, but whose opposition to various forms of popular culture was well known and whose

eye was sharp for egregious profits taken at the expense of rational entertainment, went on in a spirit of independent-mindedness to adjudicate the
claims of both sides.[21] He hoped that the council would "tell the Puritans"
that prostitution cannot be decreased "by harrowing prostitutes." These
people must be told, he insisted, "that if they wish to prevent girls going on
the streets they must not object to pay good wages and allow their employees a short rest." Prostitution, "a deep-seated social evil," can be eradicated
only by changes in economic conditions. On the other hand, Burns
explained, the fact is that the council has done much to eradicate prostitution, and it must now resist the intimidation being practiced by the Empire
directors. A long-declared proponent of enlarged powers for the county
council and an eloquent spokesman for the working class, Burns concluded
by arguing for parity between east and west: the decision of the council to
uphold the recommendation of the committee, he said, will do for the West
End of London "what has been done for the sailors' music-halls in the East-
end." He sat down to loud cheers of support.[22]

The series of speeches by advocates of one amendment or another had
the effect of bringing the issue full circle. Lord Farrer said he had never
felt more anxious about his vote than at the present moment. He could
not possibly support the Routledge amendment to remove all restrictions, since that would have the effect of endorsing the present Empire
management. At the same time he was worried that the committee recommendation was too unconditional; he would have much preferred to
see the management itself improve the mode of conducting the Empire
rather than respond to some arbitrary act of the council.[23] An eleventh-
hour amendment on this same theme was then proposed by Councillor
Westacott, who considered the licensing committee's recommendation
"too severe" and who reminded the council that a satisfactory solution to
a similar problem dealing with the Aquarium and the Trocadero had
been found through the council's requirement simply that those places
give an undertaking "that they would in future be conducted with due
regard to propriety." Accordingly, Westacott proposed the following
amendment: "That the application of a renewal for a music and dancing
license in respect of the Empire be granted on the distinct understanding
that the applicant do give his undertaking, to be prepared by the Solicitor of the Council, that everything in the establishment shall in future be
conducted with due regard to propriety, and on condition that the promenade be altered to suit the requirements of the Council." It was best,

Westacott explained, for the council that day to act in a spirit of compromise. Mingled shouts of "No, No!" and "Hear, hear!" erupted. On a show of hands, the Westacott amendment was defeated by the slim margin of fifty-four against to forty-nine for. The mostly reticent *Daily Telegraph* reporter commented the next day that this vote constituted the "crucial division."[24]

Without exception, the amendments proposed had the clear purpose of negating or diluting the conditions on the license recommended by the licensing committee. Without exception, the amendments were defeated, the Routledge amendment to remove all conditions going down to a resounding vote of seventy-five against to thirty-two for.[25] The original question was then put, divided, and carried in two separate votes: for the abolition of the promenades, the council voted forty-four to twenty-two; for doing away with the sale of drink in the auditorium, the vote was forty-three to twenty-one.[26] Neither the *Telegraph*, which published an accounting of votes that coincided with that in the council minutes, nor any other source commented on the baffling discrepancy between the total numbers of councillors voting on the amendments and the considerably smaller number who voted on the final two questions. The prospect of nearly even division of the council raised by the show of hands over the Westacott compromise may have frightened some councillors into decisive defeat of the Routledge hands-off proposal and then, as they realized what consequent strictures that vote might oblige them to impose on the Empire, sent them scurrying into silence. Such a large number of abstentions must have been due to a complex of factors, perhaps including worries about going on record in such controversial circumstances, concerns that in retrospect might have been shown to be all too real in the shift of power that occurred in the next council elections. Whatever the reasons for such differences, in the final analysis the bare margins produced by the original votes of the Theatres and Music Halls Committee had been supplanted by a weighty two-thirds majority of the council itself—that is, of those council members who possessed the courage or resolve (or what others might have deemed foolhardiness) to vote. From its beginnings the council had been concerned to establish ideal codes of civic conduct and proper social behavior. When push came to shove, the council's original devotion to effecting the moral improvement of music hall fare was officially reaffirmed, but by only something like two-thirds of the councillors who were present.[27] Ideals and realities appear to have run uneasily shoulder to shoulder in Spring Gardens that morning. The recorded votes were, finally, nonetheless decisive.

## THE EMPIRE CLOSES

That same evening, as the act curtain fell on the end of the new ballet *On Brighton Pier*, George Edwardes walked onto the stage of the Empire and announced to an overflow audience filled with expectation the immediate closing of the theatre. A larger-than-life figure for many of his auditors, he enjoyed a great measure of their affection and knew he could count on their sympathy. "I have merely to announce to you," Edwardes said to the crowded house, once it allowed him to speak, "that owing to the decision of the County Council" — at this point he was drowned out by "passionate anathemas of the Council," wrote the reporter for the *Star*, along with "cries of 'The dirty dogs!' 'Out with them!' and 'Foul bigots!' mingled with renewed cheering 'for the Empire.'" "I have merely to announce," Edwardes eventually went on, "that in consequence of that decision the Empire will close after tonight." The announcement was greeted with cries of "Shame!" Taking the tone of a practiced stage orator, a sort of latter-day Antony delivering an impassioned yet calculating eulogy over the bleeding remains of his noble enterprise, Edwardes continued to speak above the din. "I say this in sorrow rather than in anger"; there has been no time or opportunity to answer "all the unfounded charges" leveled at the Empire at the meeting of the council. But there was one great consolation, nonetheless — "that we have your sympathy, and that of the London people." The house resounded with cheers for Edwardes and the Empire directors and with more execrations leveled against the county council. The *Star* reporter, catching Edwardes's accents, cast the climactic moments of the announcement in the extreme terms of a melodramatic crisis: "Strong men went pale and ghastly with rage, while dilettante youths tried to emulate their demonstrativeness, and succeeded to the extent of a shrill cry of 'Dem'd shame.'"[28]

A notice inserted in the Empire program for that night verified that the theatre would be "Closed, owing to the action of the London County Council, From Saturday, October 27th, until Friday, November 2nd, 1894, (inclusive)." In his announcement from the stage Edwardes had omitted — for reasons best known to himself, but perhaps not beyond scrutiny — the fact that the closing of the Empire was not to be permanent but was to last only a week, as the theatre moved to initial compliance with the county council's conditions. It was, after all, a moment to be seized and exploited, not explained. Edwardes had not said the Empire would never reopen. Those who cared to read would know.

As Edwardes retired, the orchestra rose simultaneously with the audience and played the opening bars of "Rule Britannia." The house took up the refrain, laying special emphasis on the phrase "Britons never will be slaves." The national anthem followed, the cheering continuing incessantly, until Edwardes came back on, leading the Empire ballet mistress, Madame Lanner. Still the cheering went on; Edwardes and Lanner went off, and the curtain rose again on a cleared stage on which, the *Daily Telegraph* recorded, were massed "the entire stage staff of the Empire" — carpenters, scene shifters, ladies of the corps de ballet, and artistes. In the center stood Edwardes "surrounded by workmen shaking him cordially by the hand as the sincere friend in whom they had perfect confidence."[29]

As the excitement became more intense and calls for another speech rang out, Edwardes signaled for the curtain to descend. Further speeches of a more impromptu kind were addressed to the audience from the promenade, but the audience would hear nothing except from the stage. A polite hint from the stage manager, George Capel, that it was time to go had no effect. Finally, the lowering of the lights and Capel's discouragement of a workingman who came on and began a speech himself finally ended the occasion. As the house emptied out into Leicester Square, "the lights of the Empire faded one by one," the *Telegraph* writer observed in elegiac tones. The closing of the theatre was greeted with indignation by cabmen and others outside.[30]

Earlier that day, only hours in advance of the last performances at the Empire, the *Daily Telegraph*, its editorial posture having been lately vilified as "libertine," expressed its deep displeasure with the county council in a leading article accusing the council of "gross favoritism and inconsistency" for closing the Empire promenade while allowing those at the Alhambra and the Aquarium to remain open. The meaning was clear: "for men or women to walk about at any public resort is henceforth to be regarded as an offense against public decency." It seemed an elementary truth that driving out "improper characters" while doing nothing that would reduce their number merely reproduces the same situation elsewhere; "the Piccadilly, the Regent-street, and the Strand promenades continue whether licensed or unlicensed." Ignoring, as almost all writers to the *Telegraph* over the past few weeks had done, the arguable relationship between the lack of regulation of prostitutes and their fulsome presence on the streets of London (and elsewhere in Britain), the *Telegraph* maintained that it was "inane" to interfere in other "marts of vice" while the evils present on the streets were not dealt with.[31]

Three days later, the *Telegraph* made sure to note the crowded condition of certain parts of the Alhambra, which had suddenly experienced "a large accession of public favour and patronage." For the moment, in a city of some five million people, it was the only home of ballet. In addition, the Alhambra was now featuring a new set of living pictures, reaffirming the accepted staple of the variety house, namely, "a light, bright, sparkling, and constantly changing succession of cheerful and care-relieving performances, free from offence and moral censure." In one tableau a "shocked prude" was introduced, investing that presentation with "special significance at this juncture." The cheering of spectators "had a ring of meaning," the *Telegraph* concluded, driving home the point.[32] The *Music Hall and Theatre Review* joined in the chorus of disapproval, asserting that the only real result of the council decision was an invitation to "the class they apparently consider should be denied any amusement to cross Leicester Square and patronise the Alhambra, where all the features they considered so objectionable are in full swing — that is promenades and drinking bars."[33]

Responses, editorial and otherwise, to the actions of the county council and the events that would swiftly follow were predictably widespread, and wide-ranging in attitude. The *Morning Post* expressed a strong negative reaction to John Burns's speech upholding the licensing committee's recommendation, taking the council and Burns in particular to task for its decision to endorse it. Burns "prefers other places of entertainment," and he and his fellow councillors have exploited their position "to crush an enterprise which is patronised by the wealthier classes." And yet such "class animosity" is only part of the lesson taught by yesterday's performance, the *Post* writer explained; the more practical question is whether proprietors of such places are to be permitted "to conduct their own business subject to recognised conditions, or are to be subjected to continual interference of the most capricious kind."[34] A cartoon in the *Entr'Acte & Limelight* depicted Burns and Mrs. Chant dancing exultantly together (fig. 32).

A hastily convened meeting of the Playgoer's Club at St. James's Hall created a "sardine-like squash," noted the reporter for *To-Day*. In a debate mostly lacking in vigor, two speeches stood out. Henry Hyndman, the

THE FATE OF THE EMPIRE.

MR. JOHN BURNS AND MRS. ORMISTON CHANT JOIN HANDS IN A DANCE
OF EXULTATION.

32. *"The Fate of the Empire: Mr. John Burns and Mrs. Ormiston Chant
Join Hands in a Dance of Exultation."* Entr'Acte & Limelight,
*3 November 1894, 8. Harvard Theatre Collection, Houghton Library.*

socialist, "set the blood tingling and the pulse beating, his enthusiasm and vigour were contagious, and you felt that if ever *his* promenade were invaded he would protect it with a Maxim gun, instead of a mandamus." The best speech of the evening came from W. H. Jennings, a playgoer from Yorkshire who took a philosophic view, observing that every man of sanity knew about the prominence of vice in the Empire promenade, but knew also that "vice had also been prominent since the beginning of things." "Nations had risen and fallen, kingdoms had passed away," yet vice had remained. Was this not an argument for thinking that what is called vice is "something other than the mere corrupt edge of our social system?" Jennings thought it was.[35] Mrs. Chant, who also attended the meeting, wound up the debate by identifying what she believed was really at the heart of the matter. It was against "*systematic* vice" that she was fighting, she explained — "against the bully, the introducing house, the public procuress, and the rich man's private pimp." She had given twenty years to rescue work, she added, and knew more about these things than "many men about town." The reporter for *To-Day*, abandoning journalistic neutrality and inserting himself into the action, applauded her motives but cautioned her "Purist Party" to be "as temperate as they are enthusiastic," lest they jeopardize success.[36]

Adverse reaction to the council's decision took a number of forms, including a growing interest in transfering the licensing authority from the council to the Lord Chamberlain, who already had jurisdiction over the licensing of plays. If this transfer were to take place, a writer in the *Morning Post* said, it would carry with it a "guarantee for liberty," such that a public official "would make it his business to follow public opinion instead of attempting to lead it."[37] In a rambling rodomontade a commentator in *Reynold's Weekly* inveighed at length against the absurdity and danger to freedom represented by the council's decision, pronouncing it "an admirable subject for comic opera," were its consequences less serious. The cast of characters would be extremely colorful: "A motley collection of briefless barristers, advertising Nonconformist ministers, M.P.'s eager to belong to many bodies, and conspicuous in none, and adventurers of one kind and another." They sit in conclave, hearing the complaints of leisured women, "fluent busybodies" with "unbounded vanity." Their names are never connected with Women's Trade Unions; they carry on no reformation work in the slums. All they care about is a chance "to air their fluent nonsense." The operetta soon becomes serious. Will the reformers find work for women who have lost employment? Will Mrs. Chant open her Gower Street house and Lady Henry Somerset her Reigate mansion for "those of their own sex whom they are preventing from attending places of public entertainment, where they found their living?" Comparisons of Empire prostitutes and "their female maligners" redound in favor of the former. Some "are as well educated as the Chants and the Somersets," most "are much more bright and interesting as human beings," and all are "more attactive" than the "middle-aged interlopers" whose husbands pine away at home "while they are promenading among the girls at the Empire." The whole business is not only cruel but useless. One wonders why "these harridans" married, sinced they are so often from home. They call themselves Christians and believers in the Bible. Solomon, the wisest of men, "had as many women for his pleasure as would fill a small town. Why are these elderly females so regardless of God's opinion?"[38]

Writings of this sort, undistinguished by any mark except their proximity to panic, swelled the columns of newspapers after the council's decision, generating more heat than light and articulating deep-seated, if unreasoned, views representative of what was evidently a large, outraged, and frightened cohort of Londoners and Britons.

### MRS. CHANT'S CONTINUING ACTIVISM

Even as the results of the attempts to shut down the Empire were pending, the *Woman's Signal*, a weekly publication in the vanguard of women's rights and with close links with the National Vigilance Association, edited by Lady Henry Somerset, the well-known president of the British Women's Temperance Association, and Annie B. Holdsworth, was celebrating ahead of time the licensing committee's recommendation and subsequent endorsement by the county council.[39] The council, asserted a leading article in the 18 October issue of the *Signal*, had acknowledged "the fitness of women to report on and criticise the conduct of public entertainments." The next step ought to be for the council to insist on "a woman police inspector being appointed to every music-hall in London."[40] It was clear now that there was "a County Council conscience as well as a Nonconformist conscience."[41] In the view of the *Signal* it was the Social Purity Department of the British Women's Temperance Association that was the driving force behind the opposition to the Empire licensing — a convincing assertion, coming from the president of the BWTA. Allying themselves implicitly with what they perceived as a common effort, the editors of the *Signal* appeared to sense an accession of power and momentum on the part of the various groups of women and men devoted to the reaffirmation of principle in public life. Now that the Empire had been put on notice for its blatant improprieties, the *Signal* cautioned, other places, such as the Alhambra, the Pavilion, and the Aquarium, will be "carefully and systematically watched."[42]

Meanwhile, Mrs. Chant continued to exploit the momentum she herself had created by continuing a full schedule of public speaking, making clear that her efforts stemmed from a principled stand against indecency and not from any mere antitheatrical bias. On 29 October the *Pall Mall Gazette* reported on services conducted by Mrs. Chant at the New Tabernacle Congregational Church in Old Street, St Luke's, where in her opening prayer she "thanked God for the complete victory gained on behalf of decency" in the county council's decision.[43] In late October she took time for an interview in her Gower Street home with Sarah A. Torley, a reporter for the *Signal*, in which she described what life was like in the aftermath of the council's decision (see fig. 10). She had received 187 letters that morning on the Empire controversy, she said; in them, abuse was outweighed by messages of kindness from sympathetic friends. All the same, she had been threatened with "vitriol, stabbing, dynamite, running over, shooting," and the exploding of her house. On the previous Saturday, fifteen unfortunate women had sought her help, having read accounts of the Empire controversy. "I am no Puritan," Mrs. Chant insisted, repeating a theme prominent in her testimony before the licensing committee and again before the council: "I want to see more gaiety in London, only of an innocent kind, such as men will like to take their wives and daughters to see."[44]

Regarding the considerable confusion over what she wore to the Empire when she went to investigate it, Mrs. Chant explained that since the age of twenty-one she had "abjured bare neck and arms." All the same, she had worn "such a pretty dress" to the Empire, "the same dress I spoke in at the Women's Suffrage Festival at Boston — black lace over coloured silk, with an opera jacket and a pretty little bonnet to match." But she did have her head covered, and so "after all there was not much evening dress about it." The issue of proper clothing was evidently of great importance to Mrs. Chant, as her comment on some of the tableaux at the Palace makes clear: "I object *in toto* to the nude, and I also feel very strongly against the want of clothing shown in the dress of the ballet girls."[45]

Mrs. Chant was clearly taking the opportunity provided by publicity in the *Signal* to reiterate the main points of her testimony before the licensing committee and again before the full council, focusing on what she habitually identified as the twin evils of contemporary life, intemperance and impurity. Only "stimulants," not "refreshments," and no eatables of any kind were sold at the Empire, she pointed out; and she did not hesitate to acknowledge her "rigid" ideas about "the abolition of intoxicating drinks from all places of amusement." She also seized the occasion to air her radical ideas about prostitution. She approved, she said, of William Stead's definition of a prostitute as a woman "hated by virtuous women because they regard her as a blackleg, selling her virtue below the trade union price — marriage!" Her own view was quite consistent: "The price of a woman's surrender should be honourable marriage"; women who offer themselves for less "are blacklegs in the trade union sense." Women, she insisted, "must maintain a high trade union standard for purity and virtue."[46] Metaphors drawn from marketing, and their implication that marriage was the money mart certain critics accused it of being, had evidently no distastefulness for Mrs. Chant.

At the Playgoer's Club in late November (a surprising venue for Mrs. Chant but an indication of how broadly her reputation extended), she resumed the theme of exploitation of women, accusing the music halls of sweating the ballet girls: these were "the poor, sweated chorus girls of the Music Halls of London, who were paid six shillings, or even nothing at all, for their week's work." "How could they live respectably," she asked, "on that kind of payment?" — implying that they, no less than the women who frequented the five-shilling lounge at the Empire, were women of doubtful virtue.[47]

As always, Mrs. Chant took opportunities to convince her listeners that she was heartily in favor of wholesome entertainment, whether in music halls or elsewhere. In a speech given in Bristol in January 1895 she called on her audience to think of what they owed to men like Albert Chevalier, famous for his music hall song about a long-term marriage, "My Old Dutch." Mrs. Chant recalled sitting in a music hall in the poorest part of London when "My Old Dutch" was sung; the audience took up the chorus and repeated it until it brought tears to their eyes and a conviction that music like this "taking hold of the public heart might be the means of introducing into lives a tenderness and a sentiment not hitherto displayed."[48]

In the days following the council's decision to renew the Empire license subject to stringent restrictions, expressions of sentiment and views pro and con proliferated in newspapers and journals, on public platforms and stages, in churches and church halls, and beyond, wherever persons with an opinion to air, a brief to argue, or an axe to grind might congregate.

Meanwhile, as announced by Edwardes himself from the Empire stage on the night of the county council's endorsement of its licensing committee's recommendation, the Empire closed the next day, Saturday, 27 October, for alterations, reopening on Saturday, 3 November. All seats had been booked in advance, and on the opening of the gates an eager crowd rushed in. Pending an appeal, the promenades remained unaltered, affording standing room for a large number of persons; but "in front of the bar," the *Standard* reported, "which was formerly visible from this part of the house, stretched a screen of stout brown canvas, fastened to a strong wooden frame." At the back of the promenade certain small tables had been taken away. In the upper circle the usual bars had been closed, except one that was now open for coffee alone. Open bars "have practically disappeared," said the *Telegraph*, but a row of cushioned seats had been set up at the rear of the main gangway in the five-shilling part of the house. The promenade itself was "packed with well-dressed men"; there were hardly any women to be seen.[49]

There were cries for "Edwardes!" The Empire manager came on and was cheered. Roars of approval followed. Toward the end of the evening, around 11:30, when only one turn was left, "a number of young men," the *Telegraph* reported, "made a sudden attack with sticks and umbrellas upon the wood and canvas partition which had shut off the Moorish bar from the dress-circle." Most of the audience having left, the assault took the establishment by surprise. The *Morning Leader* identified and deplored "the riotous element" as numbering no more than fifty and looking for "some fun"; they were "the swell mob who disgrace the West-end of London and their aristocratic and plutocratic parents." The *Gazette* thought that the well-dressed men involved in the attack were, some of them, "almost middle-aged"; they were "well-dressed youthful blackguards," said the *Era*. The *Standard* insisted they were "youths," about twenty of them, who pushed their way through the crowded promenade and made a run for the screen; another group did the same on the other side. "Ominous holes" began to appear in the screen shutting off the bar, the *Gazette* reported. The canvas was "torn away in strips, and passed throughout the crowd, every one endeavouring to secure a scrap of it as souvenir." As the covering of the framework was dismantled, the two storming parties met face to face, whereupon they joined forces and tore down the wooden frames with "vigorous kicks from both sides." One member of the assaulting forces, possibly the young Sandhurst cadet Winston Churchill, mounted a seat and called out, "Now, gentlemen, what you have to see to is that that barrier is not put up again. What is the use of pulling it down, if you allow it to be put up once more?" A loud cheer encouraged the speaker to continue. "We had two things to pull down," he went on. "The barrier is down. We have now to pull down the County Council." More cheering and laughter followed.[50]

In a reminiscence recounting his part in the riot, Churchill remembered egging on the crowd and making what he called his "maiden speech." What appeared to have infuriated his fellow Sandhurst cadets, "a good many boys from the Universities," and others was, most of all, the attempted separation of the bars in the promenade from the promenade itself. All that it took was for "some young gentleman" to poke his walking stick through the flimsy canvas that covered the temporary barricades. Others quickly followed his example, and suddenly the entire crowd of two or three hundred persons went out of control, leaving the authorities powerless to intervene. "Amid the cracking of timber and the tearing of canvas the barricades were demolished," Churchill recalled with evident relish, "and the bars were once more united with the promenade to which they had ministered so long." Attendants stood by "in helpless and amused inactivity," the *Gazette* said. "No attempt was made," the *Standard* commented, "to interfere with the destruction of the screens which involved no damage to the permanent structure beyond a few yards of fretwork, which were carried away as trophies." The manager of the Empire, H. J. Hitchens, came upon the wild scene and attempted to remonstrate but "was promptly carried off on the shoulders of the more enthusiastic of the demonstrators."[51] His speech, Churchill recalled, "appealed directly to sentiment and even passion." Reacting with great applause to his words, and having "cheered itself hoarse," the crowd "sallied out into the square brandishing fragments of wood and canvas as trophies or symbols."[52]

At a meeting of the Theatres and Music Halls Committee on 7 November, a letter from Messrs. Allen and Sons, acting for the Empire, was introduced, requesting copies of plans for the proposed alteration of the Empire's promenade. An answer from the committee drew attention to the plans prepared by the architect of the council and noted that they could be viewed at the architect's office. The committee continued to maintain its authority in the matter, pointing out to the Empire solicitors that "no suggestion is made for the filling up of the spaces behind the boxes" and insisting testily that "it will be for the management to see that these spaces are used in a satisfactory manner."[53]

For their part, Allen and Sons had also been busy manipulating the system of justice to the hoped-for advantage of their client. On Edwardes's behalf two rules were applied for on 31 October in Queen's Bench. The first would compel the county council to "show cause why a writ of mandamus should not issue commanding them to hear and determine according to law an application for a music and dancing license"; the other would quash the council's granting of a license under certain conditions, on grounds that the council was not empowered to attach conditions to a license. Edwardes had detected what he thought was a conspiracy on the part of some members of the licensing committee and the NVA. "I am informed," Edwardes said in his affidavit, though he cited no source, "that certain members of the Licensing Committee and of the London County Council were determined to oppose the granting of my licence, but as they were unable openly to do so by reason of their occupying a quasi-judicial position as members of the same council, they determined to act in concert with a Mrs. Bailhache and others, so that Mrs. Bailhache and others should appear to be the real opponents, whilst they, the said Councillors, would secretly advise the course that they should take, and give other assistance to them before the said application came before them to be heard, so that it should not be known that they were all acting in deliberation and concert together." Edwardes's affidavit went on to spin a sinister tale of secret meetings in the houses of conspirators while members of the Theatres and Music Halls Committee lurked in adjoining rooms, and of one member of the committee admitting to a conflict of interest through simultaneous membership in the National Vigilance Association.[54]

A series of affidavits then followed, including one from Mrs. Chant herself. (Evidently the NVA was monitoring events in a close and timely way and was benefiting from expert legal advice.) She had conducted the opposition to the license at the meeting of the Theatres and Music Halls Committee, she declared, adding that no member of the licensing committee had acted in concert with her and her colleagues. She had not attended either of the meetings described in Edwardes's affidavit, and no support for the opposition to the license had come from the National Vigilance Association.[55] C. F. Parkinson, a member of the licensing committee, had indeed attended the meeting at Mrs. Percy Bunting's house, but only to explain committee procedure. Emma Bailhache, Mrs. Chant's colleague, stated that the meeting at Farringdon Hall was only for the purpose of gaining solicitor's advice on evidence they would present.

James Torr's affidavit added important substance to the opposition to Edwardes's case. Torr said he had not known of the opposition to the Empire license and did not attend any related meetings. In fact, he did not retire with the licensing committee or vote on the Empire license at the committee meeting. A member of the committee since 1889, Torr cited precedents of previous treatment of other music halls by the Theatres and Music Halls Committee: the Palace Theatre of Varieties was licensed in October 1892 on the same terms now imposed on the Empire, and nearly identical conditions had been imposed on the New Olympic and the Tivoli. The established practice of the committee, Torr explained, is not to pass plans of any new music halls that propose drinking bars in the auditorium; moreover, "promenades are now expressly prohibited in any new music halls" by regulations of the council established on 9 February 1892, under the authority of the Metropolis Management Building Acts Amendment Act of 1878.[56]

The next day the justices handed down their decision. Unfortunately for Edwardes, Mr. Justice Charles's judgment, for himself and his colleague Mr. Justice Wright, was to the effect that the charges against the council "entirely fail," as did the charges against C. F. Parkinson, who may have acted imprudently but who did not involve himself so deeply in the litigation as to disqualify himself on grounds of bias.[57] Reporting on the outcome, the *Standard* reviewed the seriousness of the Empire case, which amounted almost to a charge of conspiracy between the opponents of the license and certain well-known members of the county council — Messrs. Lidgett, McDougall, and Parkinson. The Empire brief had alleged that those persons had allied themselves so closely with the allegations made by Mrs. Chant, Mrs. Bailhache, and their friends as to disqualify them from judging the matter and even "to vitiate the decision of the tribunals on which they sat." But Edwardes was mistaken, the *Standard* said, in making such an indictment, for his arguments came down to the solitary fact that Mrs. Bailhache had invited Mr. Parkinson to attend a meeting of the opponents of the Empire license; upon hearing discussed some of the evidence they proposed to adduce, Parkinson merely remarked that if the facts were true they should be put before the licensing committee.[58] And so Edwardes's appeal was lost.

### STRUCTURAL ALTERATIONS AND MORAL ISSUES

The outcome of the suit in Queen's Bench was duly noted by the Theatres and Music Halls Committee at its meeting on 14 November. The deliberations of the committee, which now proceeded, over the alterations to be accomplished in the audience spaces of the Empire comprise a record of remarkable and persistent attention to detail.

Frank T. Verity, architect and son of the designer of the Empire, Thomas Verity, served like his father before him as consulting architect to the Lord Chamberlain; Verity now appeared and made verbal proposals on behalf of the Empire Theatre of Varieties, whose management had retained his services.[59] He offered a comprehensive plan of alterations: (1) at the stalls and pit level, "to convert the present cloak room into a refreshment room and remove the two bars in the stalls and the bar in the pit"; (2) at the dress-circle level (the "Five Shillings promenade"), "to place two additional rows of seats and provide a rail at their back and divide the existing promenade into three sections"; and (3) at the grand circle level, "to place two additional rows of seats and enclose the bars."[60]

The committee accepted all of Verity's proposals, apparently with some enthusiasm, its members having effectively if unofficially gotten into the business of architectural design themselves. Regarding the five-shilling promenade, the committee passed a motion "that the floor in front of the proposed rail be raised at least one step in height and that the gangway at the rear be not more than 9 feet in width." It further required that "all settees" on the grand-circle level "be abolished." The chair requested that Verity send in his drawings, showing how he planned to carry out the committee's wishes, and at the same time send "an undertaking signed by Mr Edwardes and endorsed by the Directors of the Theatre to the effect that every precaution should be taken by the management to prevent the spaces being used as promenades and that the premises should be properly conducted."[61] Architect Verity quickly drew up the required plans and sent them to the committee on 19 November; three sheets of plans and the required letter from Edwardes were noted as received by the committee at its meeting two days later.

Frank Verity's plan for the renovation of the Empire dress circle called for by the Theatres and Music Halls Committee offers a striking comparison with his father's original plan for that segment of the theatre. Thomas Verity, who had passed on to his son an enthusiasm for things Francophile, had trained in the years of the Second Empire and was responsible for the detailing of the Albert Hall. His specialty the design of restaurants and theatres along Parisian lines, he originated the plans for the conversion of the Royal London Panorama into a "lavishly Parisian" theatre for the Pandora Theatre Company in 1883.[62] Those designs presented a dress circle comprising four concentric rows of stalls seating a total of 158 persons. An ample promenade behind the stalls varied in width between 13 and 15 feet, augmented by a 20-foot passage at the entrance to the tier (fig. 33).[63] In contrast, the younger Verity's plan for accommodating the requirements of the Theatres and Music Halls Committee shows a major extension of the seating area backward, away from the stage, invading the area of the promenade. It is noteworthy that the younger Verity's plan is drawn on an original that significantly modifies the elder Verity's earlier design: since that second plan was put into effect, a radical foreshortening of the stalls seating at either side of the tier had evidently been effected in order to accommodate the introduction of twelve spacious private boxes (it remains unclear when this alteration was carried out) (fig. 34). Enlargement of a section of Frank Verity's proposed plan (fig. 35) reveals in even more vivid terms the addition of two new rows of stalls, further amplified by a raised platform behind them, accessible only at the sides or the center by a step or slope; behind the platform a barrier is indicated. Additional barriers are shown right and left, at the beginnings of the private box areas, reducing the area open for free passage at that point by a good two-thirds. Rows of chairs added left and right along the walls of the passage opposite the private boxes further reduce the space available for promenading. And, finally, a contiguous bar has also been enclosed, cutting it off from the audience in the promenade and promenade stalls.

A power struggle, once covert but already intermittently in evidence, between the Theatres Committee and the Empire management had now

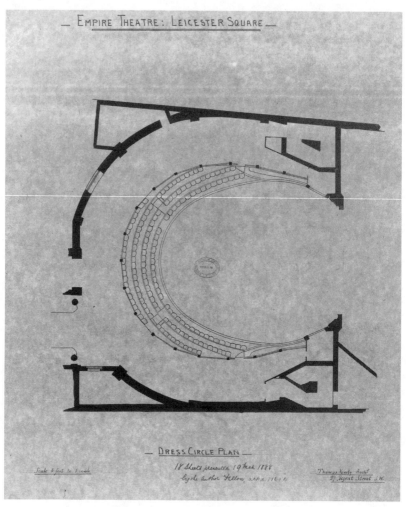

_ DRESS CIRCLE PLAN _

33. *Design by Thomas Verity for the dress circle of the Royal Pandora Theatre, 1883.*
*Ref. W2 / 39.*
*Royal Institute of British Architects Library, Drawings Collection.*

broken out into the open. Two weeks previous, the committee had gone on record, if only in a general way, about the uses to which the spaces behind the boxes might be put. Now the committee was "not at all satisfied with the assurances" given by Edwardes in the letter it had required of him, for he apparently did not mention the promenades specifically. In retaliation, the committee refused to consider Verity's plans until a satisfactory letter

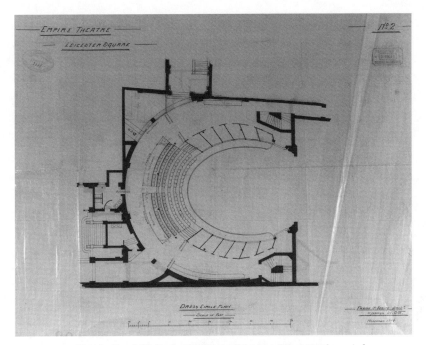

34. *Plan by Frank Verity for the Empire Theatre of Varieties dress circle, showing proposed alterations. Stamped "21 Nov. 94." London County Council Theatre Plans 102. Ref. GLC/AR/BR/102. Corporation of London, London Metropolitan Archives.*

with undertakings regarding "the promenades and other matters" was received. The committee's resolution, to be passed on to the Empire directorate, read as follows: "A letter is required from the management saying that if the spaces behind the seats on the 1st and 2nd tiers are left as proposed in the plans submitted they will take care that they are not allowed to be used as a promenade but will see that they are used in a satisfactory manner."[64] Edwardes clearly had no choice but to capitulate. Stealing precious moments from the last, lengthy rehearsals of his latest Gaiety musical, *The Shop Girl*, about to open on 24 November, on the twenty-third he put in writing, in downright obsequious tones, his undertaking "that the spaces your Committee have conceded to us shall not be used for promenading, and that the whole shall be conducted with due regard to propriety and in accordance with the wishes of your Committee as expressed in their letter of the 7th instant." He added his assurances that the work of

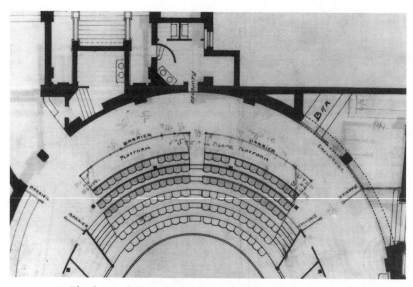

*35. Plan by Frank Verity for the Empire Theatre of Varieties dress circle,
showing proposed alterations. Detail. Stamped "21 Nov. 94."
London County Council Theatre Plans 102. Ref. GLC/AR/BR/102.
Corporation of London, London Metropolitan Archives.*

alteration would be speedily carried out as soon as the architectural plans
were finally approved.[65]

The county council had thus once again deftly sidestepped whatever
inclinations it may have had toward censure on moral grounds by means
of the material euphemism of required structural alteration. Of course, it
was true that the Theatres and Music Halls Committee, in collaboration
with the LCC Superintending Architect's Department, had been continually busy inspecting the Gaiety, the Olympic, the Royal Agricultural Hall,
and numerous other venues for conformance to fire and safety regulations — a straightforward and necessary duty in itself; out of a total of
1,299 superintending architect's inspections in the period 1890–1893, 167
alterations had been required by the council.[66] The council's licensing
committee had nonetheless a proven record of using a call for alterations
as a ruse for controlling or even shutting down venues it viewed as objectionable on other grounds. In 1890–91 the committee was successful in its
attempt to close the Angel and Crown and the Rose and Crown, two pub
music halls in the East End. The Angel's and the Rose's proprietors, John

Akkersdyk and Pedro Femenia, were served notice that improvements to their structures were required as a condition of relicensing. Having each spent £1,000 or more on repairs, the proprietors then found their licenses would not be recommended for renewal because of alleged toleration of prostitutes on the premises, even though they had not had prior warning of such offenses and even though the responsible police inspector was unable to confirm the allegations. In fact, the inspector disputed the presence of prostitutes at these places and attempted to explain to the committee certain cultural differences involving other standards of respectability relating to unmarried couples. The council nevertheless upheld the committee's denial of licenses. A large-scale lawsuit ensued, and when the committee and the council were found at fault for irregular procedures they repeated the process correctly and still found the licenses deniable. Much bad publicity resulted, precipitating broad discussion of LCC licensing practices and an internal purge of the licensing committee, including Charrington.[67]

Three years later, in April 1894, the committee had an interview with Secretary of State Asquith, who proved critical of both the committee and the council. Asquith pointed out that the committee had failed to shut down the halls by invoking powers of moral censure; instead, seemingly preoccupied with public safety, it called for structural changes. Such requirements turned out, on the committee's own admission to Asquith, to reflect its real intention: attacking London's ground landlords. "The great bone of contention," the committee said to Asquith, "is the structural alterations. What the proprietors resent is the spending of money."[68] An important component, a latter-day observer has said, of the great consensus achieved by the LCC was "the suppression of the rapacious spirit of the propertied in the person of the hall owners."[69]

Edwardes's behavior, and his and his solicitors' actions after the committee's recommendation had been made, become more understandable in light of the emergence of the committee's latent hostility toward landlords. That hostility would now seem to have come out in plain view, to judge from the incensed reaction of "G. N.," who in a letter to the *Daily Telegraph* in October had pointed out that the committee's actions exemplified the hostile spirit in which the council from the very moment of its existence "has treated London property owners of every description." Property "is not represented" on the council, the writer explained, because the council is itself the chief product of the Progressive Party, whose only progress runs toward "the appropriation or injury of that which belongs to somebody else."[70] Members of the Theatres and Music Halls Committee were in any case incompetent meddlers, according to a letter from "Observer"; although unable to distinguish a window from a door on an architect's plan, they possessed "unbounded power" to force "vexatious and unreasonable changes" in the carefully considered plans of able, practical men.[71]

Meanwhile, afforded space by the *Telegraph* for airing their views, members of the county council commented freely and frankly on the controversy still raging. J. F. Torr, who had been forced to abstain from voting on the day of the licensing committee's deliberations because of his membership in the National Vigilance Association, took the opportunity to explain his convictions about the efficacy of government regulation. If the licensing committee's recommendation is adopted by the full council, Torr asserted, the Empire will simply be on the same footing as the Tivoli and the Palace, which have survived stringent restrictions. The only reason the Alhambra is licensed without contingency is that no complaints have been brought to the licensing committee about it. As in the case of the Empire, the committee required alterations at the St. James's Hall and Restaurant in order that licensed premises be "structurally severed" from other places of entertainment, "which run like a rabbit-warren from Piccadilly right through to Regent-street." The only alternative to close supervision of the entire area is to bring about "a structural severance" comparable to that insisted upon some years back for the Gaiety Bar and Theatre.[72] Structural alterations were evidently the strategy of choice for efficient regulation of public places of entertainment, a strategy freely acknowledged by council members, who were nevertheless understandably more reticent about voicing the adverse opinions regarding arrogant landlords that they privately admitted underlay their actions—opinions inseparable from the conviction that such arrogance, when it came to questions of vice tolerated and even encouraged, was plainly insufferable.

In fact, Secretary Asquith's comment on the relationship between structural alterations and issues of morality had illuminated a central preoccupation of the Theatres and Music Halls Committee, one that emerged again the very next day after the conditional relicensing of the Empire. C. F. Gill, representing the St. James's Hall Company, responded to Shilton Collin's intemperate condemnation of the St. James's Restaurant, contiguous with the Hall, as like the Empire: a "reeking, seething hell."

Gill pointed out that the law allowed "even dissolute women" to visit licensed premises "so long as they did not misbehave themselves." The committee recommended the Hall for relicensing but called for a clearer distinction between it and the restaurant connected to it, requiring the St. James's Hall Company to give an undertaking "to structurally separate, to the satisfaction of the Council, the premises in regard to which the music and dancing license is used from the adjoining premises used for restaurant purposes."[73] Again, the committee had employed the modification of space as a solution to a seemingly intractable moral problem.

The question of architectural alteration, now taking on considerable added significance, had in fact been important from an early point. On 17 October "A Lover of Right, Not Rant," knowledgable of things architectural, had written to the *Telegraph* to explain in detail why the Empire would have to close if its promenade were not allowed to remain open. A simple reason why seats cannot be added to the second-tier promenade was that "it forms the approach to the private boxes, which open on to it." What is more, seats placed on the level floor there would afford no satisfactory view of the stage and so would not be occupied. On the other hand, if seats were constructed tier upon tier, as is the usual way, there would still be no view of the stage, for the following reason:

> At the Empire Theatre the ceiling of the box circle promenade cannot anywhere be more than 10ft above its floor, and the lowest part of the sloping portion under the seats of the circle above cannot be more than 3ft or 4ft higher than the floor, both being taken from a common datum line. As a matter of fact, the highest of the existing seats reaches the limit at which seating accommodation is practicable with a full and proper view of the stage. To alter this would necessitate the rebuilding of the different circles, approaches, stairs, &c., i.e., for all practical purposes, the entire theatre, and this would also mean the destruction of most costly decorations and fittings.

The writer added a comment that recapitulates the basic idea behind the design of such theatres, both British and Continental. One of the Empire's principal attractions is that it does not compel the choice of either sitting or leaving the building; instead, you can watch whatever interests you and otherwise "walk about, have a smoke and a drink, and again return to view the performance when you please."[74] The noted architect Walter Emden, a member of the county council, might have made such views more apparent had he been a member of the Theatres and Music Halls Committee, but, as Sir Henry Irving pointed out in his testimony before the 1892 parliamentary committee, Emden had been rejected for membership on it—a fact of which James L. Graydon, manager of the Middlesex Music Hall, and Edward Terry, manager and proprietor of Terry's Theatre, also complained, to no avail.[75] In his own testimony for the parliamentary inquiry, Emden charged that the Theatres Committee was much more interested in eliminating bars than in promoting safety.[76]

## ALTERATIONS AT THE EMPIRE

Sealing off one section of a theatre from another might at first appear as simply an effective method of crowd control. A tradition of theatre architecture dating back to the time of the first purpose-built Elizabethan theatres effectively reified the class distinctions of London society by rendering some seats more advantageous than others and charging more for the privilege of a better situation. Traditionally, prostitutes and other classes of persons more tolerated than welcomed made their way in at the several entrances along with other patrons, paying what they liked or could afford and mingling with the rest.[77] As pressures toward social respectability grew, however, in the course of the late eighteenth century, exclusivity became a highly prized commodity, and theatre architecture began to reflect social distinctions, requiring that each class of playgoer have a separate entrance and staircase.[78] Benjamin Wyatt's 1811 Drury Lane Theatre continued the practice of Wyatt's predecessor, Henry Holland, in including so-called basket boxes, by then the principal resort of "Women of the Town," behind the first tier of dress boxes; but Wyatt provided separate passageways to each so that more respectable women, discouraged from attending by the previous arrangement, could do so without having to "run the gauntlet of those who hung around the prostitutes in the basket boxes, the coffee rooms, and the surrounding passages."[79] What was good for respectability was good for business too. Proposing terms for taking over the management of Drury Lane, the highly respectable Victorian tragedian William Charles Macready, who would have preferred to drive prostitution out of the theatre altogether, proposed in a letter to the *Times* to bar prostitutes from all parts of the theatre except the gallery, which could be reached only "by a separate pay-office, and by passing through a dismantled lobby."[80] Implied in all these provisions was an implicit acknowledgment of the inevitable presence in the theatre of certain women who used it as a marketplace more than as a source of entertainment.

Segregation of audiences was in fact as old as purpose-built theatres themselves. The architect of the original Empire, Thomas Verity, had applied to these ancient and now commonplace ideas more advanced standards of construction and equally advanced late nineteenth-century social standards of respectability, allowing the strata of society that could afford the considerable sum of five shillings or more (for private boxes) to move easily up the wide central staircase of the Empire to the box stalls and the promenade on the second tier, where they could claim the privilege of mixing with their "equals" (see fig. 13). Others not so affluent had to be content with less, as in the extreme case of the gallery tier, approached by a separate corridor from Lisle Street leading to a single flight of stairs.[81]

Plans for the substantial structural changes to the Empire promenades were going forward with dispatch, as evidenced by current departures from original designs by the elder Verity for the pit and stalls and the dress circle, and by a longitudinal plan, preserved in the archive of the Royal Institute of British Architects.[82] The original dress-circle plan shows a large unobstructed promenade area completely encircling the stalls, complemented by four rows of stalls. The plan for the pit and stalls indicates ten rows of stalls and twelve rows of pit benches; there is also a promenade completely encircling the pit and stalls. These were apparently the plans carried out in the construction of the theatre that opened on the site of the old Savile House, itself succeeded by the Pandora Theatre, which soon changed its name to the Empire Theatre. The elder Verity, architect of the theatre that opened on 17 April 1884, was succeeded by the firm of J. and A. E. Bull, 35 Charing Cross, whose names appear on the plans submitted to the Theatres and Music Halls Committee in November 1894 by the younger Verity, who himself had designed a new foyer for the Empire erected in 1893.[83]

This second set of plans, now in the Greater London Record Office, comprises an underlying comparative basis for viewing the extensive alterations required in 1894 by the Theatres and Music Halls Committee. Plan No. 6, a longitudinal section showing the main entrance leading to the vestibule, indicates a broad staircase up to the "Promenade" and balcony. The "Balcony & Promenade Plan," No. 3, shows a spacious promenade encircling the entire balcony, with only three or four rows of seats and, as yet, no bar. As for the "Dress Circle and Plan of Boxes," Plan No.

2, a relatively narrow circular corridor is shown, within whose circumference are boxes and, below them, the seats of the dress circle. Plan No. 1, "Pit and Stall Plan," also shows a promenade — from the first, there were two promenades at the Empire, not just one — and also indicates a pit, pit stalls, and orchestra stalls, each section sealed off by a barrier from the others.[84]

At its weekly meeting on 28 November the Theatres and Music Halls Committee considered Frank Verity's detailed summary of his proposed alterations, along with the plans by J. and A. E. Bull on which the alterations were shown as a series of overlays.[85] Ever vigilant, the committee accepted the proposals for the stalls and pit level but added some requirements for the two circle levels. Mindful, very likely, of the riot that took place on the reopening of the Empire on 4 November and the ease with which the flimsy temporary barriers were pulled down by crowds of angry patrons, it called for the barriers dividing the promenade at dress-circle level to be "of solid construction, and be not less than 4 feet high." In addition it required that there be "only one opening to the refreshment bar, and that such opening do not exceed 4 feet in width, and that the additional opening by the doorway leading to the stalls saloon, now shown on the plan, be blocked up to the satisfaction of the Council." As for the grand circle, it was resolved "that the screens to the bars be 6 feet 6 inches high with openings at either end, not exceeding 4 feet in width, and that they be constructed to the satisfaction of the Council." The committee approved the plans, subject to the agreed stipulations, and sent them on to the council on 4 December.[86] In the form in which they reached the council, the committee's recommendations now included the desiderata that the enclosures to the bar on the dress-circle level "be carried up to the ceiling of this part of the premises" and that "the settees behind the boxes on either side of the tier be removed."[87]

Verity's plans embody in lucid graphic terms the verbal proposals he made to the committee on that date. They have an additional, independent significance for the extent to which they throw into bold relief the changes, not simply architectural but social, and even moral, called for explicitly or implicitly in the far-reaching recommendations of the committee. The most perspicuous changes occurred, not surprisingly, in the five-shilling promenade. Prepared in the form of a series of overlays on earlier plans, Verity's plans in the instance of the second-tier promenade reveal with unmistakable clarity the fundamental connection in the eyes of

the committee itself and also of numerous witnesses and commentators —
including the British Women's Temperance Association, whose social
purity wing had been conducting an assiduous crusade against prostitution in London — between prostitution and alcoholic drink.[88] On the
overlays the bars throughout the premises are marked for enclosure; at the
same time the number of seats has noticeably increased. In the second-tier
circle the seating capacity has effectively doubled and the opportunity for
walking has been correlatively reduced: seats proliferate back into the area
once open to promenaders, six rows of them now instead of three; behind
them, a sloping platform circumscribed by a barrier effectively demarcates
a reduction by fully one-half in the amount of ambulatory space. That
space is itself further interrupted by the insertion of barriers, leaving a
scant four feet for passage through. So long as such barriers remained in
place, the spaciousness of the promenade and its encouragement of the
free circulation of patrons would be drastically curtailed.

An additional consideration that might have obtruded itself into the
committee's deliberations remained, unaccountably, unmentioned. Not
once during the entire series of discussions about effective ways to cut
down on prostitution in the promenade, along with its alleged encouragement by the proximity of bars serving alcohol, did any participant call the
attention of the committee to the question of fire safety. "There is a fire-
proof exit from the Gallery on the opposite side [of the staircase], carried
right across, but not communicating in any way with the Stage," the
Empire Theatre program for opening night in 1884 had explained; it was
to be used only as an additional exit. The detailed explanation included
the assertion that if necessary the entire audience might "leave the Theatre without inconvenience in the space of about three minutes." The
result was that no theatre in the entire city could be found "safer or more
easily understood in regard to its exits, than the Empire Theatre."[89]
Despite the high safety standards touted in the opening-night program,
and despite the self-assured statement of the Theatres and Music Halls
Committee on the eve of the council meeting that "a great advance has
been made in the safety of licensed places frequented by the public," one
wonders, once the required additional seats and barriers were put in place
throughout the auditorium, what would have happened to the estimated
1,800 spectators, sitting or standing, had fire broken out.[90]

Writing in the *Illustrated London News* in November 1894, its theatre
reviewer Clement Scott lodged a protest over that very point, inveighing

against the safety hazards created by the structural alterations called for by the Theatres Committee (and echoing a complaint made earlier by Walter Emden). Scott's charges are quite specific: to carry out the prohibition of alcohol in the auditorium, he explained, "it has been necessary to erect temporary swing-doors, in order to divide the auditorium from the refreshment-rooms." The council, he pointed out, has previously opposed such doors, especially if they open inward, as is now the case at the Empire. Curtailing the promenade even by an inch, Scott warned, blocking up clear spaces with seats, and installing dividing doors or partitions between the amusement part and refreshment part of the theatre would add to the risk. Ironically, what is acknowledged to be "the safest and most convenient theatre in London" is now faced with the threat of "a very grave and serious danger, in case of fire, panic, or accident." Much more important than the physical safety of Empire audiences was, presumably, their moral well-being. Having left the task of "looking after the lives of her Majesty's subjects" to the Building and Construction Committee of the LCC, the Theatres and Music Halls Committee, Scott concluded, is now "most gratuitously looking after their souls."[91] One could speculate that their spiritual condition now depended partly on the elimination of opportunities for providing alcoholic beverages to promenaders. The Empire was simply not to be let alone on this subject, by the Theatres and Music Halls Committee or the county council itself.

Others in official positions took the same dim view of the moral evil symbolically represented by the existence of a bar in close proximity to a promenade. In early January the Honorable Spencer Ponsonby Fane, K.C.B., an official in the Lord Chamberlain's office, reiterated the point in a letter to the Empire scene and costume designer C. Wilhelm. "Also pray remember," he wrote, "that H.L. [His Lordship the Lord Chamberlain] will not sanction Bars open to the Auditorium, nor what is known in these days as a 'Promenade.'"[92]

### NYMPHS AND SATYRS

As the process of effecting alterations at the Empire, first on paper, then physically, went slowly on through the autumn and into the winter of 1894, the controversy that had raged throughout October and early November seemed to subside almost as quickly as it had arisen. The slow progress of draughtsmen, carpenters, and painters did not make for sensational journalism, and the Empire's helpless capitulation to the requirements of the county council and their aggressive interpretation by the Theatres and Music Halls Committee was not exactly news. It began to appear that people were growing tired of the whole business. The *Daily Telegraph* itself, having marched, banners flying, in the vanguard of public outrage throughout the month of October and into November, admitted in early December to considerable ennui when it came to the more general subject of prostitution in public places, complaining in a leading article (written, perhaps, by Clement Scott, the voice of the *Telegraph*'s reactionary response to Ibsen and Pinero) that the "oppressive nightmare of the fallen woman" was being kept continually before the public and that audiences were "hunted by the harlot from theatre to theatre." Every new drama, it seemed, could be found to contain "the same dreary and disgusting tale of female impurity and masculine imbecility."[93] In the context established by the events of October and November, the "harlots" of the Empire five-shilling lounge were left not entirely unimplicated by the remark, but the notoriety with which they had been visited at the height of the controversy had lately much diminished.

Meanwhile, in a situation both anomalous and seemingly inevitable (and even comical), the Empire Theatre of Varieties was still operating without a license. At the meeting of the council on 13 November, licensing committee chair Richard Roberts was asked whether a license had yet been delivered to the Empire. It had not, Roberts replied; there had not been sufficient time for compliance with the attached conditions, and it was the practice of the council to keep back licenses until such conditions had been fulfilled.[94] By 24 November no license had yet been issued, the *Era* reported, adding that the question of whether the county council had the right to impose conditions on a license had not been taken up.[95] The issue of the range and efficacy of the council's authority was evidently up in the air, but when, in December, the council was queried by one of its members, Lieutenant Colonel Ford, as to whether the council was exceeding its "power to grant conditions" when "sitting as licensing body," the council declined to take up the question.[96]

In fact, it was not until early March 1895 that the *Era* could report that the required alterations at the Empire were effectively in place. (The license was then, presumably, issued.) Everything in the front of the house is managed in the best way, it said, and the Empire is well attended, the additional seating and "standing-view" accommodation in the dress circle being "eagerly taken advantage of."[97] By mid-March the *Era*'s regular

"Music Hall Gossip" was able to cite the report of the Empire board of directors declaring a net profit, after expenses including the defense of the license, of £17,276. The three most recent quarterly dividends amounted to £15,625; no final dividend would be paid. Instead, the Empire would carry forward credit to meet expenditures necessitated by "structural alterations required by the County Council."[98]

By the end of the month the *Era* reported that at a general meeting of the Empire proprietors George Edwardes had been reelected to the board of directors (having relinquished his position as managing director two or three years before, he was now coequal with the others). A self-indulgent tone of heroic long-suffering would seem to have prevailed among the proprietors. J. C. Collier, a member of the board, explained sympathetically that Edwardes had been through "a trying ordeal" but had protected the interests of shareholders in ways that merited "hearty thanks." He defended the Empire against the charge of indecency leveled by some investors, commenting that those who profited from investment in the Empire enterprise were not in a position to complain about the fare. In a speech on the occasion Edwardes said he had been contemplating resigning from the Empire directorate owing to the press of other business, but the attack on the Empire had caused him to stay on "in order to combat those designs." He admitted that the Empire had not done very well recently, but now that the requirements of the county council had been carried out, the management would, he assured his auditors, bring the Empire "once more to the front."[99]

Meanwhile, by the middle of January, a new drop curtain painted by Burchardt of Vienna had been placed in service on the Empire stage. Representing a Bacchanalian festival, it featured as central figures a nymph and satyr dancing, with a statue of Priapus prominent in the background.[100] The more things changed at the Empire Theatre of Varieties, it seemed, the more they remained the same.

# 5 : Why They Attacked the Empire

### THE OUTCOME OF THE CONTROVERSY

After weeks of commingled outcry and exultation over the recommendation of the Theatres and Music Halls Committee and its overwhelming endorsement by the London County Council, together with the wearied capitulation of the Empire management to the stipulations linked to its license (which had not yet been delivered), the air itself might well have been redolent of the scent of victory for the advocates of purity in social life, or acrid with the smell of defeat for those whose pleasures, or profits, had been compromised. On 4 December the Theatres Committee had been officially informed by the county council of its approval of drawings encapsulating the alterations the Empire management had agreed to make in order to carry out the council's conditions for the renewal of its music and dancing license. Further, the superintending architect had informed them that the council's requirements had been carried out satisfactorily.[1] For the moment, the militant forces campaigning for an end, or at least a curtailment, of immorality in and around the five-shilling lounge of the Empire would seem to have emerged triumphant.

And yet the victory proved to be short-lived. On 24 September 1895, the Theatres and Music Halls Committee received notice that George Edwardes's application for renewal of the annual license for the Empire Theatre of Varieties would be filed on 2 October — weeks later than the required interval between filing and action, and perhaps an indication of some time-consuming testing of the waters. The notification took the form of a letter from Edwardes's solicitors Allen and Low informing the committee that the application would be for "an ordinary full Music and Dancing License, unhampered by the restrictions or conditions imposed last year, or any other restrictions or conditions; in other words, we shall ask for the renewal of the License in the form in which it was originally granted in 1887 and regularly renewed until last year."[2]

The transcript of shorthand notes taken by its clerk during the licensing committee session of 2 October 1895 records C. F. Gill's long speech of justification on Edwardes's behalf. Edwardes was then called and examined. It was "absolutely untrue," he said, according to the *Era* reporter, "that women were admitted free." Great care was always taken, and a large staff was present to keep order. He said he had lost "nearly £20,000" as a result of the restrictions of the previous year; asked to clarify, he explained that this meant "a less sum made" — that is, "less money taken at the door." He went on to complain of an effective handicap imposed by those restrictions, consisting of the freedom of potential customers to go to other halls a short distance from the Empire and take a certain kind of refreshment "in a private box"; such clients no longer had this privilege at the Empire.[3] Edwardes's reference was clearly to the Alhambra, a two-minute walk diagonally across Leicester Square to the southeast, and the implication was, just as clearly, one of unfair competition underwritten by government fiat.

Asked about the dividends paid to shareholders in the last year, Edwardes replied that they were 30 percent or 40 percent, compared with 75 percent the year before. These percentages, he was careful to note, were on the old stock value; anyone buying it now of course pays "a very large premium." Edwardes added that, because of the financial losses he had described, the Empire had also not been able to provide the same quality of entertainment. In particular, he complained, the last three months of 1894 were "absolutely disastrous for the Empire." For all that, he went on, the sale of intoxicating liquors in the house was the same, the only difference being that many more people were now congregating around the bars, since drink was no longer available in the auditorium, and "causing greater obstruction." The number of casual patrons, on whom the Empire had greatly relied in the past, had considerably diminished, he said. And as for the structural alterations imposed by the county council at the recommendation of the licensing committee, he thought they resulted in keeping the promenade from being used as intended. A member of the committee, Mr. Jerome, asked, "It is a sort of gangway now?" "Yes," Edwardes replied, "and rather dangerous."[4] Evidence was presented, as memorialized in later printed council records, that there had been no change in the character of the audience since the promenade had been removed and the drinking in the auditorium discontinued and, further, that every effort had been made to maintain the respectability of the place.

The police had testified to the excellent way in which the premises were conducted.

The paucity of questioning of Edwardes by the committee this time around, along with its perfunctory tone, is particularly striking in comparison with the tone and events of the previous October and in view of the easy availability, from Edwardes or from other sources, of fuller, more salient information. Edwardes himself, as quoted by Hollingshead in a hostile article on oppressive government control of music halls, "Molly-Coddling Regulation," would later set the Empire's alleged financial misfortunes in the larger context provided by the distance of over a year after the events of October 1894. Regarding the current fiscal situation with regard to the music hall, Edwardes explained that, whereas shares of theatres are either stable or discounted, music hall shares command, "in most cases, enormous premiums." There were at the time twenty-eight principal halls or "theatres of variety," as some like to call them, representing "in capital over two millions sterling, in debenture investment nearly four hundred thousand pounds, and in mortgage commitments between four and five hundred thousand pounds, or about three millions sterling."[5]

Edwardes's summary corroborates the testimony of Henry Newson-Smith, fellow of the Institute of Chartered Accountants, before the 1892 parliamentary select committee on theatres and music halls. Asked to give information on the value of the Empire Theatre of Varieties, Newson-Smith offered some revealing figures. Although the Empire management paid a high ground rent of £6,000 per annum, and its share capital had the relatively small total of £31,250, "the shares stand at a very high premium," much higher than those of its competitor the Alhambra, namely at some 300 percent, yielding an actual value of £93,750. Given a capitalization of the ground rent over a twenty years' purchase of £120,000, the total value of the enterprise can thus be estimated at £245,000. Newson-Smith thought, given the small amount of paid-up capital, Empire dividends were to be valued at "something approaching 80 per cent."[6]

Evidently, the Empire was continuing to participate advantageously in the highly profitable business of popular entertainment in London, experiencing hardly more than a temporary downturn as a result of the events of late 1894. Almost as evident was an implication consistent with the point that Queen's Counsel Murphy had emphasized on the day of the council's decision: that capitalization on this scale entails huge risk on the part of investors and therefore must not be arbitrarily threatened or circumvented by governmental authority.

When questioning by the licensing committee had ended, the committee retired for a mere quarter of an hour (one-third the time it had spent the previous October on the Empire application) and then returned with its decision. Speaking for the whole, the chair, Richard Roberts, announced: "In the case of the Empire Theatre the Committee have considered the application & decided to recommend the Council to grant the license."[7]

Neither the National Vigilance Association nor any private persons such as Laura Ormiston Chant had submitted objections in advance or had attended the committee meeting itself. Just as significantly, no questions had been asked by the committee members about either of the two great issues raised by Mrs. Chant and her colleagues at the licensing session the year previous: the presence of prostitutes plying their trade in the five-shilling promenade and the indecency of some of the costumes in the ballet. (The closest such questioning came was an inquiry as to whether certain persons were admitted without charge.) In the view of Daniel Farson, a historian and biographer of Marie Lloyd, Mrs. Chant, a proud and sensitive woman, had sailed for America in late 1895 rather than face another round of perhaps futile protests, having accused the press of abusing her "in every conceivable manner, almost entirely ignoring that I was but the chosen representative of others."[8] She had been through a difficult year, to be sure. Effigies of her were burned in the streets, her granddaughter Marjory Lester has explained, her house had been mobbed, and police protection was required, including escorts for the children on their way to school.[9] The patently angry tone of her reminiscence, *Why We Attacked the Empire*, is not difficult to account for, given the repercussions on Mrs. Chant herself and her long-suffering husband, Thomas, and their family that occurred as a result of her efforts. Moreover, the deliberations in camera of the Theatres and Music Halls Committee in October 1895 produced a healthy endorsement of Edwardes's bid for an unrestricted license: the vote was nine to two in favor.[10]

For reasons best known to himself, Edwardes subsequently gave it out that the vote had been much less decisive. "It is an open secret," he explained, looking back on the October 1895 proceedings, "that, in Committee, the Empire obtained its unrestricted licence by the narrowest possible majority, while the Palace got the same privilege by a majority at least six times greater." Adding irony upon irony, the full council, Edwardes went on to point out, confirmed the Empire's freedom "by a majority of seventeen," but the Palace was "sent back into Bondage by a majority of one" — that one the tie-breaking vote of the council's own chair.[11]

Citing a comment in the *Era* on the results of the county council elections the previous spring, Farson attributes the change to the music hall proprietors' "very strong ally," the public, which expressed its views "in no uncertain voice" at the ballot box.[12] What had happened was that the Progressives — most of them activist Radical Liberals[13] — already amounting to almost two-thirds of the first members of the county council at its beginnings in 1889, had increased their majority in the 1892 election; but in 1895 the Moderates, allied with Conservatives, had drawn even with the Progressives (at fifty-nine apiece), even while the Progressives kept marginal control of the council through their election of enough aldermen (twenty in all, elected by the council members themselves) favorable to their views (twelve, outnumbering the seven Moderate aldermen).[14] One may infer that the climate of the Theatres and Music Halls Committee had modulated in correlative ways. Evidently, the interests that had coalesced around the efforts of Edwardes and his fellow entrepreneurs to provide the kind of entertainment and ambiance available since the Empire began conducting its present policy of entertainment in 1887 had once again prevailed.

The proof, as before, emerged in material terms, in the form of a resolution of the crucial issue of alterations of the Empire promenade and contiguous spaces. Committee and council minutes from this point on record a deliberate, decisive process of structural reversal. On 13 November 1895 the committee agreed to meet with Frank Verity to review plans for proposed alterations. Nine days later Verity sent in completed plans consisting of two drawings whose import was unmistakable. The declared intention was, first, "to remove 12 seats on the upper circle level, to re-instate the coffee bar in the rear of the seating and to remove the iron screens enclosing the refreshment bars at the sides of the circle." As for the all-important dress-circle level, the proposal was "to substitute one long row of easy seats or lounges for the two back rows of armchairs which were added last year; to remove the barriers and the raised platform in the rear of the seating, to re-instate the refreshment-bar on the prompt side of the circle, and to widen the entrance doorway in the screen enclosing the refreshment-bar at the south-west angle of the auditorium to 8 feet." When Councillor McDougall, still a member of the committee, attempted to have added to the report to the council certain particulars "showing the premises as they were previous to October 1894, as they are at present, and as they will be if the plans above referred to are approved by the council," he was effectively silenced by the rest of the committee.[15] And when the council's superintending architect, having surveyed the results of the latest round of alterations, sent in his report on 15 January 1896 calling attention to the presence of "a row of seats placed against the back wall of the upper circle which was not shown on the approved drawings," far from pouncing vindictively, as was their wont, upon a brazen departure from what they had previously approved, the committee decided that "no steps be taken in regard to the rows of seats mentioned in the Superintending Architect's report" and that the council simply be informed that the alterations at the Empire "have been completed."[16]

A tone of weariness with an overattenuated issue is nearly palpable in the record of the committee's latter-day proceedings. For a committee that, a little over a year before, had been rigidly bent on implementing structural alterations patently intended to discourage prostitution and the consumption of spirituous liquors at the premier resort of its kind in the British Isles, the turnabout was no less than stunning.

### A RETROSPECTIVE VIEW

Looking back at the controversy over the Empire license from the near vantage point of 1895, Laura Ormiston Chant assessed the most recent battle of the righteous against the vicious in a vituperative thirty-one-page pamphlet entitled *Why We Attacked the Empire*. Her intended readership evidently comprised an audience much different from powerful members of the county council; moreover, the time for reticence and tact had long since passed, while the gravity of the social problem she and her colleagues had addressed had not diminished in the least. No longer in evidence were the calm, patient words and altruistic sentiments of her testimony the previous October before the Theatres and Music Halls Committee or her sunny, measured oratory before the London County Council itself. Adopting the strident tones of the militant platform orator, sometimes sarcastic, sometimes self-congratulatory, she recounted the true history of an attempt by responsible citizens to "elevate the amusements of the people."

Early in *Why We Attacked* she answers the question of why the attack on the Empire caused such a tremendous outcry by identifying four classes of persons who perceived their interests to be endangered by it. There were those for whom money is "the be-all and end-all of life," for whom the dividend no matter how earned is sacrosanct. The second group were hedonists for whom the pursuit of amusement and pleasure was everything, no matter at what sacrifice of character; these persons were "almost panic-stricken with anger and fear, at any interference with amusement or sport." A third category embraced those who dwell in the centers or suburbs of art, literature, and science and who live under the illusion that the "grapes of Beauty, Life, and Wisdom" may be gathered "from the thorns of impurity, cruelty, and greed." The fourth group — clearly pimps and procurers, though Mrs. Chant does not identify them as such — comprised members of "the sad mournful army who minister entirely to the demands of lust, and who love darkness and secrecy because their lives and deeds are evil." An additional class of persons was composed of those who cried out against "bigots and fanatics" who, they charged, were trying to close down music halls and theatres and to interfere with liberty. Against all of these rose the voice of righteous public opinion — "the Non-Conformist conscience," as it is sometimes called.[17] Mrs. Chant had pointed words also for the attitudes of certain members of the press who, she claimed, were no more than mouthpieces for England's three great enemies, "Drink, Vice, and Gambling." She went on to expose the cant and hypocrisy of those who spoke up on behalf of the outcast woman, at the same time condemning what they viewed as the puritanical harshness of those who were thrusting her out of the haven of the Empire promenade onto the cold pavement outside. Even worse were those who fought to maintain a place where "successful vice" earned a large dividend and where "unsuccessful vice" in the form of streetwalker and outcast were "rigidly excluded *by order of the management.*"[18]

At the end of the pamphlet, in a section entitled "The Social Gethsemane," Mrs. Chant narrated another of her poignant tales based on personal observation, the story of "Pearl" — a narrative in the bold magdalenist genre encapsulating, as Michael Mason has explained, a view of "the trajectory of the prostitute's career as steeply descending into social dereliction and chronic illness or death."[19] Once "the gayest, youngest, and most attractive of the bedecked and painted crowd" that flocked nightly to the Empire and Alhambra promenades, after two or three months Pearl succumbed to the wearing effects of too much drink, late hours, excitement, and fatigue; she became "very thin, pale, and hysterical." One night when a man she had secured for herself rejected her and went off with someone else, she flew into such a passionate fury that she was summarily turned out of the Empire promenade and hustled into a four-wheeler by "friends" and a policeman. Now she sells matches and "picks up" what she can, is frequently drunk and seldom out of pain, often cold, wet, and hungry. Attempts to reclaim her had failed, for reasons not far to seek, considering the disappearance of her father long before and the vicious influence of her mother, who had introduced her to a life of prostitution at the age of fifteen. From there it proved an almost inevitable step to dressing in a silk frock, rouging her cheeks, and going to a place of amusement where she could be introduced to new men and persuade them to go home with her.[20]

Like Josephine Butler's stories of female victims of male power and lust, Mrs. Chant's pathetic accounts of virtue destroyed, or of women rescued from disaster at some eleventh hour by a persistent crusader like herself, embody a powerful fantasy of redemption whose variants, shining success or unhappy failure, were in some ways equally probative.[21] In numerous melodramas of the period the same fantasy is reified in the form of a suffering, patient father who at length discovers and, sometimes, redeems his errant, long-lost daughter — or, on occasion, his much younger long-lost wife, as does the elderly north-country miner Job Armroyd in Watts Phillips's sensational Adelphi drama *Lost in London* (1867). After a relentless search Job finds his beloved Nelly dying, in the company of her now-remorseful seducer Gilbert Featherstone. Manfully refraining from taking the life the guilty Featherstone offers him, but resigned and sorrowful, Job leaves Nelly to heaven, as the silvery beams of a limelight moon fall on her figure, *"flooding it as with a glory."*[22] As Judith Walkowitz suggests, Butler and other women writers in the genre of social purity narrative substitute themselves for the critically absent father, taking his wrongs upon their own shoulders and becoming an "avenging mother who presents the magdalen's case to the dastardly seducer."[23] Mrs. Chant's own early experience of being expelled from her family home by a proud, remorseless father who condemned her choice of the nursing profession as a fall from respectability may have lain behind her readiness to take the place of the no longer protective father and become the "indignant English mother," as she did in her story of the rescue of a servant girl from a seducer in the Underground.[24]

Another, later melodramatic treatment of the fallen woman, Henry Pettitt and Augustus Harris's Drury Lane "sensation drama" *A Life of Pleasure* (1893), adapts the familiar magdalenist agenda to the popular stage, reiterating yet another instance of the classic tale, so well known to theatre audiences in the near-immortal *East Lynne* (1866), of a woman who succumbs to the lure of evil sensuality and falls victim to the machinations of a heartless upper-class, pleasure-loving seducer. The arrival of Pettitt and Harris's long-suffering father, who determines to help his unfortunate daughter Norah to "forget," is no novelty, after so many instances; but their setting of a crucial, champagne-in-the-face encounter between seducer and seduced in the promenade of the Empire Theatre itself points up just the kinds of connections that Mrs. Chant was attempting to make, early and late in her life, as a writer and crusader on behalf of women and purity.

Pettitt and Harris brought out *A Life of Pleasure* at Drury Lane just over a year before Mrs. Chant made her case against the Empire. Having resigned in anger from the board of the Empire, Harris took the opportunity for a sweet, if vicarious, revenge by featuring an actual scene set in *"The Promenade at the Empire"* and calling for *"Realistic detail."*[25] The play revolves around the varying fortunes and contrasting personalities of two women who once were friends, Norah Hanlan and Phyllis de Belleville. Norah has been so badly treated by a faithless lover, Colonel Chandos, that she is resolved to ruin herself just to make an example of him. Phyllis, employed at the Empire, encounters Norah, hears her pitiful tale, and attempts to rescue her. Pettitt and Harris spare no efforts in depicting the extreme nature of Norah's feelings. "I have become reckless of what happens to me now!" she tells Phyllis. "He shall see me dressed in the raiment that is the uniform of my shame — decked in the diamonds that are the price of my soul. . . . My love for him has but brought the misery — I'll forget it all in a life of pleasure." Hence the title of the play and its loudly resonant ironies. In answer, Phyllis responds with an action-stopping speech of her own, a tale not unlike Mrs. Chant's cautionary story of Pearl. "Hear me," Phyllis exhorts her despairing companion; "let me tell you what the life of pleasure means." She had a sister with whom she lived happily, though both were poor and friendless; but the sister, sorely tempted by luxury, soon traded gainful employment for "a life of pleasure!" Phyllis, working hard as a singer and laughing off the men who would purchase her love with diamonds, saw nothing of her for over a year. But then "one night my sister came back to me. Not the beautiful girl who had gone away; only the wreck of a woman — praying for death. There was no light in the once bright eyes — no colour in the once beautiful face — no music in the once sweet voice. Her thin and wasted arms with the blue veins marbled in them — she placed round my neck — and died. That was the end of her life of pleasure."[26] Pettitt and Harris's heavily moralized action then proceeds to Norah's critical encounter with the heartless Colonel Chandos. Publicly accusing him of having seduced her and then taunting her with her shame, she dashes in his face the champagne he has ordered "to gratify the heart of woman!" In the last scene she is rescued by her father, who has found her at last and who determines to "spend my life in helping her to forget."[27]

Mrs. Chant had her own, even more cautionary view of the significance of the Empire promenade. Rescue work, laudable as it is, is not the real answer, she explains in *Why We Attacked*, any more than is the indiscriminate clearing of the streets. The places of entertainment and the streets are integrally connected, and the streets can be cleared only "by stopping the sources of supply." The immediate sources, she implies, are the Empires and Alhambras of London and other metropolises, but the full list of causes of prostitution is a long one: "Unfair wages, over-tasked strength, inadequate preparation for the duties of life, unhappy home-life, betrayed love, amusements that corrupt, the many snares set for inexperience by cunning hands, and a low estimate of women on the part of men" — these, Mrs. Chant explains, are "some of the sources from which the dark stream of human ruin on the streets is supplied."[28] The indictment is grave and comprehensive, reaching far beyond the lure of music halls and theatres and the danger presented by the unprincipled seekers of pleasure and profit who frequent them or do business there. It extends to an exploitative economic system and, beyond that, to failures of education and upbringing, the chronic ills of domestic life, the fragmentation of the family, and the deeply flawed relationships of women and men, within and without the all too unsafe fortress of the home — that cherished place John Ruskin had piously idealized, in 1865, as "the place of Peace; the shelter, not only from all injury, but from all terror, doubt, and division."[29]

An unengaged reader of Mrs. Chant's succinct but far-reaching analysis of modern society as source and abettor of prostitution might wonder whether, in view of the very comprehensiveness of her indictment, any specific strategies taken against the Empire or its alleged institutional coconspirators in vice could lead to permanently useful results. No amount of hope for "a purer, sweeter, happier London" could gainsay the enormity and intractability of the problem, so large as to transcend the powers not only of licensing committees or even governments but also of human beings collectively and en masse. And yet, perhaps it was because of the staggering dimensions of the problem itself that the "crusade," as Mrs. Chant and her followers enthusiastically characterized their protest, was undertaken and, within the range of its influence, left almost no one unaffected or uninvolved.[30] For the Empire was viewed by the crusaders as the premier place in London where vice of this kind was to be found. Just as important, as Mrs. Chant's depiction of the "social Gethsemane" makes clear, the Empire was seen as the principal feeder of street prostitution, despite the voices that argued quite the contrary — argued that the Empire promenade performed the salutary service of keeping fallen women off the streets. It was no wonder that in his 1892 account of the history of Leicester Square John Hollingshead — no prude on the prowl, but aware of the extent that unregulated street prostitution could hurt theatre business — could complain that the north side of the square is currently "the prowling place of *demi reps*" and that authorities and owners of west-side properties "appear to be unable or unwilling to remove this Metropolitan disgrace, which has existed and developed for at least a dozen years."[31]

In the heat of the fray, such sober voices as Hollingshead's would have been only barely audible above the shouts of success uttered by the *Vigilance Record* and its sympathizers, who as early as mid-November 1894 had come to believe they had won what the *Record* headlined "The Battle of the Music Halls." The real issue, said the *Record*, had been "whether the libertines were to be allowed to go their own sweet way, indulging to the full their evil propensities without let or hindrance," or whether the London County Council would so control the halls "as to make it possible for decent and respectable men and women to visit them without having both the eye and the ear subjected to most immoral influences." The battle had been "one of the fiercest fights" ever waged "by Purity against lust, by righteousness against iniquity," and it was in great part owing to Mrs. Chant's "fidelity and womanly courage" that "a most decisive victory" had been realized.[32]

In 1899, to satisfy a French visitor's curiosity, Max Beerbohm revisited the expansive arc of the Empire five-shilling promenade. "I asked my friend to walk slowly," he recalled, "and to observe carefully the throng's demeanour":

> Everything was the same as it had ever been. The same glare, and the same music; the same congestion of silk hats and swallow-tails, pressed against the barrier of the circle, watching the ballet; the same slow and serried procession of silk hats and swallow-tails, billicocks and racing-coats, moodily revolving along the space between the ballet-gazers and the long row of large-hatted ladies who, bolt upright on the crimson settees against the wall, conversed with one another in undertone; the same old absence, in fact, of any gaiety, of any semblance of gaiety, of any wish or effort to contrive any little hollow semblance of gaiety. I saw that my friend was puzzled, disappointed. Around him were all the common ingredients for revelry —light, glitter, youth, money, beauty, dancing, alcohol; all those things without which revelry is, indeed, quite possible, but with even a small measure of which revelry would seem, to the child of a Latin race, quite inevitable. I was amused by my friend's disillusionment. We loitered, contemplative. There was no need to clinch my previous argument by pointing for him with words the moral of the Promenade. As we descended the staircase to the stalls, "My brave," he said to me simply, "you had reason."[33]

For all of Beerbohm's melancholy conclusion that the Empire and its cavernous lack of true gaiety remained unchanged and intractable, and notwithstanding the outcome of the licensing controversy in the short term, leading within a year to the restoration of the unimpeded reaches of the Empire promenade and the renewed availability of alcoholic beverages there and elsewhere in the auditorium, the efforts of Mrs. Chant and her colleagues had achieved, in practical terms, an undeniable effect on the business and art of theatrical entertainment in London (and elsewhere). Dagmar Kift, who has written authoritatively and comprehensively on the British music hall, has pointed to the anticapitalist aspect of the controversy, an aspect she believes remains neglected, although both Mrs. Chant and John Burns took special pains to emphasize it during the county council's deliberations. Mrs. Chant's campaign introduced new elements into the controversy, Kift believes, demonstrating the division that had occurred, because of recent developments, between the more traditional music hall and the newer theatre of variety. No longer were the music halls exclusively working-class institutions, as many think them to have been in their earlier phases, and as such were no longer clearly deserving of working-class support in their hour of need. "Capitalist variety-theatre impresarios" therefore had no right to depend on the "automatic solidarity of the workers," Kift points out. The reform movement of which both Mrs. Chant and John Burns were a part was now adding to its more traditional moral and doctrinal concerns a newer interest in criticism of the capitalist system itself, Kift concludes.[34] At the same time, the canny strategy of George Edwardes, reflecting a skill rare among managers and landlords, to co-opt the support of the hundreds of Empire workers who had willingly joined him, massed on the stage of the Empire the night of the London County Council's decision, to deplore what they clearly realized was a threat to their very livelihoods should not be overlooked. The hypothetical solidarity of a working-class audience was one thing; the solidarity of the workers behind the scenes or in the front of the house, engaged in occupations that now might suddenly disappear, was quite another. The Empire "was theirs," Kift points out, "only because they were directly employed by the management or in some other way economically dependent on it."[35]

All the same, beyond the heightened awareness of the Empire workers themselves, an estimable impact had also been made on the consciousness of many persons who before had blithely taken the situation in the Empire promenade, together with its underlying social conditions, for granted. In 1912 W. R. Titterton looked back with sorrow at how much improved the variety stage had become — "improved as a Gothic cathedral would be by the hacking off of gargoyles." The fact was that "open vulgarities have, by County Council edict, been ruthlessly suppressed."[36] A year earlier, S. L. Bensusan's *Souvenir of London* reported that a change for the better had occurred over the previous decade. The council's vigilance has proved to be "very effective," Bensusan judged, and although "a few of the leading variety houses are still the hunting-grounds of the demi-monde, behaviour is perfectly decorous and drunkenness unknown." A measure of the increased respectability now characteristic of variety theatres was that some popular favorites were now able to earn, "in return for a few hours' work each night, the salary of a Cabinet Minister."[37] Bensusan's comment, strikingly condescending and sexist, together with its premise that respectability may be measured in terms of income, reflects a familiar belief characteristic of late Victorian life and values and carrying over into the Edwardian period. At the same time, its novel attribution to the results of the efforts toward reform in local government hints at the presence of a new matrix of political forces more characteristic of the twentieth century than of the nineteenth.

As that earlier century was drawing to an end, those forces had suddenly and spectacularly come to the fore. Mrs. Chant's testimony before the Theatres and Music Halls Committee in October 1894 had been persuasive enough to divide the committee almost down the middle. The Empire's license nearly failed to survive on the very first vote, and the restrictions imposed on the Empire promenade spoke unambiguously and eloquently of the committee's perception of the real nature of the problem — one that at least some members might well have preferred not to acknowledge. Once compelled to do so, they dealt with it in draconian fashion and with a certain measured vindictiveness. Once the committee members had launched themselves on the arduous course of moral reform through structural alteration and reconstruction, the momentum generated by their collective will became, at least in the short term, virtually irresistible. "The austerely-virtuous regard for the public's morals which is the particular characteristic of the LCC is apparently an irrepressible quantity," the *Financial News* complained in 1893: "no rebuff dampens its Pecksniffian ardour; no criticism, however mordant, disturbs its smug equanimity."[38]

All the same, the efforts of the Empire management to avoid compliance with the council's ruling and then, when required to comply, its cynical tolerance of the riot led by a scrappy young Winston Churchill and his peers — only some of whom, said the newspapers, with no little amusement, were approaching middle age — were costly only in terms of legal expenses and of architects' and builders' fees. They were not costly in terms of takings at the doors, despite Edwardes's remarkable talent for crying poor after the fact. The two ballets on at the Empire in October 1894, *La Frolique* and *On Brighton Pier* — "A New Ballet Divertissement in one Tableau" (fig. 36)[39] — "are in the height of their success," said a writer in the *Illustrated Sporting and Dramatic News* in late December, "and will not be changed for some time to come." Moreover, the *Illustrated* pointed out, "the abolition of the promenade has not affected the popular-

*36. "The New Empire Ballet, 'On Brighton Pier'."*
Illustrated Sporting and Dramatic News, *20 October 1894, 236. Harvard University,*
*Houghton Library.*

ity of the Empire in the slightest."[40] In an earlier issue, for 13 October, a
reviewer of the new ballet observed that the Empire directors were "noted
for their generous and lavish outlay in all they do" and that the ballet
played to an "immense audience."[41]

Beyond the immediate, tremendous uproar over the Empire licensing
controversy itself, what had emerged to claim attention was the clash of
contrary cultural forces that reverberated in the committee's and the
council's deliberations and decisions and echoed further in the extraordinary range of opinion on an entire spectrum of related issues. Some members of the committee, and of the council itself, must surely have felt that
Mrs. Chant was — to use some contemporary commentators' terms — a
"fanatic," that she and her colleagues were surely to be described as
"prudes on the prowl," and that, so long as they behaved themselves, prostitutes in the promenade were neither desirable nor possible to exclude.[42]
To be sure, some opposition took an even more extreme form, bordering
occasionally on hysteria. The anonymous author of "Chanterism" in the
*Sketch* for 17 October 1894 took Mrs. Chant to task for returning to the
Empire for another visit "gaily dressed," after having previously called too

much attention to herself in her customary muted garb. Mrs. Chant and her followers were "indecent females," the writer insisted, for "it is indecent of women to stand up in public and say what these women have been saying." All the same, the judgment of such women who assert that the dancing at the Empire excites impure thoughts and passions was, the writer concluded, finally "so warped, so prurient, so exaggerated, and so very ugly, as to become absolutely disgusting."

That such adverse opinion against the kind of thinking and behavior demonstrated by Mrs. Chant and her colleagues was nearly pervasive in the culture, in the last decades of the century, is evident in the cliché invoked by Charles Harrison in his handbook *Theatricals and Tableaux Vivants for Amateurs*, published in 1882, in offering advice about dressing a character representing "Woman's Rights." Keying his description to a labeled illustration of the character and costume, Harrison explains: "a large tortoiseshell back comb, the largest that can be procured, should be worn at the back of the head. . . . The costume should be made in the form of a tightly fitting paletot of a light brown (LB) material, with dark brown (DB) trimmings. The bottle which is suspended by the strap over the shoulders should be labelled 'Smelling Salts,' and the small reticule should be red (R) with black trimmings. . . . Old-fashioned spectacles would greatly add to the effect, and if a large green (GN) umbrella of a past age can be procured so much the better" (fig. 37).[43] Cartoons in the *Illustrated Sporting and Dramatic News*, *Punch*, and other journals captured the popular hostility toward Mrs. Chant and her followers in tones more cruel than laughable (figs. 38, 39). Mrs. Chant's keen intelligence and iron will were no less proof against the ravings of self-contradictory extremists of a pseudoliberal stamp than against the excesses of cartoonists who strove to ridicule those "females" campaigning for women's rights and decency. Her and her colleagues' assiduous efforts in the cause of social purity were strikingly noteworthy, but no less prominent were the recalcitrant facts of contemporary social conditions. Undeniably, the Empire promenade exhibited the virtue of its gravest moral defect: it was, Mrs. Chant was forced to acknowledge, "the best place" where prostitutes "can carry on their trade." Nothing, it would seem, could undermine or controvert that fundamental fact.

Bernard Shaw's later comment on his character Mrs. Warren's defense of herself to her daughter Vivie adds a context to Mrs. Chant's point and partly corroborates her own analysis of the causes of prostitution — a

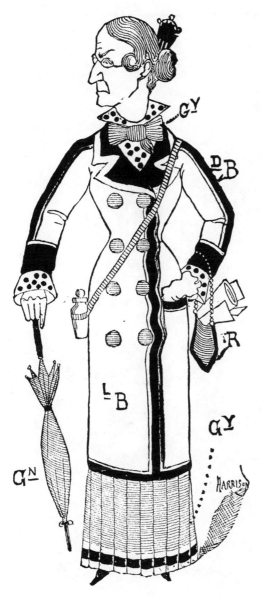

37. *"Woman's Rights Costume."* *Charles Harrison*, Theatricals and Tableaux Vivants for Amateurs. *London: L. Epcott Gill, 1882, 85. Harvard University, Houghton Library.*

*38. Leighton Ward. "The Empire — Another Living Picture."*
Illustrated Sporting and Dramatic News, *3 November 1894: 303.*
*Harvard University, Houghton Library.*

MRS. PROWLINA PRY.—"I HOPE I DON'T INTRUDE!"

THOUSANDS OF FELLOW-CREATURES FLUNG FROM WORK      THAN *PUNCH* IMAGINES, OUR NEW BUMBLE-BAND,
AT THE MERE PEN-STROKE OF A HASTY CENSOR!—      IF MISTRESS PRY'S DECISION THEY ABIDE BY;
AN UNCONSIDERED TRIFLE ZEAL MAY SHIRK!      BUT SHOULD THEY FAIL US, *PUNCH* THROUGHOUT THE LAND
BUT SENSE MAY NOT, NOR JUSTICE! THEY ARE DENSER      WILL WAKE THE PEOPLE PRUDES AND PRIGS ARE TRIED BY!

*39. "Mrs. Prowlina Pry. — 'I hope I Don't Intrude!'"*
Punch, *27 October 1894, 194. Smith College.*

central issue in Shaw's early "Unpleasant" play *Mrs Warren's Profession*
(written just a year before the Empire controversy erupted). Mrs. Warren's sister Liz had encountered her working in the bar at Waterloo Station and had taken Mrs. Warren into her business. They soon bought a
house in Brussels, "real high class — a much better place for a woman to

Why They Attacked the Empire ::: 209

be in" than the factory where another sister of theirs, Anne Jane, had contracted lead poisoning. The scandalized Vivie allows that her mother in doing what she did was "quite justified — from the business point of view." "Yes; or any other point of view," Mrs. Warren retorts, and she asks the unanswerable question: "What is any respectable girl brought up to do, but to catch some rich man's fancy and get the benefit of his money by marrying him? — as if a marriage ceremony could make any difference in the right or wrong of the thing!"[44] Such is the hypocrisy of the world and, hence, the hypocrisy of the institution of marriage, which is hardly more than legalized prostitution, Mrs. Warren implies. "The only way for a woman to provide for herself decently," she concludes, "is for her to be good to some man that can afford to be good to her." "Though it is quite natural and *right* for Mrs. Warren to choose what is, according to her lights, the least immoral alternative," Shaw commented in his preface to the 1902 edition of the play, it is "none the less infamous of society to offer such alternatives. For the alternatives offered are not morality and immorality, but two sorts of immorality."[45]

Ever alive to the shortcomings of lesser minds, in a letter to the *Pall Mall Gazette* at the height of the controversy over the Empire license Shaw had called attention to what he believed was Mrs. Chant's naïveté in believing an Empire prostitute's declaration that she earned "£20 and £30 a week" plying her trade in the promenade. Shaw's analysis of the economic implications of prostitution, in the Empire lounge and on the streets, was by any standard uncommonly perceptive — though NVA secretary Coote himself could make a similar point, observing that "the women who parade our streets are not there from choice, but because they have been driven into the life by hard economic conditions, and once there they are kept there by the cruelty of society."[46] Yet neither Shaw nor Mrs. Chant, despite their complementary insights into the springs of human viciousness and the recondite origins of social debilitation, were capable of recommending a clear and certain resolution of the problems these deficiencies created.

As the London County Council had prepared to take up the matter of the Empire's annual license, the question of how to deal with the apparently ineradicable presence of prostitutes in public places, along with the issues — economic, political, moral, and artistic — that their presence generated, would seem to have been hanging in the balance. Councillor John Burns admitted that "harrying women" who carry on the illicit trade amounted only to a "superficial palliative" that probably led to its increase. Yet many contemporaries would have agreed with a writer in the *Liberal* who insisted that "state regulation of vice" had "no place" and found it intolerable that government should in effect provide "convenient and luxurious accommodation for male and female loveless love."[47] Another question of a different kind also remained: would the decision of the county council do anything more than express a political majority view, overdetermined by myriad factors, social and individual, for the moment asserting its members' collective influence? If the decision did not (as it surely could not be expected to) resolve all the questions present in thoughtful observers' minds, might it at least frame those questions perspicuously enough to encourage useful answers over time?

Short of providing such answers, certain commentators were nonetheless able to set the major issues in useful perspective. In March 1895 William Archer, drama critic, translator and champion of Ibsen, and collaborator with Shaw in an earlier "blue-book" play, *Widowers' Houses*, about slum landlords and ill-gotten gains, published in the *Contemporary Review* a commonsense critical overview of the controversy in an essay entitled "The County Council and the Music Halls." Drawing on Elizabeth Pennell's masterful historical account of the halls in an earlier issue of the same journal, Archer pointed out that the music hall as it was now known was "an alliance — nay, a fusion — of the music hall and the publican" (a fact that had not escaped the notice of the council). The county council, he complained, was "capricious and sometimes vexatious in its demands for structural alterations" and furthermore was "open to the influence of Puritan bigotry and busy-bodyism." And yet people were panicking unnecessarily, Archer thought. The fact remained, if electors disapprove of the council's actions in a previous session, now was the time to say so.[48] The actions of "certain private societies and individuals" had created a "shriek of indignation and terror" in the press, but the process was eminently democratic: the licensing committee recommends a course of action to the council; time is allowed for public opinion to be expressed; if opposition emerges, the question is reopened and put to the vote of the whole body. Thus, the process is an "open, deliberate, above-board procedure." Still, in the case of the Empire license, the process had been denounced as "tyrannical" by those same persons who were content to see the legitimate theatre at the mercy of "a single individual appointed by Court patronage" — Archer's reference is to the Lord Chamberlain's Examiner of Plays — "from whose secret and silent tribunal there is no appeal!" Archer therefore encouraged his readers to view the dispute in a larger context, as a "battle between the democratic and oligarchic theories of government — between the organic and mechanical conceptions of society."[49]

As for the "ignoble and foul-mouthed outcry" of the previous autumn, echoes could still be heard, Archer acknowledged, but it was clear that the Empire management's bluff had been called and no real harm had been done. In fact, the structural alterations called for by the council had not yet been carried out in December 1894 when he had last visited the Empire, and a new series of "Living Pictures" at the Palace indicated that its management "had not taken too much to heart the warning it had received." And so it could be said that the London County Council's directives remained effectively moot. The main point, in Archer's view, was that the community should be aware of its "powers and responsibilities in the matter of public amusements; that it should possess a recognised machinery for the exercise of these powers; and that managers and performers should know it."[50]

In calling attention to the council's preoccupation with structural problems, Archer had put his finger on a critical factor in the controversy. The Theatres and Music Halls Committee's consistent recourse to requiring structural alterations as a means of reducing or eliminating immorality in places of public entertainment illuminates a crucial aspect of the history of the conflict over the Empire license. In fact, the events of 1894 provide a compelling instance of the close relationship between theatre architecture and social life. Dagmar Kift has pointed out that the change in interiors of music halls earlier in the century from longitudinal rows of tables, with patrons seated at right angles to the stage entertainment, to rows of seats facing the stage had the effect of inducing a fundamental change in audience behavior. Tables had encouraged conversation and mobility, but the installation of closely ranged seats in new halls and the even newer variety theatres had forced audiences to resort to the bars for convivial purposes. A resulting alteration occurred in the relationship of performer and audience, Kift argues: performers no longer had to vie for the attention of their audience, but could play directly to those in their seats and count on their attention.[51]

The point is true enough, but it slights the importance of the presence of hundreds of persons circulating in the promenades and around the contiguous bars of variety houses such as the Alhambra and the Empire, where it was possible to pay scant attention, or none at all, to the entertainment onstage while favoring another, quite unofficial but nonetheless real performance taking place closer in, of which the promenaders themselves were a part as great as the whole. Georges Bourdon reasserted the point astutely in his 1903 study of the English theatre in observing that, at the Alhambra or the Empire or some comparable house, the end-of-evening grand finale of some ballet or other marks no real stopping point, for the spectacle continues unabated on the other side of the footlights. In a reverse reflection, the performers in their gilded palaces who have been the subject of the audience's gaze become themselves spectators; looking out into the house, Bourdon explains, they see before them "a parterre full of low-necked dresses in a palace of genuine gold."[52] The Theatres and Music Halls Committee, well aware of the nature of the alternative and all too licentious "entertainment" available on the audience's side of the footlights, had sought to diminish or eradicate it altogether by introducing practical physical barriers in the form of additional seats and other obstructions intended specifically to impede the free circulation of those who chose not to sit and orient themselves toward the onstage entertainment but, instead, to become an unofficial, unacknowledged entertainment of their own devising.

And so the Empire licensing controversy had effectively resulted in the imposition of a kind of "overlay," at once graphic and symbolic, on the architect's original plans for a theatre building that afforded expansive interior vistas combined with spaces that paradoxically conferred an aura of intimacy and a simultaneous sense of detachment — a building that offered the opportunity for anonymous spectatorship and, at the same time, an amplitudinous, luxuriant access of leisure. That overlay had the effect of reifying with sharp-edged clarity the prevailing features and special conditions, at once architectural and social, that made the Empire the mutual resort of ladies of the night and gentlemen of the town and, for a time, marked it out for notoriety.

## THE PROBLEMATIC GOSPEL OF SENSUOUSNESS

One of the most significant layers of controversy that had marked the attack on the Empire concerned the character, more centrally than the costume, of the ballet dancer, with ramifications that penetrated far out into the surrounding matrix of cultural values and beliefs, well beyond any arena of direct concern to either George Edwardes or Laura Ormiston

Chant. The artist Selwyn Image, present at the October 1889 meeting of the Church and Stage Guild, followed the dancer Julie Seale's paper on the life and reputation of the ballet girl with commentary that in effect redefined "the battle of the music halls" more expansively in the larger terms of art in general. In fighting for the ballet, he said, he was fighting not only for the dancers themselves but also "for my own position as a painter; for Mr Irving's position at the Lyceum, and Sir Frederick Leighton's at the Academy; for every man's position, who practises any form of Art." If one thinks things through, Image explained, "opposition to the ballet is radically an opposition to Art." The perpetrators of such deeds are persons with no understanding of art, or with some understanding and are nonetheless radically opposed to it. Essentially the battle now being waged was between two classes of persons. One group is convinced that human life in its highest form is to be grasped, "not merely in the education and discipline of the senses, but in their destruction." The other group believes that life at its highest pitch "depends immensely upon the frank acceptance and cultivation of the senses, upon the joyous and exuberant life of the senses." The latter is the artist's ideal. Between the two sets of people he describes, Image concluded, "no compromise is possible."[53] In a letter to his friend and sometime colleague Herbert Horne, Image, a devoted student of John Ruskin, described his impromptu speech delivered at the guild as one in which he set forth "the gospel of sensuousness, as the very foundation of all fine art." Stewart Headlam, founder of the guild, had called the speech "an eye-opener" and begged him to write it up for the *Church Reformer*. Image was growing "more and more irritable," he confided to Horne, in the face of the "impudent creatures, who oppose and seek to rule us." "We must exterminate" them, he said, "or be ourselves exterminated."[54] In the face of what seemed to him fearful threats so uncompromising and absolute, and at the same time so dire that they even might threaten his livelihood, Image had little room for nuanced perception of gradations of difference. Mrs. Chant's repeated assertions, for example, that she was no enemy of pleasure and that she loved music and dancing had either not reached him or failed to penetrate.

Yet the fact remained that, while other writers of a more theoretical bent like Image saw the ethical and aesthetic conflict in which the Empire controversy had emerged in an even wider perspective, they found it no less absolutely a battle of opposites. In a fortuitously well-timed article in the *Fortnightly Review* in March 1894, the prolific scientific and sociological writer and novelist Grant Allen, who a year later would publish the notorious "New Woman" novel *The Woman Who Did* (1895), offered his view of the conflict under the title "The New Hedonism." Only two theories of the origins of human action have ever been advanced, Allen asserted. One is hedonism, a rational theory acknowledging "that pleasure and pain are and must ever be the sole guides of voluntary acts for all sentient beings." The other theory was, in effect, Calvinism, an irrational construct holding that the universe was created by "one or more superior beings, who hate pleasure and love pain, or who dispense them by caprice, and who desire that some or all of their creatures should suffer abundantly." The need now, Allen declared, is for a "new hedonism," a set of ideas and beliefs already espoused "by evolutionary moralists." Because "supernaturalism" has fallen, under the pressure of these new evolutionary ideas, and dragged asceticism down with it, this new hedonism remains as the only rational choice.[55]

The test case, Allen contends, for determining the validity of the new hedonism as opposed to the ascetic conception of life is the case of parental and marital relations. Ascetics argue that if religion ("supernaturalism") is taken away, we are "on the verge of a moral cataclysm"; such persons fear that removing religious restraints would "inaugurate an era of unbridled licentiousness." Asceticism has always considered human sexuality and the sexual instinct as "something to be despised, repressed, vilified, slighted" — "a mark of our 'fallen' condition." Allen argues to the contrary that from the sexual instinct arises "everything high and ennobling" in human nature, including our aesthetic sense, which is "a secondary sexual attribute." Offering an extended paean to human responsiveness to the beauty and multifariousness of the world, Allen argues that these responses, like "all the finest feelings," are prompted by the sexual instinct. "The sense of beauty, the sense of duty; parental responsibility, paternal and maternal love, domestic affection; song, dance, and decoration; the entire higher life in its primitive manifestations; pathos and fidelity; in one word, the soul, the soul itself in embryo — all rise direct from the despised 'lower' pleasures," he insisted. In contrast, asceticism hates "social life, wide sympathy, broad thought, intellectual freedom," hates "painting and sculpture, nude limbs of classic nymphs, romance and poetry, the drama, the dance, innocent love, innocent pleasure."[56]

The world at large is of course far from perfect, Allen acknowledges. The existing system of "harlotry and marriage" is not a "divine institution";

our sexual relations need extensive remodeling. Walk, on an evening, from Charing Cross by Leicester Square to Piccadilly Circus and one will discover the proof. The present system, one that "culminates in the divorce court, the action for breach of promise, seduction, prostitution, infanticide, abortion, desertion, cruelty, husband-poisoning, wife-kicking, contagious disease, suicide, illegitimacy, unnatural vice, the Strand by night, the London music hall," could surely be improved, Allen believes. The new hedonism, he concludes, may have the effect of introducing a superior system.[57]

Such views as Image's and Allen's, of an irreconcilable opposition between the ascetic and the aesthetic, were certainly thought-provoking but too simplistic and tending toward a naïve idealism, on the one hand, or a rigid fanaticism, on the other. Moreover, they failed to consider variation occurring in sometimes surprising quarters. The audience of W. A. Coote's speech, "Episodes of the Work of the National Vigilance Association," given under sufferance before a meeting of the Church and Stage Guild early in 1895, might well have been surprised to hear what Coote had to say on the subject of the nude. On the one hand, he categorically condemned exhibitions of "nude and semi-nude women as a means of amusement for a mixed audience"; on the other, he felt entirely receptive to the idea of the nude in painting, which has not, he thought, the slightest demoralizing effect. "The artist's soul so consciously pervades the work," he explained, that "the beauty of the form and pose" disguises what would otherwise "mar or vulgarise" it, and so the subject "becomes an inspiration for good and lovely thoughts."[58]

All the same, Coote had unequivocally condemned the tableaux vivants at the Palace in that same speech, soon printed in the *Church Reformer*. Even as the Empire controversy continued to simmer, Bernard Shaw, drawn to the Palace tableaux by that publication, found them "not only works of art" but "excellent practical sermons," he reported in the *Saturday Review*, urging the father of every family unable to afford the Haymarket and Bond Street picture galleries to take his daughters, and their brothers too, to the Palace. As for Coote's view that there was no art in the Palace tableaux, Shaw invited him to substitute himself for W. P. Dando, the arranger of the Palace tableaux, and try to "produce a single tableau that will not be ludicrously and outrageously deficient in the artistic qualities without which Mr. Dando's compositions would be hooted off the stage." As for Coote's assertion that the true artist's soul spiritualizes his work and inspires "good and lovely thoughts," Shaw asserted that there were very able artists "whose souls exactly resemble those of some members of the National Vigilance Association in debauching every subject, and finding in it an inspiration for obscene and unlovely thoughts." It is not nudity or semi-nudity, Shaw insisted, that by itself produces indecency. Shaw concluded that Coote should be categorized among persons "morbidly sensitive to sexual impressions, and quite insensible to artistic ones." Coote gave himself away, Shaw contended, when he pleaded that the living pictures were "so very obviously *living*. Human nature is so very much in evidence." In that view "you have the whole of Mr Coote's pessimistic, misanthropic philosophy," Shaw concluded. "Human nature and the human body are to him nasty things. Sex is a scourge. Woman is a walking temptation which should be covered up as much as possible." It was important to be clear about where Coote went wrong: his error lay not in his insistence that society should "suppress indecent exhibitions," but rather "in his attempt to make nudity or semi-nudity the criterion of indecency."[59]

Finally, both the matter-of-fact pragmatism of a Seale and the high-blown idealism of an Image or even a Coote failed equally to acknowledge the problematic eroticism of the dancer, onstage and, it would seem, off-stage as well. The ambiguously erotic quality of the performer exhibiting her body, often scantily clad, with or without a skirt, even seemingly nude or nearly nude, was evidently a troublesome one to a great many people. William Etty, preeminent Victorian painter of nudes, unwittingly acknowledged the complexity of the aesthetic situation in declaring, in his "Autobiography," that "where no immoral sentiment is *intended*, I affirm that the simple undisguised naked figure is innocent" — effectively shifting the locus of meaning from the painting to the moral character of the artist's intention and leaving unclear whether that intention could be inferred from the work itself.[60] Nudity in art, even for some who considered themselves knowledgable and sophisticated observers, also had its difficulties, even where the medium was the painting, a form traditionally concerned with (among other subjects) the unclothed human body.

In a letter written in 1877 the Bishop of Carlisle mentioned that he had had considerable mental exercise that season "by the exhibition of Alma-Tadema's nude Venus" (fig. 40). Undoubtedly there were "artistic reasons" justifying the "public exposure of the female form," but it was unclear what principles were involved. The art historian Richard Jenkyns has

40. *Lawrence Alma-Tadema.* Venus. A Sculptor's Model. *Opus CLXXIX, 1877.*
*Frederic George Stephens, ed.* Laurence Alma-Tadema, R. A. *London: J. S. Virtue,*
*1895. Sterling and Francine Clark Art Institute.*

explained the uncertainty by identifying Alma-Tadema's model as the Esquiline Venus, a copy of a lost fifth-century statue. Possessing a far from perfect form, the model was thus all the better for Alma-Tadema's purpose. "His girl is a model for the goddess; she is thus both a Venus and not a Venus," Jenkyns observes: "As Venus, she carries with her all the respectable association of high art; as an ordinary girl, photographically painted, she becomes an object of desire." The lack of ideality in the model and consequently in the figure represented by the artist "is all too pleasant, rendering the girl more appealingly real." The question remains, how far did the artist know what he was doing? The Victorians, Jenkyns concludes, appeared to have achieved precisely that "balance of knowledge and ignorance which would give them freedom to indulge their fantasies and yet stay respectable."[61] Brian Bailey has made the same point about the nudes of William Etty, another devotee of the image of Venus. The *Observer* critic accused him of painting unclothed women so convincingly fleshlike that, at an exhibition at the Royal Academy in 1835 that included Etty's *Venus and Her Sattelites*, several ladies were forced to stay away from the corner in which the painting was exhibited "to avoid the offence and disgrace Mr Etty has conferred on that quarter." Etty retorted that there was no indecency in what he painted, "only in the vile notions people may bring with them."[62] Again, the difficulty lay in the ambiguous figure of the model. Etty's Greek goddesses "have divine figures," Bailey points out, "but too often look like the London barmaids and shop assistants who posed for him." Unlike the "pure, innocent and timeless" nudes of Lord Leighton, Etty's were "real women — part-time models who had taken their clothes off."[63]

A persistent duality of just this sort existed, as the dance historian Amy Koritz has explained, in the late Victorian perception of the dancer, viewed at once as a symbolist ideal and a highly erotic flesh-and-blood woman. Arthur Symons's complex ambivalence on the subject is a case in point, creating a tension between his "celebration of the dance as art and his interest in the dancer as flesh."[64] In his essay "The World as Ballet" Symons described the simultaneous physical presence and fleeting quality of the dancer and the dance itself; its "possession and abandonment" are "the very pattern and symbol of earthly love." As spectators we look at the dance onstage, and there are "all these young bodies" offered to us like a bouquet, "living flowers" with all the glitter of artifice. As they move in rhythm, they define the simultaneous presence of the ethereal and fleshly dancer, "so human, so remote, so desirable, so evasive."[65] Holding such views, Symons and observers similarly inclined had gone well beyond the simple freshness of beautiful movement described by Ruskin in *Modern Painters*: as with the bough of a tree in motion, producing a felt loveliness, we may perceive, "when a girl dances rightly, that she moves easily, and with delight to herself, that her limbs are strong enough, and her body tender enough, to move precisely as she wills them to move."[66] Evidently, the seemingly simple etherealism encapsulated in Hake's poem "The Dancing Girl" created problematic reverberations for many of his contemporaries. In that poem Hake himself had suggestively observed of his subject, "None dare interpret all her limbs express." The line resonates ambivalently, suppressing the erotic possibilities of meaning while still acknowledging their recondite presence. Audiences of a less repressed, more libertarian stamp, perceiving such ambivalence as effective hypocrisy, believed that efforts to block the Empire Theatre license were naïve and hopeless, in view of the irremediable proclivities of human nature itself — or of male human nature, at any rate.

Undeniably, in attempting to control or even eliminate what was viewed in some quarters as unacceptably licentious behavior, the London County Council had made itself the butt of jokes and even of more serious satire on the theme of hypocrisy, some of it in the pages of the premier comic journal of the age, *Punch*. In a series of satirical pieces first published there and collected in 1892 as *Mr Punch's Model Music-Hall Songs & Dramas*, F. Anstey included a ribald satire with serious overtones entitled "Conrad; or, the Thumbsucker." Obviously based on *Der Struwwelpeter*, the German physician Dr. Heinrich Hoffmann's picture book for children, dating from 1845, Anstey's modern blank-verse fable tells the story of Conrad, age six, a clandestine thumbsucker, and his mother, age forty-seven, "one of London's County Councillors."[67] Her bill filed in "the sacred cause of Nursery Reform" was passed, after patient lobbying, by a bare majority. Through her efforts infants' toys are now carefully inspected once a month. Nursery songs and tales "Must now be duly licensed by our Censor, / And any deviation from the text / Forbidden under heavy penalties." Her crowning achievement is now upon her, a bill curbing the lawlessness of children "So lost to every sense of decency / That, in mere wantonness or brainless sloth, / They obstinately suck forbidden thumbs!"[68] Rejecting half-hearted remedies such as compulsory woolen gloves or bitter aloes, Conrad's mother's bill appoints a new official, the

"London County Council Scissorman," who will summarily cut off the appendages of young offenders. "Thus," she triumphantly exclaims, "shall our statute cure while it corrects, / For those who have no thumbs can err no more." Her self-congratulation is short-lived, however, for a knock at the door announces the arrival of "the Official Red-legged Scissorman," who has come to enforce the new law by snipping off her own Conrad's thumbs. Unfortunately, as Conrad ashamedly admits, he has been a "Suck-athumb" (his shocked mother's term) "from birth!"[69] Conrad's mother remorsefully offers her own thumbs for Conrad's, but the Scissorman is unmovable. Conrad stoically accedes to the inevitable, but, having lost his thumbs, he now takes his mother severely to task. Her endearments will not replace "the thumbs your County Council took from me." Where was the sin in sucking them? he asks. Nature is nature: "The dog will lick his foot, the cat her claw." No law restrains them, but "your rage for infantine reform" has resulted in "this most ridiculous enactment," and its first victim has proved to be her own hapless child.[70]

The superevident moral of Anstey's gruesome satire emerges: no overzealous county council can legislate out of existence fundamental human instincts for pleasure and self-gratification. The examples of the dog's foot and cat's paw suggest that indulgence of self, instinctive and quite normal, has a cleansing and therefore salutary effect. Whether or not Anstey's readers might have grasped the connotation of castration in the mutilating actions of the council's red-limbed Scissorman, emphasized in Conrad's mother's determination that "those who have no thumbs can err no more," Anstey clearly means to identify a basic, healthy, and inerad-icable human urge; any attempt to curb it will prove futile and in fact counterproductive — and, in basic human terms, damaging.

Lest there be any doubt of his purposes, in his introduction Anstey inveighed against "those active and intelligent guardians of middle-class morality, the London County Council," and their "moral microscope." Anstey was evidently concerned about additional censorial powers the council might gain through application to Parliament for "clauses" enabling them to require every proposed performance to be submitted "to a special committee" for advance approval. He offers in illustration a brief prophetic sketch, "Poetic Licenses: A Vision of the Near Future," drama-tizing a scene in which a perfectly innocent song, "Molly and I," is torn apart by the "Sub-Committee of the Censors," who intend to save the music hall audience from itself. The chair of the subcommittee explains:

"Not that I consider the words particularly objectionable in themselves, but we are men of the world, . . . and as such we cannot shut our eyes to the fact that a Music-hall audience is only too apt to find significance in many apparently innocent expressions and phrases."[71] From Anstey's libertarian perspective it is the knowingness itself, the self-confident "man of the world" quality of males in the music hall audience, that is under attack by the purists of the world.

A graphic epitome of that audience appears as a frontispiece to Anstey's introduction. Captioned "Music Hall Proprietor," the image shows a well-dressed, venal-looking man in a fur coat and top hat, sitting in his auditorium at his ease and smoking a cigar, his head turned toward the stage, where a woman in a low-cut bodice and a skirt pulled up to her knee is dancing the can-can and kicking one leg high in the air (fig. 41). The image articulates the familiar link between the practiced male eye and the indecent posture, as some characterized it, of the dancer. If a girl is "young, and pretty, and poor," observed a writer in the *Vigilance Record* in 1889, there is little chance for her on the stage unless she becomes, as it is sometimes put, "acclimatized from childhood in the atmosphere of the green room." The more difficult the actress's calling, "the more careful should the community be to prevent any additional obstacles being placed in the way in the shape of compulsion to wear indecent dresses, to sing indecent songs, and to use language which can only have one meaning." It was a matter of puzzlement for this writer that while conventional morality dictated that a woman's virtue should be "to her more sacred than life itself," the sacrifice of the modesty that protects that virtue "is enforced every night as an element in popular entertainments."[72] It would do no good, Selwyn Image told the members of the Church and Stage Guild in October 1889, if they could convince the reformers tomorrow that "every ballet-dancer was, in the conventional sense, as pure as the driven snow"; the next day "the battle would rage as fiercely as ever."[73] Although it was unclear what distinction Image was making, in using that hackneyed phrase, between the "conventional" idea of physical virginity and other, perhaps less obvious ways of defining womanly "purity," his allegation of permanently hostile camps, intransigently opposed, is difficult to discredit. A near-Manichaean conflict between the forces of good and evil, the lovers of the world and its visible, tangible beauty ranged against those who denied the intrinsic saving power of the human body, had emerged over the ostensibly particular battle being waged over the

41. *"Music Hall Proprietor."* F. Anstey, Mr. Punch's Model Music-Hall Songs and Dramas. *London: Bradbury, Agnew, 1892, 2. Harvard University, Houghton Library.*

Empire license. Image's perception that neither side was amenable to persuasion by the arguments of the other appeared to be all too true.

And so, mounted from a variety of vantage points, the argument that human nature is what it is — perhaps irredeemably so — had proved a powerful one in the context of the controversy over the Empire license, for it joined the questions of alleged indecency on the stage and immorality in the five-shilling promenade just as surely as did the double-barreled attack of Mrs. Chant and her followers on those two luminous targets of righteous indignation. The perceived indecency of the ballet dancer's costume and the eroticism profoundly implicit in her movements, even in her very presence before a disengaged audience, were, finally, inseparable from the surmise, deeply imbedded in contemporary culture, that the ballet dancer was a person of questionable morals. Who could wear such a dress and remain pure? The very costume defiled its wearer. In the popular imagination the evils of the profession were notorious, and conclusive.

### OUR EMPIRE

Among the many visitors to the Empire around the time the controversy over its license arose, two in particular stand out. As a radical analytical thinker and fearless platform orator, Bernard Shaw could bring to his subject perspicacious, keenly articulated insights into the obscure but linked realities underlying a given set of disparate social or artistic phenomena. Somewhat ironically, Shaw kept sociological analysis for his plays and prefaces and letters to editors, and went to the Empire for the sheer aesthetic pleasure of its stage performances. Although her agenda was much more specific and her mental sphere of operation seemingly more circumscribed, Laura Ormiston Chant, equally adept at platform oratory, saw a good deal more of interest at the Empire than did Shaw, and was in certain ways Shaw's equal in her ability to uncover the hidden connections that give all too poignant meaning and coherence to the generally fragmentary experience of modern social life.

Appropriately, both Shaw and Mrs. Chant had their evening out at the Empire. While Shaw spent his in looking exclusively (so far as his reportage indicates) at the stage, Mrs. Chant, from her perspective in the five-shilling promenade, could look in more than one direction, and did. Her position there, quietly taking notes on both the stage performances and the activity closer at hand and refraining, for once, from interfering in behavior she judged objectionable, becomes emblematic of the significance of the Empire controversy itself. For at the Empire Theatre of Varieties the gaze of the interested was drawn simultaneously to performances onstage and off; to art and entertainment as both distinct from and connected with their social milieu; and to the representation of what a Theatres and Music Halls inspector and even George Edwardes himself appreciatively called "the female form divine" — celebrated by the secular saint William Etty as "God's most glorious work"[74] — as an ethereal, even spiritual image or, conversely, as vibrant human flesh highly painted or indecently exposed, the very sight of which could compromise the chastity of any virtuous woman and corrupt the morals of every man. Analyzing the phrase "painted women," Arthur Symons captured the systemic connection between the actress or dancer and the prostitute in their common use of cosmetics and all that such use implied: "to have put paint on her cheeks," Symons explained, "though for the innocent necessities of her profession, gives to a woman a sort of symbolic corruption."[75] The cyprian's rouge, identified thirty-five years before by the remorseful reporter for the *Peeping Tom*, remained definitive of any woman who used it.

That these issues and their multifarious implications all arose from what may seem to later eyes an obscure controversy over the renewal of an annual music hall license says something important, even crucial, about the nature of public entertainment and its place and status in modern life. It also underscores the increasing importance of leisure in the late Victorian period and, hence, the value of a study of leisure activity for identifying some of the generative characteristics of modern culture. In a study of this kind the Victorian music hall now appears to loom large in interest and significance.

For, as the century neared its end, the centrality of the music hall, as well as of its higher-toned younger sibling the theatre of varieties, to the life of the people of London (and of urbanites elsewhere in Britain and beyond) was becoming ever more evident. In a retrospective account posthumously published in the *Encyclopaedia Britannica*, Hollingshead pronounced the "rise and progress of the music hall and variety theatre interest" to be "one of the most extraordinary facts of the last half of the 19th century."[76] Earlier, in November 1894, during the protracted height of the controversy over the Empire license, a writer in the *Saturday Review* called attention to certain incontrovertible facts. The great actor Henry Irving had tried to dissociate the theatre from the music hall by condescending to the latter collectively as "places of public entertainment"; but the music halls are here to stay, the writer insisted, and indeed are a fact of life that cannot be ignored. The most popular of the variety halls has been paying more than 70 percent (clearly, a reference to the Empire), a profit greater than that generated by the long-running comedy *Charley's Aunt*. The music hall appeals to the public "with extraordinary force," said the *Review* — a claim with which Mrs. Chant herself would have agreed; it is "the best form of entertainment," she had asserted, "for tired and hard-working people." It was for this reason that she had put on her prettiest evening dress, "black lace over coloured silk, with an opera jacket and a pretty little bonnet to match," to "investigate the morals," or the dividends, as she told the Playgoer's Club, of the Empire.[77] Irving's attitude, no different from that of the average conservative playgoer, was therefore "impossible," the *Review* concluded, and must be abandoned, for the music hall is "as certain, as serious, a fact as democracy" and must be treated the way a fact must be treated: "seriously, reasonably," and with "courteous openmindedness."[78]

J. A. Hobson would very likely have concurred. Perhaps less openminded, but more deeply concerned with social consequences and more admittedly critical of the effect of the music hall on public life, Hobson explained in his probing near-contemporary study *The Psychology of Jingoism* (1901) that the "gradual debasement" of what had once been a wholesome popular art, the ballad, had raised the music hall to the status of being "the most powerful instrument of such musical and literary culture as the people are open to receive."[79] Hobson makes no distinctions of class within his sweeping general category of "the people." Percy Fitzgerald, writing in 1890, took a comparable if less intellectual interest in the psychology of the music hall audience but preferred to return the form to its working-class roots. There he discovered a power comparable to what Hobson would identify and a universal human value as well. The East Ender who has glimpsed at bars the kind of gentleman, or "gent," who fulfills his fantasies of prosperity and respectability finds that image reified perfectly at the music hall. The reason, Fitzgerald explained, is that the music hall, for all its "spurious gentility," betokens "an actual craving in the human character": the "crowd" or "mob" assembled in the hall "find their own ideal of gentility, nobility, virtue, humour, fashion, and the rest" presented in easily accessible and deeply meaningful form on the music hall stage.[80] The views of Fitzgerald and other contemporary sympathetic observers run well at odds with those of such modern historians as John MacKenzie, who sees reflected in the music hall "the dominant imperial ethos of the day in topical and chauvinistic songs, royal fervour, and patriotic tableaux."[81] But they see eye to eye on its centrality.

In his reminiscence of London nights in the 1890s, Shaw Desmond paid similar but fonder attention to the music hall and had much to say about its variety and vitality. The large claim Desmond makes for its significance — "The story of our English people in our day is written in its music-halls"[82] — seems less exaggerated once we realize how extensively and deeply the Empire controversy engaged the attention and feelings of contemporary Londoners and Britons in general. Finally, the reason very few contemporaries may have been left unaffected by the events, centered in Leicester Square, of the autumn and winter of 1894 was that the controversy engendered such a powerful sense of disenfranchisement on the part of those who felt offended and excluded by the entertainment and other activity on view at the Empire, and a comparably passionate sense of ownership and belonging on the part of others who considered themselves an integral element of the Empire audience. It was "the best informal club in the world," as the publisher Grant Richards described the lounge at the back of the dress circle at the Empire; "indeed, it was described as *the* club of the world and as The Cosmopolitan Club of Empire."[83]

J. B. Booth, a prolific if unreflective student of popular entertainment, could explain why. Up to the end of his day, Booth recalled in 1924, the Empire "was club as well as music-hall." Men attended the Empire more for companionship than entertainment, he said, and specifically the companionship "of other men." To such habitués "the feminine lure of the promenade" had little appeal, he insisted. Two decades back, people said there were only three places where one could, with sufficient patience, encounter "the returned wanderer from the waste places" — "the Salon Carré of the Louvre, Charing Cross Station, and the Empire Promenade." When one bade goodbye to a friend outbound to some remote corner of the world, the chances were heavily in favor that his parting words would be, "So long, old man, see you in London again. Sure to run across you in the Empire." And so, in a sense, Booth explained, the Leicester Square theatre "was not ill-named; it was a gathering and meeting place for the men of the Empire."[84]

Desmond catches a precise, vivid image of that insider's sense of possession in his description of Albert Chevalier, "the great coster comedian," who had gone to live in the East End to acquire an authentic sense of local color and had brought his insights back to West End music hall patrons. "He had a way of doing a double-shuffle and of strutting with stiffened thigh muscles and tautly curved back" that was all his own, Desmond recalled, "the very last thing in John Bullish *joie de vivre*. The way he plunged his hands into the cross-pockets of a trousers made on the principle of a trap-door front, was a liberal education in owning the earth."[85] That feeling of ownership seemed primary, almost visceral, as in the example of a complaint communicated in the midst of the controversy to the *Telegraph* by a writer who had just returned from a long residence in Australia to find "my amusements" interfered with.[86]

The sense of possession, and its correlative instinct of possessiveness, went far toward explaining the complex attractiveness of tableaux vivants as well, whether of ostensible nudes, as at the Palace Theatre of Varieties, or the sumptuously well-clothed subjects on view at the Empire. Over the course of the century, tableaux had acquired a certain patina of respectability when performed by amateurs in domestic or other fastidious surroundings; and yet a comparable psychology underlay even the most decorous of efforts. In Edith Wharton's novel *The House of Mirth* (1905), for example, living pictures become the calculated means of attracting eligible bachelors. The heroine Lily Bart's "vivid plastic sense . . . found eager expression in the disposal of draperies, the study of attitudes, the shifting of lights and shadows," Wharton wrote; "but keenest of all was the exhilaration of displaying her own beauty under a new aspect: of showing that her loveliness was no mere fixed quality, but an element shaping all emotions to fresh forms of grace."[87] Wharton's description of her central character's enthusiasm for these home entertainments nicely captures the erotic quality of the enterprise, along with the crass values of the marriage market that these presentations could simultaneously embody.[88] In a sense the presentation of a tableau can be understood as conferring an opportunity on its audience for appropriating the body of the performer, and so during the performance it substitutes for the painting or sculpture itself. The result is a sort of "vicarious ownership" of the work of art conferred on the audience, endowing them with the prestige and status of the collector, as Robin Veder observes, and bestowing on them the pleasures of a virtually acquired possession.[89]

The same phenomenon applied in the case of the music hall experience itself, whether of tableaux vivants, of other types of entertainment, or simply of entering and traversing the public spaces of a building designed to cater to the gratification of its audiences. Even the inclusion, in the dramatis personae of the ballet, of the cross-dressed female dancer miming the male hero performing opposite the première danseuse contributed to the pervasive opportunity for feelings of possessiveness. George Edwardes offered a blasé but accurate explanation of this curious phenomenon to a naïve inquirer: "Don't you see, dear boy, that every man in the audience is her partner?"[90] "By casting women in the parts where the male spectator would, in imagination, cast himself," Amy Koritz has explained, "the management insures that no potential competitor will interfere with his fantasy of possession."[91]

Beneath this impassioned yet easy sense of ownership, reflecting in some cases an almost compulsive need to hold on at all costs to what is "ours," lay some even deeper feelings of entitlement, and of correlative dispossession, in the minds and hearts of contemporary Britons. Keith Thomas's seminal essay "The Double Standard" makes a pair of observations pertinent to the subject. One concerns the pervasive traditional conviction on the part of men that they "have property in women," property whose value is diminished if the woman "has sexual relations with anyone other than her husband."[92] That prohibition clearly did not apply at all, or at least with no corresponding rigor, to men, who were "free" to engage in infidelities so long as they did not, in the view of the law and their peers, threaten the sanctity of marriage and the family. Because the Empire promenade was one of the most advantageous and pleasurable grounds for engaging in such transgressive but widely condoned behavior, assaults by purists against the privileges it represented and, worse, the foreclosure of those privileges by government agency itself produced extremely strong protests from "Englishmen" and "gentlemen." Explicitly or by implication, in letters to newspapers or in other expressions of outrage, these men advanced the fact of their nationality and class as an irrefutable reason why the Empire promenade was by rights their hallowed preserve. In this sense, the "crusade" conducted by Mrs. Chant and her colleagues cast the crusaders, in a curiously ironic and quite unintentional way, as infidels engaged in a blasphemous, unpardonable invasion of holy ground.

The second of Thomas's observations regards the pervasive Victorian view that, except in the case of the "fallen," sexual desire in women "remains dormant." Such was the case, W. R. Greg's review essay of 1850 in the *Westminster Review* explained, until or unless a woman was "excited by undue familiarities" or by actual sexual intercourse. Consequently some women might "pass through life without ever being cognizant of the promptings of the senses."[93] That belief is poignantly illustrated by a report in the *Telegraph*, during the height of the controversy, of a meeting in Glasgow of the Central Conference of Women Workers. These "workers in the cause of womanhood," meeting in the Queen's Room, felt sensible of the queen's personal influence. "When every woman in the realm," observed the presiding officer, Mrs. Mirrlees, "has equally learned when and where to smile and where to frown," hope may emerge that public opinion "will tend not only to keep down the base in man, but to teach high thoughts and amiable words and courtliness, and the desire of fame and love of truth and all that makes a man."[94]

The assumptions on view in this program addressing the amelioration of contemporary sexual arrangements between women and men, and concerning also the presumed sexual character of each group, reveal much about the ways in which late Victorian society often fell short of achieving healthy sexual relationships. In the view of the Central Conference of Women Workers, women have both the right and the responsibility to approve or disapprove of — "to smile" or "to frown" at — the sexual behavior of men; theirs is simultaneously a prescriptive, a proscriptive, and an educative function. Assuming such a burden would be no easy matter in any age, but it appears an especially onerous imperative in a period when women themselves were not allowed to acknowledge the possession of any motives or inclinations of their own that could be characterized, however adversely, as "base." Even allowing for the more radical (if infrequently expressed) egalitarian views of such analysts of the contemporary scene as the U.S.-trained physician Elizabeth Blackwell, it is sobering to find that ideals of social transaction between women and men in the age of Victoria were marked by the nearly ubiquitous presupposition that it was a woman's duty to set an example of unwaveringly virtuous behavior for men, whose "baser" instincts might otherwise overwhelm the operation of a chivalrous courtliness that ideally and by rights should govern all their dealings with "the fair sex." "Men are very much what women make them," an anonymous provincial actress wrote in her diary, published in 1885: "If all women were good and true, what a different world this would be. That is a woman's true mission, to influence men for good."[95] "When women are bad," Eliza Linton explained in no uncertain terms, "all is bad. Their vice poisons society at its roots, and their low estimate of morality makes virtue impossible."[96] Despite some improvement in appearances, the world had evidently not fundamentally changed from the condition described by George Drysdale at midcentury in his dense tract *Physical, Sexual, and Natural Religion*, which found "the poor perishing in their squalid homes, the forsaken prostitutes wandering in our streets, the sexual victims pining in solitude and bitterness," a condition that led Drysdale to look down "into the fearful abyss of our social miseries and wrongs."[97]

Consequently, the admonitions of John Stuart Mill and a few other writers, female and male, that ideas of chivalry were not only outmoded but pernicious in their effect on the relationships of modern men and women fell, for the most part, on deaf ears.[98] The argument of Mill's treatise *On the Subjection of Women*, published in 1869, had turned on his identification of the principle that regulated existing social relations between men and women as "the legal subordination of one sex to the other." The power conferred by this legal advantage on the male may have extremely deleterious, even vicious, results, Mill believed. He condemned it as wrong and proceeded to argue for its replacement by "a principle of perfect equality, admitting no power or privilege on the one side, nor disability on the other."[99] Another, equally clear-sighted observer called attention to the economic consequences of such inequalities. In *Purchase of Women: The Great Economic Blunder*, a pamphlet published in 1887, Elizabeth Blackwell explored the ways women become "the subjects of trade." Basing her argument on the principle that the "consent" of willing women is not genuine and explaining that a social contract requires the equality of the two parties, Blackwell insisted that no true consent was possible in the current context of relations of capital to labor. Following, up to a point, Mill's arguments regarding the subjugation of women, Blackwell faults him for not realizing that the clandestine earnings of women must be factored into the calculus of unequal competition and compensation. In the present scheme of things, she explains, "the wages given by vice are allowed to supplement the underpayment for honest work, and the street door key makes up for the deficient salary." The upshot of it all was the deplorable lack of "trust, freedom, and sympathy" at the base of relations of men and women. For in present-day society the man who buys a woman to gratify lust helps to create what Blackwell calls, in a memorable phrase, "the irresponsible polyandry of prostitution." The purchaser thus buys into a moral double standard, departing from the "Unity of the Moral Law" and ignoring the great truth, which women are now learning, that "every man should be chaste." Adapting the argument from inversion of terms so prominent in the speeches of Mrs. Chant and other feminist reformers, Blackwell insists that "without male chastity female chastity is impossible."[100]

The principle of equality, and its negative corollary, injustice, made its way deeply into Mrs. Chant's own thinking, as a later brief essay, "Women and the Streets," published in 1903 in James Marchant's collection *Public Morals*, reaffirmed. Mrs. Chant had long held that protecting virtuous women from knowledge of what was going on in the public street only resulted in "the foul social atmosphere of interested silence." What was even worse, the spectacle of street prostitution had become a kind of tourist attraction, drawing many men and not a few women as sightseers to "gaze on the bedizened victim plying her shameful trade among men who are there to buy what she is offering for sale." The great desideratum was therefore the clearing of the streets, in despite of overzealous defenders of the vicious from unjust treatment. Such persons had forgotten "that vice is in itself a colossal injustice, an infringement of the liberty of the subject more dire than any that can be perpetrated in suppressing it." A further injustice consisted, in Mrs. Chant's view, in the inability of decent working women to go to and from work "without being ogled and stared at in the unspeakable manner that is a deeper outrage than any words." Many men might not understand the power and intrusiveness of the male gaze, she acknowledged, for it was difficult for any man "to realise the sting and insult of that same stare." All the same, that gaze and, beyond it, any other injurious behavior violated a principle that could be clearly articulated: "possession of liberty is relative, and I forfeit my right to liberty in proportion as I use it in a way injurious to my fellow-beings."[101] Mrs. Chant had evidently read her Mill — and could apply this insight with equal force from the lecture platform or from a vantage point in the promenade of the Empire Theatre of Varieties.

All the same, a quarter century later (and beyond), despite the protests of Dr. Blackwell and many others, the condition of inequality that Mill had so deplored remained the law of the land; and one of its most poignant manifestations was the conviction that women, unlike men, who had thicker skins, must be kept free from contact with depravity, actual or alleged. Late Victorian society was in fact deeply conflicted over the issue of uncleanliness. Implicit in the requirement that good women keep themselves pure and undefiled by the world was the imperative that they not consort with women who had committed sexual sins. On the one hand, Mrs. Chant had argued in her testimony before the Theatres Committee that the mere sight of indecency on the stage was inappropriate and dangerous for a respectable, pure-minded woman; on the other, she had actually gone to the Empire promenade on more than one occasion intentionally to view such indecency for herself, and had invited fallen women into her home. Neither Solicitor Gill nor any other person present at the committee hearing had apparently thought to point out this blatant inconsistency of word and deed. And yet exposure of this sort was evidently no novelty for Mrs. Chant, who had begun her career as a nurse by ministering to women pure and otherwise and had not flinched from hearing and repeating the sad stories of unfortunate women who had "fallen." Surely such exposure had not compromised her own virtue? But, if not, then why was exposure such a threat to others? Angry men wrote letters to the editor of the *Telegraph* and other journals to protest, not merely the behavior or motives of such visitors to the Empire promenade as Mrs. Chant, but their very presence in those licentious precincts. That she could deliberately expose herself to the sight of an indecent spectacle, whether on or off the stage, to say nothing of allowing herself to become liable to its possibly unmentionable consequences, was one of the root objections of those who complained about her intrusion there. Her presence in the Empire lounge produced an unintended irony, consequently, for Mrs. Chant herself took the same view about the damage incurred by virtuous women in seeing indecency exposed to public view. Even worse, that women could lower themselves, as she believed they did, to acts of indecent behavior, even for the sake of earning money to keep themselves and their loved ones alive, whether through the exhibition of their bodies in revealing costumes on the Empire stage or through far more reprehensible behavior than exhibition itself in the Empire promenade and beyond, imposed enormous burdens on persons who believed that members of the "fair" sex should be true exemplars of virtue for errant (if reformable) men.

These are some of the valences that, to a remarkable extent, control and invigorate the perceptions and views both of women like Mrs. Chant and of men who called for her to abandon her naïve ideals and come to terms with the fact, as they perceived it, that men will be men and that it is hopeless to think of reforming them entirely. It was only women who could be rescued — if not too deeply mired in depravity. Assumptions of this kind are to be found virtually everywhere, if often only implicitly or even subliminally, in the social transactions of the period and, more particularly, in the onstage entertainments and offstage encounters on view at the Empire.

There is no little genuine pathos, with regard not only to women but to men as well, resonating in this highly charged moment of history. In reproaching women like Mrs. Chant for exposing themselves to indecency and unchastity, men were exercising a chivalrous protective instinct on behalf of the female sex instilled in them, as Mill well recognized, from a young age. At the same time, other men — or, paradoxically, perhaps even the same men, in some instances — were taking Mrs. Chant and her peers to task for their misplaced idealism and touching naïveté in thinking that men could be moved to abandon their self-gratifying and self-aggrandizing motives and become pure, like them. Judith Walkowitz, a discriminating latter-day observer of the complex social and sexual arrangements of women and men in the Victorian period, identifies a mixed message being sent to men by advocates of social purity, demanding "that men control their own sexuality" but at the same time giving them "power to control the sexuality of women as well," since they called upon men "to protect their women and to repress brothels and street-walkers." Social purity advocates' attacks on male vice and male dominance had an unacknowledged problematic aspect, for they "involved no positive assertion of female sexuality," Walkowitz wryly observes. Only a small minority of feminists were interested in the issue of female sexual pleasure. The vast majority of women in the vanguard of female rights still seemed to subscribe to the ideology of a "separate sphere," whose clear implication was that "women were moral, 'spiritual' creatures who needed to be protected from animalistic 'carnal' men."[102]

That a large component of possessiveness of women lurked behind these male impulses toward protectionism made the situation only more fraught for everyone concerned. Fundamentally, as Keith Thomas explains, female chastity has traditionally been viewed as a matter of property — "the property of men in women."[103] Such values seem so nearly akin to the protocols of protection and possession that characterize the imperialistic policies and impulses of Britain as a nation, in this period and before, that the analogy seems impossible to deny. The more the comparison is pursued, the more perspicuous the mirror image becomes. In his inaugural lecture of 1870 John Ruskin, Slade Professor of Art in the University of Oxford, put it all too plainly, as Edward Said has pointed out. What imperial England must do, Ruskin explained, is to "found colonies as fast and as far as she is able, . . . seizing every piece of fruitful waste ground she can set her foot on, and there teaching these her colonists that their chief virtue is to be fidelity to their country, and that their first aim is to be to advance the power of England by land and sea."[104] That the social purity activists and reformers might have balked at the notion of property as applying to themselves — to their own persons — and not simply to the world in which they hoped to exercise greater sway does not disturb the relevance of the notion to the condition of men and women at this time, as well as to the more particular instance of the conflict over the possession of the promenade and the stage itself of the Empire Theatre of Varieties. As Ronald Hyam has argued in his far-reaching study of imperialism and sexuality, "sexual dynamics crucially underpinned the whole operation of British empire and Victorian expansion," even as a campaign by social purity advocates gradually reduced the opportunities for extramarital sexual satisfaction beginning in the 1880s, first at home and then abroad.[105]

From a later perspective a century on, the details of the Empire licensing controversy, important in themselves as part of the fabric of the historical record, are significantly complemented by their pointed indication that the component elements of a society — not just classes, broadly speaking, but other, sometimes much smaller and more specific groups — have each their own need to possess themselves as individuals and, simultaneously, to hold in common the culture they believe to be theirs, especially if it is felt to be under threat from a hostile outside force. In the period of the 1890s when Mrs. Chant and her colleagues undertook their attack, the lights of the Empire, shining alluringly through the gloom, night after night, at the top of Leicester Square, came to symbolize for everyone concerned a possession so valuable that it could not willingly be relinquished; it had to be fought for and fought over, tenaciously, joyously, or bitterly, as the case might require (fig. 42, and see frontispiece).

In *The Psychology of Jingoism*, a rare example of competent contemporary social analysis written from the near perspective of 1901, Hobson explains how the psychological phenomenon of jingoism worked to forge a tightly bonded community, much to its discredit. How, an exasperated Hobson asks, does one explain the transformation of the wholesome collective love of one's own country into "the hatred of another," accompanied by a "fierce craving to destroy the individual members of that other nation"? In such a matter it is important to distinguish between the actual impulse to fight, to join in the fray, and a separate impulse to feed "a neurotic imagination." The term "Jingoism" defines "the passion of the spectator, the inciter, the backer, not of the fighter; it is a collective or mob passion which, in as far as it prevails, makes the individual mind subject to a control that joins him irresistibly to his fellows."[106] What Hobson found most deplorable was the ability of music hall singers to appeal, through

*42. "The Empire by Night in 1895." M. Willson Disher, Winkles and Champagne.*
*London: B. T. Batsford, 1938. Opp. 65.*

"coarse humour or exaggerated pathos," to "the animal lusts of an audience stimulated by alcohol into appreciative hilarity."[107] G. H. McDermott's irresistibly provocative and, by this time, universally familiar song "We Don't Want to Fight" and its rallying phrase, "By Jingo," inspired extreme reactions, Laurence Senelick observes in his study of music hall songs; audiences would rise en masse and roar out the chorus:

> We don't want to fight, but by Jingo if we do,
> We've got the ships, we've got the men,
> We've got the money too.
> We've fought the Bear before, and
> While Britons still are true
> The Russians shall not have Constantinople.[108]

Behind this phenomenon, Senelick explains, was an element that would occur with growing frequency in music hall songs from this time on, an element of "possessiveness."[109] Although Hobson had little to say about the reemergence of the age-old phenomenon of xenophobia at a crucial moment in the recent history of British imperialism, the implications of his analysis must have been obvious to the more thoughtful readers of a nation deeply embroiled in the current war in the Transvaal.

If not for such persons, then for others less reflective, the theatre of varieties offered a welcome respite from purposeful work and even from the normal pursuits of a gentleman, as Oscar Wilde's Algernon Moncrieff understood perfectly well. In offering his friend Jack Worthing the opportunity to drop in at the Leicester Square venue after dinner — to "trot round to the Empire at 10.00?" he proposes — Algy would have intended it as a happy chance for them to immerse themselves in the amusements of another, less genteel class without revealing their identity or compromising their status in any way. In the opening scene of Act 1 of *The Importance of Being Earnest* (produced at the St. James's Theatre in King Street on 14 February 1895), having held his own in a dialogue with his master about the limited attractiveness of the married state, Algy's manservant, Lane, goes off, leaving Algy to muse over the transaction. "Really, if the lower orders don't set us a good example," he remarks, "what on earth is the use of them? They seem as a class to have absolutely no sense of their moral responsibility."[110]

Wilde's clever inversion of the more expectable view that the upper orders of society are the ones that set the moral standard points by implication to the paradoxical character of modern urban life. In places like the Empire Theatre of Varieties, where the upper orders seemed to hold sway and where a high level of decorum, normally unmixed with any hint of rowdiness, was the rule, the habits and values of the "lower orders" were nevertheless on continual, colorful display and could be consumed as an attractive commodity. Although theatres of variety were categorically different and geographically removed from the working-class halls that served loosely as their prototype, the fare available at the West End luxury palaces of entertainment combined ballet, an essentially upper-class and aristocratic amusement having origins in court entertainments and the elite form of grand opera, with "turns" drawn from much less pretentious venues. The same mixture of high and low applied across the whole range of such entertainment. Arthur J. Munby had self-consciously reveled in the fantasy of possession of upper-class taste available to him in the working-class halls, where "Trovatore singing" enabled him to ape his betters at no cost whatever to self-esteem or convenience. An inversion of that same fantasy was available every night in the mirrored reaches of the higher-toned theatres of variety, where a much more aristocratic and prosperous middle-class clientele aped the working-class's love of boisterous music and song and indulged themselves in its reputed predilection for licentious sexual pleasure. But they did so vicariously, by assuming an anonymity that afforded scope for a temporary, selective departure from upper-class and middle-class tastes and from the social obligations and standards of behavior that accompanied them. That departure entailed a delicious opportunity for distanced connection, for a perspicuous vantage point, and for a sophisticated, subtle, but real selfdistinction. In this way the five-shilling lounge became the true epitome of what the Empire had to offer: an enlarging, satisfying sense of simultaneous connection and disengagement and an amplitudinous feeling of well-deserved leisure. In so doing it offered a first-class ticket of entitlement to and possession of property of several kinds, with no requirement to produce the deed.

In retrospect, the ballet divertissement called *La Frolique*, playing at the Empire as the controversy over the license began, proves to have been paradigmatic of the type of entertainment, both onstage and off, available there and, by extension, indicative of the subtly collusive nature of Empire entertainment in general. The plot of *La Frolique* danced out on the Empire stage demonstrated that what is ostensibly risky with respect to established mores, or even patently offensive in the strict eyes of the law, may turn out to be permissible after all because, on closer inspection, the law is shown to be a willing, complicitous partner in activities that threaten to transgress officially established boundaries. It was this larger fact of implicit collusiveness, and not merely the alleged indecency of costume onstage or of indecent activity offstage, that made the Empire promenade "the battle-ground of the Nonconformist party," as H. G. Hibbert so aptly characterized it.[111] It was this same collusiveness that fostered and nurtured the fantasies of empire — of imperialism itself and of sovereign sway in private as well as public life — whose lure drew patrons to the Empire night after night and so made possible the nearly obscene profits, as Mrs. Chant and her followers rated them, enjoyed by George Edwardes and his partners and by all who owned shares in the enterprise.

Little wonder, then, that such a compelling fantasy of possession, available in exchange for a few shillings at the pay box at the top of the grand staircase or at some other exalted point, attracted hundreds of well-dressed men and women nightly to the glittering venues in Leicester Square and elsewhere in the West End, and most of all to the Empire. Ultimately, "Our Empire" proved to be much more than the title of a ballet divertissement that drew crowds to the theatre of varieties on the north side of the square for months on end, and much more than the building itself, the theatrical venue in which classical ballet, the more up-to-date ballet divertissement, variety turns of every description, and attention-commanding living pictures competed at the level of the stage with the erotic, semi-illicit spectacle of gorgeously dressed, strange-faced young women promenading in the five-shilling promenade, in arousingly close proximity to the men who might wish to become their customers or were content with experiencing the frisson of possibility. "Our" Empire had proved to be an icon highly charged with the fantasies of appropriation, of possession, of respectability, of protection, of empire itself, powerful fantasies brought to the licensing controversy by everyone whose desires and fears were raised by it.

As a result, during a brief but momentous time, the Empire became the collective, metonymous scene on which the metaphors of an aggressive, expansive colonial policy were reified and performed; the battleground on which "British pluck," in both military and civilian modes, was spectacularly demonstrated; an arena in which idealism and cynicism, sensualism and asceticism, love of the arts and love of another world, came to blows; and a field on which opposing notions of human nature and human growth and decline were asserted, exemplified, and tested. It became, as well, the stage on which an ordinary, or extraordinary, evening's pleasure came to take on far greater meaning than most seekers of entertainment might have been prepared to acknowledge — or might even have been able to understand. From the distance of a century and more, that stage, and the deeply fraught moment it epitomized, remains to compel our attention and challenge our understanding.

# NOTES

### ABBREVIATIONS IN THE NOTES AND WORKS CITED

clp = clipping

*DNB* = *Dictionary of National Biography*

*DT* = *Daily Telegraph*

HTC = Harvard Theatre Collection

*ILN* = *Illustrated London News*

LCC = London County Council

LCC/MIN = London County Council Minutes, Greater London Record Office

M&M = Raymond Mander and Joe Mitchenson Theatre Collection

*PMG* = *Pall Mall Gazette*

*PMLA* = *Publications of the Modern Language Association*

PRO = Public Record Office

*Report* (1866) = *Report from the Select Committee on Theatrical Licences and Regulations*

*Report* (1892) = *Report from the Select Committee on Theatres and Places of Entertainment*

*TLS* = *Times Literary Supplement*

TMHC = Theatres and Music Halls Committee, London County Council

### PROLOGUE

1. *Athenaeum*, 3 February 1849, 118, qtd. Smith, *Victorian Nude*, 51.

2. Qtd. Altick, *Shows of London*, 349; Senelick, ed., *Tavern Singing*, 218; see Nicholson, *Rogue's Progress*.

3. Bill inscribed "Augt. 1855" in Disher, *Winkles*, 8.

4. G. Boase, "Lord Chief Baron Nicholson," 4–5. A bill for the Coal Hole Tavern annotated "July 1856" advertised "Poses Plastiques" "By the most exquisite female models, at half-past seven, and after the Theatres," featuring Mrs. Roberts, "of the late Royal Italian Opera House," Mrs. Lyons from the Theatre Royal Haymarket, and Madame Fatima Betsina of Astley's Royal Amphitheatre, along with other less illustrious performers (rpt. Busby, *British Music Hall*, 9).

5. E. Duranty, "Aspects de Londres," *Revue Libérale*, 10 May 1867, 442, qtd. Smith, *Victorian Nude*, 52 (author's translation).

6. *John Johnson Collection*, 56, item 178.

7. Mayhew, *London Labour*, 4: 254; see Howard, *London Theatres and Music Halls*, 245.

8. *London Encyclopedia*, s.v. "Eros."

9. Taylor, *Leicester Square*, 471–73; Altick, *Shows of London*, 464–67.

10. Busby, *British Music Hall*, 12.

11. F. Boase, *Modern English Biography*, 6: 792–93. Alfred Joseph Woolner's contemporary painting *Lady Godiva* (ca. 1856), depicting the subject's naked ride through Coventry, captured the idea of the English nude in the 1850s, Alison Smith explains, "by virtue of its theme of redemptive nakedness": Lady Godiva had pleaded in vain with Leofric, Earl of Mercia, to reduce heavy taxation on the citizens of Coventry; he said he would do so if she would ride naked through the streets. She took his dare, riding at night, commanding that all residents close their shutters. All did except one, a "peeping Tom," who was struck blind in consequence of his voyeurism (Smith, ed., *Exposed*, 67). The risks associated with gazing at forbidden sights are nicely — and ironically — epitomized in the legend.

12. For information on Madame Warton, sometimes spelled "Wharton," and the painter William Etty see Baker, *History of the London Stage*, 344; F. Boase, *Modern English Biography*, 6: 792–93; Gaunt and Roe, *Etty and the Nude*, 62; Farr, *William Etty*, 107; and Altick, *Shows of London*, 345–49.

13. Hibbert, *Fifty Years*, 87.

14. The date of the tableau is probably fixable at 1860, since the ballet seems to have been imitative, the dance historian Ivor Guest has suggested, of an upper-class attraction, the opera *The Night Dancers*, based on the ballet *Giselle*, revived at the Royal English Opera in 1860 (Guest, *Ballet in Leicester Square*, 80 and n.) A good notion of what Madame Warton's exhibitions were all about may be inferred from the publicity they commanded in the popular press. In the issue for 17 October 1846 the *Illustrated London News* carried the first advertisement for tableaux and poses at "THE WALHALLA" by "Madame Wharton's" new troupe:

> Madame WHARTON begs to inform the Nobility, Gentry, and the Public that she has
> OPENED the above spacious Gallery with a series of Tableaux Vivans [*sic*] and Poses
> Plastiques; having, during her recent visit on the Continent, engaged a Troupe of
> Eminent Artistes, and been favoured with admissions to the studios of several celebrated painters and sculptors. She is enabled to produce in a classical and authentic
> manner this truly popular exhibition.

A daily matinee at 3:00 P.M. was to be followed by an evening performance at 8:30 (*ILN*, 254).

15. Altick, *Shows of London*, 347.

16. Bills and advertisements cited in Altick, *Shows of London*, 347.

17. *Survey of London*, 34: 464.

18. "Cafe du Globe," 1–2. All quotations descriptive of the Cafe du Globe are taken from this source.

19. Sala, *Gaslight and Daylight*, 177.

20. A brief overview of the controversy itself, with quotations from primary sources, may be found in Cheshire, *Music Hall in Britain*, 38–42.

21. The Licensing Act of 1737, though far from being the first attempt by the English government to regulate theatres and other places of amusement, became the bedrock on which successive legislation in the eighteenth and nineteenth centuries kept or attempted to keep in check the allegedly riotous or immoral tendencies of audiences and the instinctive attempts of theatre proprietors to take profitable advantage of them. For useful accounts of the long history of governmental regulation of theatres and audiences, see Conolly, *Censorship of English Drama*; Kift, *Victorian Music Hall*; and Pennybacker, *Vision*.

22. Letters from Collin et al., 22 September 1894, 10 October 1894, 404 [LCC/MIN 10,717]; Theatres Committee Papers, LCC/MIN 10,803.

23. Morton and Newton, *Sixty Years' Stage Service*, 160.

24. Gänzl, *Musical Theatre*, 1: 398. Ursula Bloom, Edwardes's biographer, for reasons best known to herself, sets his birth date exactly three years later (*Curtain Call*, 27). See also Hyman, *Gaiety Years*, 16–18.

25. Hyman, *Gaiety Years*, 17; *Catholic Who's Who*, 107; undated clp., *New York Herald*, HTC.

26. *Dramatic Peerage, 1892.*

27. And to differentiate himself from another George Edwards on the Savoy payroll (Hyman, *Gaiety Years*, 30).

28. Hollingshead, *Gaiety Chronicles*, 434–35; "Men of the Day"; Jupp, *Gaiety Stage Door*, 198.

29. Lamb, *150 Years*, 116; MacQueen-Pope, *Carriages at Eleven*, 103.

30. Hyman, *Gaiety Years*, 40; Thomas Postlewait, "George Edwardes: Musical Productions from 1885 to 1915," unpub. table. Unfortunately for Edwardes, *Dorothy* ran so poorly at first that he had to cut his losses and sell out, to the Gaiety accountant Henry J. Lesie, who put a new, unknown actress named Marie Tempest into the leading role and made a fortune (Hyman, *Gaiety Years*, 42), teaching Edwardes a lesson he would never forget.

31. Bloom, *Curtain Call*, 87, 136; Hyman, *Gaiety Years*, 105.

32. Hyman, *Gaiety Years*, 88–89.

33. Hyman, *Gaiety Years*, 68, 83.

34. Hyman, *Gaiety Years*, 74–76; Mander and Mitchenson, *Lost Theatres*, 51–54; Lamb, *150 Years*, 121–22.

35. Pigache, *Café Royal Days*, 39.

36. *Illustrated Sporting and Dramatic News*, 18 May 1895.

37. Hibbert, *Fifty Years*, 254–55.

38. Jupp, *Gaiety Stage Door*, 208–13.

39. "Death of Mr George Edwardes."

40. Reeve, *Take It for a Fact*, 78.

41. Jupp, *Gaiety Stage Door*, 199, 20.

42. Guilbert, *Song of My Life*, 142.

43. "Men of the Day."

44. Hibbert, *Fifty Years*, 254–55.

45. *DT*, 5 October 1915, clp. HTC.

46. Reeve, *Take It for a Fact*, 78.

47. "George Edwardes and the Stalls."

48. Unidentified clp. HTC.

49. P. Bailey, "'Naughty but Nice,'" 39. Bailey's indispensable studies of the music hall and popular culture may be conveniently consulted in his two books *Leisure and Class in Victorian England* and *Popular Culture and Performance in the Victorian City*.

50. Walvin, *Leisure and Society*, 36–41.

51. Lester, "Family Histories"; Pratt, *People of the Period*, 1: 216.

52. Lester, "Family Histories"; Pratt, *People of the Period*, 1: 216.

53. Pratt, *People of the Period*, 1: 216.

54. Lester, "Family Histories."

55. Bristow, *Vice and Vigilance*, 111.

56. "Mrs Ormiston Chant in Canada."

57. Journal of Mabel Loomis Todd, 13 May 1890, qtd. Gay, *Bourgeois Experience*, 1: 98.

58. *Who Was Who*.

59. Hearing of 1888, International Council of Women, reported in *History of Woman Suffrage*, chap. 8, 139.

60. Lester, "Family Histories."

61. *Union Signal*, qtd. "Mrs Chant in America"; "Mrs Ormiston Chant in Canada"; Pratt, *People of the Period*, 1: 216; *Who Was Who*.

62. "Death of Mrs Ormiston Chant"; *Who Was Who*.

63. Banks and Banks, *Feminism and Family Planning*, 12.

64. Trotter, *Cooking with Mud*, 268–69.

65. *Vigilance Record*, January 1895, 40.

66. On Butler, Bristow, *Vice and Vigilance*, 83.

67. Chant, *Social Purity Alliance*, 2–4.

68. Chant, *Social Purity Alliance*, 4.


### 1. MRS. CHANT AT THE EMPIRE

1. Except where otherwise indicated, for facts and information about Mrs. Chant's attendance at the Empire Theatre and for her own description of and comments on her visits I draw on her presentation before the Theatres and Music Halls Committee on 10 October 1894, taken down verbatim in shorthand at the time by

the clerk of the committee and later transcribed; see Donohue, ed., "Empire The-atre." This information is supplemented by Empire Theatre of Varieties programs for 30 July 1894 and other relevant dates, as indicated. In responding to the public-ity given to Mrs. Chant's testimony before the Theatres Committee, Chevalier, known as "the Costers' Laureate" (Stuart and Park, *Variety Stage*, 196), later protested in a letter to the *Telegraph* that he had never sung on the Empire stage (qtd. Bloom, *Curtain Call*, 146). The most pertinent and detailed account to date of Mrs. Chant's attack on the Empire appears in Faulk, *Music Hall*, chapter 3.

2. Torley, "Empire Theatre," 273–74.

3. *Round London*, 100.

4. Sachs and Woodrow, *Modern Opera Houses and Theatres*, vol. 2, ed. Sachs, 39.

5. *Survey of London*, 34: 465. The Fox Theatre in Atlanta, Georgia, is a splendid example still in existence of this fantastic "outside-in" interior, with its ceiling effect of a starlit night sky ringed by minarets and other Arabic architectural features; see http://www.cr.nps.gov/nr/travel/atlanta/fox.htm.

6. Berlanstein, *Daughters of Eve*, 20.

7. Earl, "Building the Halls," 27; Caradec and Weill, *Le Café-Concert*, 35–36, 60–61, figs. 73–74; Walker, "George Jacobi," 83.

8. Sachs and Woodrow, *Modern Opera Houses and Theatres*, vol. 1, ed. Sachs, 1, 2, 9–10; Howard, *London Theatres and Music Halls*, 8; Mander and Mitchenson, *Lost Theatres*, 15–16; Earl, "Building the Halls," 27. An advertisement of the time listed the attractions of the Alhambra: "Enlarged, Re-decorated and Re-furnished," the theatre was "Open Every Night, all the Year round, 7.45 to 11.30," at prices from sixpence to three guineas. It was a "Cool Theatre" with "Electric Light," featuring "Large and Spacious Boxes[,] Promenades, and Comfortable Seats and Fauteuils." Advertisement, bound in with front matter in Hollingshead, *Leicester Square*.

9. Advertisement, bound in with front matter in Hollingshead, *Leicester Square*.

10. Glover, *Jimmy Glover*, 138–39.

11. Qtd. Guest, *Ballet in Leicester Square*, 15.

12. Beerbohm, "An Object Lesson," 32.

13. Soldene, *My Theatrical and Musical Recollections*, 305.

14. Guilbert, *Song of My Life*, 141.

15. H. Scott, *Early Doors*, 161.

16. Hollingshead, *Leicester Square*, 60.

17. Richards, *Memories*, 323–24.

18. Wilde, *Oscar Wilde's* The Importance of Being Earnest, 184.

19. Baker, *History of the London Stage*, 344–45; "History of the Empire."

20. *Survey of London*, 34: 465. At some point soon after it would alter its name to Empire Theatre of Varieties, though continuing to do business legally as Empire Palace, Ltd.

21. Program, 22 December 1887, HTC.

22. Hollingshead, *Leicester Square*, 75; Pigache, *Café Royal Days*, 39; Guest, *Ballet in Leicester Square*, 91; Stuart and Park, *Variety Stage*, 194.

23. "History of the Empire."

24. Guest, *Ballet in Leicester Square*, 90–91.

25. "History of the Empire"; Pigache, *Café Royal Days*, 41.

26. Stuart and Park, *Variety Stage*, 191. Prominently on the program, under the name of the theatre itself, the Empire reminded visitors that it was "Lighted by Electricity."

27. *Round London*, 100.

28. Guest, *Ballet in Leicester Square*, 101.

29. *World*, 19 October 1892, rpt. Shaw, *Music in London*, 2: 168.

30. LCC/MIN 10,803, qtd. T. Davis, "Indecency," 124.

31. Other sources suggest a figure more like 470 persons, but this number would presumably encompass the nonseating capacity of both the first- and second-tier promenades.

32. "Shares of Shows"; T. Davis, *Economics*, 268. In testimony before the Theatres and Music Halls Committee, Edwardes let it be known that shares in music halls and theatres of variety typically commanded high premiums on the face value; but this was a fact generally known in any case.

33. *Builder*, 12 April 1884, 530.

34. LCC/MIN 10,803.

35. See Donohue, "W. P. Dando's Improved Tableaux Vivants."

36. Au, "Tutu," 216.

37. Programs, 11 March 1889 et seq., HTC.

38. *Round London*, 100; "Shah at the Empire."

39. Guest, *Ballet of the Enlightenment*, 43.

40. Hibbert, *Fifty Years*, 107.

41. Guest, *Ballet in Leicester Square*, 97.

42. Hibbert, *Fifty Years*, 108; the school was established at 73 Tottenham Court Road (*Entr'Acte Annual*, 79); Myers, "Lanner, Katti (Katharina Josefa Lanner)."

43. Myers, "Lanner, Katti (Katharina Josefa Lanner)"; see also Guest, *Empire Ballet*, 19–23; Bensusan, "Evolution of a Dancer," qtd. Guest, *Empire Ballet*, 23.

44. Hibbert, *Fifty Years*, 108; Wilhelm, "Art in the Ballet," 52; Pierpont, "Wilhelm, C."

45. A. S. [Symons?], "Notes from the Music-Halls."

46. Merely a "divertissement," John Hollingshead explained ("Music Halls," 89).

47. Archer, "A Napoleon."

48. T. H. L., "Chat with a Costumier."

49. Program, Empire Theatre of Varieties, Monday, 30 July 1894, "and Every Evening, at 8," HTC.

50. Program, 5 February 1894, M&M.

51. Guest, *Empire Ballet*, 104.

52. "Living Pictures at the Empire."

53. *Empire Past and Present*, 18.

54. Program, 5 February 1894, HTC.

55. Shir-Jacob, "Staging the British Empire"; Holder, "Melodrama, Realism, and Empire."

56. Holder, "Melodrama, Realism, and Empire," 129–33; see also Bratton, "Theatre of War," and Russell, "'We Carved Our Way.'"

57. M. Booth, "Soldiers of the Queen," 3.

58. Hichberger, *Images of the Army*, 111–12. Imperialism enacted on the theatrical stage has been the subject of much useful scholarship; in addition to the works just cited, see, for example, Hays, "Representing Empire," and Mayer, ed., *Playing Out the Empire*.

59. "The London Music Halls: The Empire," *Era*, 30 March 1895, 16.

60. Kennedy, *Oxford Dictionary of Music*, 329; Guest, *Ballet in Leicester Square*, 98, 102.

61. Program, 11 February 1895 "and every evening," HTC; scenario in Guest, *Ballet in Leicester Square*, 170–72.

62. Thomas Anstey Guthrie, writing as F. Anstey, "London Music Halls," 191–92; for Anstey's identity see Pratt, *People of the Period*, 1: 31.

63. Symons, "At the Empire"; Anstey, "London Music Halls," 192.

64. Summerfield, "Patriotism and Empire," 29.

65. Ziter, *Orient on the Victorian Stage*, 194–95.

66. Guest, *Ballet in Leicester Square*, 114; program, 20 September 1897, HTC.

67. Program, 22 December 1887, HTC.

68. Program, 20 September 1897, HTC.

69. *Entr'Acte & Limelight*, 22 September 1894, 10.

70. *Entr'Acte & Limelight*, 13 October 1894, 4.

71. *Les Tableaux vivants*, 160.

72. Sanger, *Seventy Years*, 334; *Vigilance Record* (March 1893), 12, cited in Bartley, *Prostitution*, 191.

73. Edwardes, "Living Pictures," 461.

74. *DT*, 18 October 1894, 3.

75. Beckson, *Arthur Symons*, 82.

76. Symons, "At the Empire."

77. Anstey, "London Music Halls," 190.

78. Hollingshead, "The Bumble Pest!" 9.

79. *Times*, 11 October 1878, 7, qtd. Kift, *Victorian Music Hall*, 138.

80. *Times*, 15 October 1881, 7, qtd. Kift, *Victorian Music Hall*, 138.

81. TMHC, *Presented Papers*, Canterbury Music Hall 1888–1904, 23 February 1891, 9 August 1891, qtd. Pennybacker, "'It was not what she said,'" 129.

82. The quality is nicely captured in Walter Sickert's music hall painting *Gatti's Hungerford Palace of Varieties* (1887–88; see *Sickert*, 71), as John Stokes has explained. There was some suggestion that the indefinite shape in the painting of a woman in the stalls was that of a prostitute. "Was the picture then 'a true reflection' of Sickert's mind," Stokes asks, "or was it rather a true representation of a social reality? Or was it both? Sickert did not record his intentions, but some people certainly thought they saw a prostitute in his picture. Prostitutes were visually ambiguous — quite literally so" (Stokes, *In the Nineties*, 67).

83. *Entr'Acte & Limelight*, 20 October 1894, 4.

84. No source given, qtd. Turner, *Roads to Ruin*, 210.

85. Beaumont, *Bookseller at the Ballet*, 82.

86. Macqueen-Pope, *Melodies*, 232; Macqueen-Pope, *Twenty Shillings*, 275.

87. Shaw, "Two Easter Pieces," 103.

88. Pascoe, *London of To-Day*, 147–48.

89. Fitzgerald, *Music-Hall Land*, 8–11.

90. Stokes, *In the Nineties*, 61–62.

91. *Sickert*, 74–75.

92. Titterton, *From Theatre to Music Hall*, 120–21. The idea of a self-conscious, self-reflecting audience was, in a sense, no novelty, given the circumstances of lighted auditoriums in purpose-built indoor English theatres since the time of Shakespeare and the opportunity they afforded of multiple perspectives during the performance, long before the advent of electricity and introduction of dimmers in theatres in the 1880s made it possible to plunge an audience into near-darkness (as the Empire regularly did when showing the living pictures). Not surprisingly, as the century moved toward its end the possibilities for revealing to an audience a mirror image of itself came to be exploited to the full — even in Henry Irving's gaslit Lyceum Theatre. As Bram Stoker recalls of Irving's revival in 1880 of Dion Boucicault's sensational melodrama *The Corsican Brothers*: "The scene of the Masked Ball represented the interior of the Opera House, the scenic auditorium being furthest from the footlights. In fact it was as though the audience sitting in the Lyceum auditorium saw the scene as though looking in a gigantic mirror placed in the auditorium arch. The scene was in reality a vast one and of great brilliance. The Opera House was draped with crimson silk, the boxes were practical and contained a whole audience, all being in perspective" (Stoker, *Henry Irving*, 1: 159–61, qtd. M. Booth, *English Plays*, 72).

93. Bailey, "Custom," 204–5.

94. Wratislaw, *Orchids*, 20.

95. Stokes, *In the Nineties*, 62.

96. Symons, *London Nights*, 3.

97. Beerbohm, "An Object Lesson," 34.

98. Program, 24 September 1894, M&M.

99. Guest, *Ballet in Leicester Square*, 110. Georges Seurat's painting *Le Chahut* (Courtauld Institute Galleries, London) is reproduced as plate 14 in West, *Fin de Siècle*. West comments that the scene of can-can dancers, far from being mere pleasurable entertainment, raised a subject "loaded with associations" for the Parisian audience and was linked with "the notion of social degeneration" (19). For social and moral issues raised by the French can-can see also T. Davis, *Economics*, 130–37.

100. Program, 3 December 1894, HTC; Hibbert, *Fifty Years*, 109.

101. "'La Frolique' at the Empire," *Daily Graphic*, 24 May 1894, 12; 25 May 1894, 4.

102. Richards, *Memories*, 114.

103. Richards, *Memories*, 323–24, 338.

104. Yates, *Edmund Yates*, 1: 161.

105. Linton, *Girl of the Period*, 1: 1–7.

106. Bourdon, *Les Théâtres Anglais*, 248 (author's translation).

107. Benjamin, *Illuminations*, 171; Nead, *Myths of Sexuality*, 99.

## 2. THE LICENSING COMMITTEE MEETS

1. Bartley, *Prostitution*, 155–56.

2. Walkowitz, "Male Vice," 85.

3. "Places of Theatrical Entertainment in London in Operation Each Year of the Nineteenth Century" (chart), Donohue and Ellis, comps., *A Handbook for Compilers*.

4. LCC, catalogue, introduction. The licensing of plays themselves remained under the purview of the Lord Chamberlain and his agent, the Examiner of Plays.

5. Pennybacker, "'It was not what she said,'" 123.

6. Waters, *British Socialists*, 139.

7. Pennybacker, "'It was not what she said,'" 122–23.

8. 25 Geo. II, c. 36; see Ganzel, "Patent Wrongs and Patent Theatres."

9. Hollingshead, "Music Halls," 88. Hollingshead's estimate is somewhat in advance of the facts. In 1851 the population of Great Britain stood at 20.82 million; by 1901 it had climbed to 37 million. In the same span of time the population of London had increased from 2.36 to 4.54 million (Woods, "Population Growth," 137).

10. Senelick, "Music-Hall," 520.

11. *Licensed Victuallers' Official Annual*, 149–50.

12. Thorne, *Great Acceptance*, 104–37; Bristow, *Vice and Vigilance*, 105–6.

13. Transcript, licensing session, 1 October 1890, LCC/MIN 10,803.

14. Transcript, licensing session, 1 October 1890, LCC/MIN 10,803.

15. Pennybacker, "'It was not what she said,'" 118–21.

16. Pennybacker, *Vision*, 217; Bristow, *Vice and Vigilance*, 209.

17. Bristow, *Vice and Vigilance*, 209–11, 117–18.

18. Saunders, *History of the First London County Council*, 59.

19. "County Council and Public Morals," 30. The phrase "gross indecency" had been a highly charged one ever since the enactment of the Criminal Law Amendment Act of 1885 — the statute under which, less than a year after the Empire controversy erupted, Oscar Wilde would be convicted. See Foldy, *Trials of Oscar Wilde*, 85–86.

20. *Licensed Victuallers' Official Annual*, 137.

21. Saunders, *History of the First London County Council*, 311.

22. LCC/MIN 10,766: 3–10.

23. LCC/MIN 10,803.

24. Hamlyn, *Manual*, 95.

25. LCC/MIN 10,766: 264.

26. Qtd. Pennybacker, "'It was not what she said,'" 127.

27. Hibbert, *Fifty Years*, 190–91.

28. *Vigilance Record*, 15 October 1890, 102, 108.

29. *Vigilance Record*, 15 April 1893, 19.

30. Desmond, *London Nights*, 42. Archetype of the narrow-minded, intolerant person, alive to the slightest breach of propriety, Mrs. Grundy was introduced to the English stage in Thomas Morton's play *Speed the Plough* (1798).

31. LCC/MIN 10,717: 272.

32. LCC/MIN 10,717: 271.

33. LCC/MIN 10,717: 271.

34. Gibbon and Bell, *History of the London County Council*, 570.

35. LCC/MIN 10,803: 3–4.

36. LCC/MIN 10,803: 2, 3.

37. LCC/MIN 10,803: 3.

38. Yeats, *Autobiography*, 101.

39. Image, *Selwyn Image Letters*, 64.

40. 17 October 1889, Image, *Selwyn Image Letters*, 66.

41. Gilbert, *Savoy Operas*, 2: 317–18.

42. Kift, *Victorian Music Hall*, 162.

43. "London Music and Dancing Licences," 11 October 1894.

44. Howard, *London Theatres and Music Halls*, 169–70; *Survey of London*, 33: 300–04.

45. "The 'Living Pictures,'" *Vigilance Record*.

46. Coote, "Episodes," 84.

47. McCullough, "Edward Kilanyi"; McCullough, *Living Pictures*; Donohue, "W. P. Dando's Improved Tableaux Vivants."

48. LCC/MIN 10,870.

49. Qtd. Smith, *Victorian Nude*, 148.

50. LCC/MIN 10,870.

51. LCC/MIN 10,870.

52. LCC/MIN 10,717: 403.

53. LCC/MIN 10,870: 10.

54. On the Canterbury, Vicinus, *Industrial Muse*, 248; on the Oxford, P. Bailey, "Custom," 185.

55. "National Vigilance Association."

56. Morton, "Living Pictures," 462.

57. Pinero, "Living Pictures," 463; Shaw, "Living Pictures," 80.

58. Mills, qtd. Guest, *Dandies*, 12.

59. Davidson, "In a Music-Hall," *Poems*, 26–27.

60. TMHC, *Presented Papers*, Palace Theatre of Varieties 1888–1904, 28 August 1897, qtd. Pennybacker, "'It was not what she said,'" 130.

61. LCC/MIN 10,717: 403; "London Music and Dancing Licences," 12 October 1894; "National Vigilance Association."

62. LCC, *Minutes*, 10 October 1895, agenda item 44.

63. Letters from Collin et al., 22 September 1894, 10 October 1894: 404 [LCC/MIN 10,717]; Theatres Committee Papers, LCC/MIN 10,803.

64. "Licensing the Music-Halls."

65. As before, unless otherwise indicated the source for Mrs. Chant's account of her visits to the Empire is the transcript of her testimony before the Theatres and Music Halls Committee; see LCC/MIN 10,803: 4–12 and Donohue, "Empire Theatre."

66. Among the daily newspapers published in London, the *Daily Telegraph* had the largest circulation, at 300,000 in the 1880s, followed by the *Standard* at 250,000 (Alan Lee, "The Structure, Ownership, and Control of the Press, 1855–1914," ed. George Boyce, James Curran, and Pauline Wingate, *Newspaper History: From the Seventeenth Century to the Present Day* [London: Constable, 1978], 120–23, cited Foldy, *Trials of Oscar Wilde*, 164n.). See also Lee, *Origins of the Popular Press*.

67. Hyde, *Oscar Wilde*, 200, 208. Gill would second Edward Carson the following April as prosecutor of Oscar Wilde in the Queensberry trial for criminal libel.

68. "Sir Charles Frederick Gill."

69. On Amos, F. Boase, *Modern English Biography*, 4: 110.

70. "County Council and Licensing"; "London Music and Dancing Licenses," 12 October 1894; "Babble," 12 October 1894: 12; "Music, Dancing, and Theatre Licences."

71. "London Music and Dancing Licences," 12 October 1894.

72. "London Music and Dancing Licences." 12 October 1894.

73. On Gwynne, Jupp, *Gaiety Stage Door*, 48.

74. "Babble," 12 October 1894, 13.

75. "Music, Dancing, and Theatre Licenses."

76. Pennybacker, "'It was not what she said,'" 125.

77. Saunders, *History of the First London County Council*, xii.

78. "Babble," 12 October 1894, 14; LCC/MIN 10,803: 140–41.

79. LCC/MIN 10,717: 405–6; "London Music and Dancing Licences."

### 3. REPERCUSSIONS

1. Notice dated 11 October 1894, Allen and Son, solicitors, LCC/MIN 10,803.

2. *DT*, 10 October 1895, 5.

3. Bloom, *Curtain Call*, 135–36; Jupp, *Gaiety Stage Door*.

4. Thomas Postlewait, "George Edwardes: Musical Productions from 1885 to 1915," unpub. table of events; Postlewait, "George Edwardes: Productions in 1892, 1893, 1894," unpub. description. (Documents in Postlewait's possession.)

5. *Guardian*, 26 August 1892, and *Examiner and Times*, 18 February 1891, cited in Waters, *British Socialists*, 147.

6. *DT*, 13 October 1894, 3.

7. *DT*, 15 October 1894, 3.

8. "Mrs Prowlina Pry. — I hope I Don't Intrude!" *Punch*, 27 October 1894, 194.

9. The reference to the owner of the freehold was to Daniel de Nicols, who, in addition to being the largest shareholder, owned the land, the estate, on which the Empire had been constructed, in contrast to shareholders who had simply put up capital to purchase portions of the enterprise conducted there. The threat was not an idle one; de Nicols stood to lose substantial sums attributable to the loss of rents scheduled to be paid him as freeholder by Edwardes and others (including de Nicols himself) as leaseholders.

10. "Statement by the Directors."

11. *Financial News*, 22 October 1894.

12. *Entr'Acte & Limelight*, 6 October 1894, 4.

13. "Empire Licence."

14. LCC/MIN 10,803.

15. LCC/MIN 10,803.

16. LCC/MIN 10,803.

17. *Report* [1892], sec. 2338.

18. *Report* [1892], sec. 4700.

19. *Builder*, 3 November 1894, 307.

20. *DT*, 13 October 1894, 5.

21. *DT*, 13 October 1894, 5; 15 October 1894, 3.

22. *DT*, 16 October 1894, 5.

23. *DT*, 16 October 1894, 5.

24. *DT*, 16 October 1894, 5.

25. *PMG*, 17 October 1894, 5.

26. *DT*, 16 October 1894, 5.

27. *DT*, 15 October 1894, 3.

28. *Saturday Review*, 13 October 1894, 405–6.

29. *DT*, 15 October 1894, 4.

30. *DT*, 19 October 1894, 3.

31. *DT*, 19 October 1894, 3.

32. *DT*, 22 October 1894, 3.

33. *DT*, 13 October 1894.

34. Stokes, *In the Nineties*, 55.

35. *DT*, 19 October 1894, 4.

36. Mill, *On Liberty*, 217, 223–24.

37. Mill, *On Liberty*, 220.

38. *DT*, 20 October 1894, 7.

39. Scott, "The Playhouses," *ILN*, 20 October 1894.

40. *DT*, 26 October 1894, 5.

41. *DT*, 19 October 1894, 3.

42. *DT*, 20 October 1894, 7.

43. "Babble," 12 October 1894, 9.

44. "Aim of the Purity Crusaders."

45. "Aim of the Purity Crusaders."

46. Shaw, "Empire Promenade."

47. Guest, *Ballet in Leicester Square*, 5n. In 1896 Katti Lanner explained that dancers' salaries at the Empire were 1s.–2s. per performance for child dancers, £4–£8 per month for older girls, £12–£18 per month for freelance adults, £20–£25 per month for seconda donnas, and £750–£2000 per year for star soloists ("What a Ballet Costs: A Peep behind the Scenes," *Sketch*, 12 February 1896, 114, cited in T. Davis, *Actresses as Working Women*, 25).

48. C. Booth, *Life and Labour*, 129–30, 129n.

49. Gilbert, "Concerning Some Actresses Encountered by the C.P.," *Fun*, 8 October 1864, in Stedman, *Gilbert's Theatrical Criticism*, 25.

50. Perugini, *Art of Ballet*, 263, 272.

51. Guest, *Ballet in Leicester Square*, 155.

52. *Church Reformer*, November 1889, 259–60.

53. "Characteristic Sketches."

54. Munby's diary, 22 March 1862, qtd. Smith, *Victorian Nude*, 56–57.

55. Ashbee, *Index of Forbidden Books*, 205. Ashbee was allegedly the "Walter" who kept the now-classic diary *My Secret Life*. Another entry in the *Index*, *The Story of a Dildoe: A Tale in Five Tableaux* (privately printed, with five photographic plates, in 1880), exemplifies the extension of the notion of the tableau into late-century pornography (402).

56. Mayhew, *London Labour*, 4: 257.

57. Carter, "Blonde," 33; Hibbert, *Fifty Years*, 108.

58. *Report* [1866] 1707, secs. 1684–86.

59. *DT*, 19 October 1894, 3.

60. Symons, *London Nights*, 21.

61. *DT*, 15 October 1894, 3.

62. *Western Daily Press*, 28 January 1895, qtd. Meller, *Leisure and the Changing City*, 165.

63. "Speech by Mrs Chant."

64. "Mrs Ormiston Chant."

65. "Mrs Ormiston Chant on Music-Halls."

66. *DT*, 18 October 1894, 3.

67. "London Music and Dancing Licences," 11 October 1894.

68. Image, *Art of Dancing*, 2, 6, 11, 14–15, 16, 18, 19.

69. Headlam, *Function of the Stage*, 19.

70. Hake, *Maiden Ecstasy*, 34, qtd. Headlam, *Function of the Stage*, 25.

71. "Statement by Mrs Chant."

72. Letter dated "London Oct 1894," received 26 October 1894, LCC/MIN 10,803.

73. Ellis, *Daughters of England*, 16–17, 28–29.

74. Lecky, *History of European Morals*, 2: 283.

75. Gay, *Bourgeois Experience*, 2: 361 and n., 362–63; Parent, qtd. Matlock, *Scenes of Seduction*, 30.

76. [Greg], "Art VII — 1," 448.

77. *Quarterly Review* 70 (1837): 20, qtd. B. Harrison, "Underneath the Victorians," 242.

78. [Greg], "Art VII — 1," 458–59.

79. [Greg], "Art VII — 1," 479–81.

80. Parent, *De la prostitution*, 2: 14, qtd. Corbin, *Women for Hire*, 4.

81. [Greg], "Art VII — 1," 493.

82. Wilde, *Lady Windermere's Fan*, 40.

83. Allen, qtd. Gay, *Bourgeois Experience*, 2: 363.

84. Grand, *Modern Man and Maid*, 62.

85. Thomas, "The Double Standard," 197.

86. Banks and Banks, *Feminism and Family Planning*, 113.

87. "Mrs Ormiston Chant in America."

88. *DT*, 16 October 1894, 5.

89. *DT*, 18 October 1894, 3.

90. *DT*, 16 October 1894, 5.

91. *DT*, 18 October 1894, 3.

92. *DT*, 18 October 1894, 3.

93. LCC/MIN 10,803.

94. "Music Hall Employees' Agitation," 17; *DT*, 15 October 1894, 3.

95. "Music Hall Employees' Agitation," 17.

96. "Music Hall Employees' Agitation," 18.

97. *DT*, 15 October 1894, 3.

98. LCC, *Minutes*, 12 March 1894.

99. LCC/MIN 10,803.

100. TMHC, *Presented Papers*, Empire Music Hall, 25 October 1894, qtd. Pennybacker, "'It was not what she said,'" 133.

101. Letter, 22 October 1894, LCC/MIN 10,803.

102. LCC/MIN 10,803.

103. Letter, 22 October 1894, LCC/MIN 10,803.

104. Letter, 24 October 1894, LCC/MIN 10,803.

105. "Protests of Ratepayers."

106. *DT*, 19 October 1894, 3.

107. "In Defence of the Empire"; *DT*, 22 October 1894, 3.

108. "In Defence of the Empire"; *DT*, 22 October 1894, 3.

109. "In Defence of the Empire"; *DT*, 22 October 1894, 3.

110. "In Defence of the Empire."

111. *DT*, 22 October 1894, 3.

112. *DT*, 20 October 1894, 7.

### 4. THE COUNCIL'S DECISION AND ITS AFTERMATH

1. LCC, *Minutes*, 1020.

2. LCC, *Minutes*, 1046.

3. Chant, *Why We Attacked*, 10.

4. LCC, *Minutes*, 1047.

5. LCC, *Minutes*, 1047.

6. Chant, *Why We Attacked*, app., 17.

7. LCC, *Minutes*, 1063.

8. "London Music and Dancing Licences," *DT*, 27 October 1894, 3.

9. "London Music and Dancing Licences," *DT*, 27 October 1894, 3.

10. "London Music and Dancing Licences," *DT*, 27 October 1894, 3.

11. Chant, *Why We Attacked*, app., 19.

12. Chant, *Why We Attacked*, app., 19.

13. Chant, *Why We Attacked*, app., 19–20; "Empire Music Hall License," 26–27.

14. Chant, *Why We Attacked*, app., 20; *DT*, 27 October 1894, 3.

15. Chant, *Why We Attacked*, app. 20.

16. Chant, *Why We Attacked*, app., 21; *DT*, 27 October 1894, 3.

17. Chant, *Why We Attacked*, app., 23; *DT*, 27 October 1894.

18. Chant, *Why We Attacked*, app., 23.

19. On Burns, Kift, *Victorian Music Hall*, 161; Grubb, *From Candle Factory to British Cabinet*, 88; McCarthy, *John Burns*, 4; Pennybacker, *Vision*, 3.

20. Chant, *Why We Attacked*, app. 22; *DT*, 27 October 1894, 3.

21. On Burns's reputation, McCarthy, *John Burns*, 2; Waters, *British Socialists*, 31.

22. Chant, *Why We Attacked*, app., 22; *DT*, 27 October 1894, 3. On Burns and the working class, Grubb, *From Candle Factory to British Cabinet*, 107–8; McCarthy, *John Burns*, 1.

23. Chant, *Why We Attacked*, app., 23; *DT*, 27 October 1894, 3.

24. *DT*, 27 October 1894, 3.

25. Chant, *Why We Attacked*, 10; *DT*, 27 October 1894, 3.

26. LCC, *Minutes* 1070–71; LCC/MIN 10,803; *DT*, 27 October 1894, 3.

27. The considerable fence-sitting that went on is not acknowledged by some historians; see, for example, Waters, *British Socialists*, 58.

28. *Star*, 27 October 1894.

29. "The Empire Closed."

30. "The Empire Closed."

31. *DT*, 27 October 1984, 5.

32. "Alhambra Theatre."

33. "Babble," 2 November 1894, 9.

34. *Post*, qtd. Chant, *Why We Attacked*, 25.

35. *To-Day*, qtd. Chant, *Why We Attacked*, 27.

36. *To-Day*, qtd. Chant, *Why We Attacked*, 28.

37. *Morning*, qtd. Chant, *Why We Attacked*, 28–29.

38. *Reynold's Weekly*, qtd. Chant, *Why We Attacked*, 29–30.

39. On Lady Somerset, Pratt, *People of the Period*, 2: 390; Bristow, *Vice and Vigilance*, 212.

40. "A Signal Victory."

41. *Woman's Signal*, 1 November 1894, 278.

42. *Woman's Signal*, 18 October 1894, 278.

43. *PMG*, 29 October 1894, 7.

44. Torley, "Empire Theatre."

45. Torley, "Empire Theatre," 273, 274.

46. Torley, "Empire Theatre," 274.

47. "Mrs Chant at the Playgoer's Club."

48. *Western Daily Press*, 28 January 1895, qtd. Chevalier, *Albert Chevalier*, 135.

49. *Standard*, 5 November 1894; "Empire Theatre: Scene at the Re-opening."

50. "Empire Theatre: Scene at the Re-opening"; *Morning Leader*, qtd. Chant, *Why We Attacked*, 26; *PMG*, 5 November 1894, 9; "Music Hall Gossip," *Era*; *Standard*, 5 November 1894.

51. *PMG*, 5 November 1894, 9; *Standard*, 5 November 1894.

52. Churchill, *My Early Life*, 71.

53. LCC/MIN 10,717: 456.

54. "Empire Theatre License"; "Empire Music Hall License," 27–29.

55. "Empire Theatre: Arguments."

56. "Empire Theatre: Arguments."

57. LCC, *Minutes*, 1894, 1215–16; "Empire Music Hall License," 29–32; "Empire Theatre: Arguments."

58. Qtd. Chant, *Why We Attacked*, 24.

59. On Frank Verity, Ware, *Short Dictionary of British Architects*, 240; LCC/MIN 10,717: 469.

60. LCC/MIN 10,717: 468–72.

61. LCC/MIN 10,717: 468–72.

62. N. Taylor, "Sir Albert Richardson," 450. The plans are now in the British Architectural Library at the Royal Institute of British Architects (RIBA); see *Catalogue of the Drawings Collection*, 92–93.

63. Plan, British Architectural Library, RIBA, Ref. W2/39.

64. LCC/MIN 10,717: 486–87.

65. Letter, 23 November 1894, LCC, *Minutes*, 4 December 1894, 1249.

66. *Report* [1892], app. 2 (G), (H), (K), (L).

67. Kift, *Victorian Music Hall*, 167–68; *Report* [1892], 494–960.

68. TMHC Proposed Legislation, 1887–1905, 17 April 1894, qtd. Pennybacker, "'It was not what she said,'" 125.

69. Pennybacker, *Vision*, 215.

70. *DT*, 18 October 1894, 3.

71. *DT*, 19 October 1894, 3.

72. "Views of Members."

73. "London Music and Dancing Licences," *DT*, 12 October 1894, 7.

74. *DT*, 17 October 1894, 3.

75. *Report* [1892], secs. 987, 30-32-34, 3470–73.

76. *Report* [1892], sec. 2317.

77. Gurr, *Shakespearean Stage*, chap. 6.

78. Leacroft, *Development of the English Playhouse*, fig. 83, 122–24; fig. 106, 168–69.

79. Leacroft, *Development of the English Playhouse*, 174.

80. 15 January 1842, qtd. Downer, *Eminent Tragedian*, 209.

81. Empire Theatre program, 17 April 1894, 6.

82. British Architectural Library, RIBA, Ref. W2/39.

83. Howard, *London Theatres and Music Halls*, 79.

84. Empire Theatre of Varieties, Plans 102, Greater London Record Office. The plan of the dress circle is reproduced in Cheshire, *Music Hall in Britain*, 38.

85. Verity's detailed summary, discussed below, reflects the presence of a master designer and craftsman pressed into urgent work for which he must have felt a profound distaste, since its requirements ran quite contrary to the spirit and purpose of his father's design.

86. LCC/MIN 10,717: 499–501.

87. LCC, *Minutes*, 1894, 1249.

88. On the BWTA crusade, Pennybacker, "'It was not what she said,'" 131.

89. Empire Theatre program, 17 April 1884, 7.

90. "Licensing Question."

91. C. Scott, "The Playhouses," 10 November 1894.

92. L.C. [Lord Chamberlain] 1 639 (f. 3): Theatres, Letters Sent, 1895, Public Record Office, Chancery Lane.

93. *DT*, 7 December 1894, 5.

94. *DT*, 14 November 1894, 4.

95. "County Council and Amusements," *Era*, 24 November 1894, 17.

96. "County Council and Amusements," *Era*, 1 December 1894, 16.

97. "London Music Halls: The Empire," *Era*, 2 March 1895, 16.

98. *Era*, 16 March 1895, 17.

99. "Empire Palace, Ltd."

100. "London Music Halls: The Empire," *Era*, 12 January 1895, 16.

### 5. WHY THEY ATTACKED THE EMPIRE

1. LCC/MIN 10,718, 26 June 1895.

2. LCC/MIN 10,803.

3. LCC/MIN 10,803; "County Council and Licensing."

4. LCC/MIN 10,803; "County Council and Licensing."

5. No source given, qtd. Hollingshead, "Molly-Coddling Regulation."

6. *Report* [1892], 3900–3906, 3926.

7. LCC/MIN 10,803; "County Council and Licensing."

8. No source given, qtd. Farson, *Marie Lloyd & Music Hall*, 63.

9. Lester, "Family Histories."

10. LCC/MIN 10,718, 2 October 1895.

11. No source given, qtd. Hollingshead, "Molly-Coddling Regulation."

12. Qtd. Farson, *Marie Lloyd & Music Hall*, 63.

13. J. Davis, "Progressive Council."

14. Clifton, "Members and Officers," 3; Davies, *London County Council*, 2.

15. LCC/MIN 10,718, 27 November 1895.

16. LCC/MIN 10,718.

17. Chant, *Why We Attacked*, 5.

18. Chant, *Why We Attacked*, 6.

19. Mason, *Making of Victorian Sexuality*, 83.

20. Chant, *Why We Attacked*, 14–15.

21. On Butler's stories, Walkowitz, *City*, 87ff.

22. M. Booth, ed., *Hiss the Villain*, 269.

23. Walkowitz, *City*, 90; see also Walkowitz, *Prostitution and Victorian Society*.

24. Chant, *Social Purity Alliance*, 2–4.

25. Hibbert, *Fifty Years*, 89.

26. Pettitt and Harris, *A Life of Pleasure*, 3:3, 33.

27. Pettitt and Harris, *A Life of Pleasure*, 3:3, 35; 5:5, 35.

28. Chant, *Why We Attacked*, 16.

29. Ruskin, "Of Queens' Gardens," 122.

30. Chant, *Why We Attacked*, 16.

31. Hollingshead, *Story of Leicester Square*, 76.

32. "Battle of the Music Halls," 25.

33. Beerbohm, "An Object Lesson," 32.

34. Kift, *Victorian Music Hall*, 163–64.

35. Kift, *Victorian Music Hall*, 174.

36. Titterton, *From Theatre to Music Hall*, 121–22.

37. Bensusan, *Souvenir of London*, 81.

38. *Financial News*, 21 November 1893, qtd. Pennybacker, *Vision*, 213.

39. *PMG*, 15 October 1894, 1.

40. *Illustrated Sporting and Dramatic News*, 29 December 1894, 600.

41. "New Ballet at the Empire."

42. *Sporting Life*, qtd. Chant, *Why We Attacked*, 31.

43. C. Harrison, *Theatricals and Tableaux Vivants*, 84.

44. Shaw, *Mrs Warren's Profession*, Bodley Head ed., 195–96. *Mrs. Warren's Profession* was first published in Shaw's two-volume *Plays Pleasant and Unpleasant* in 1898.

45. Shaw, "Author's Apology," xxviii.

46. Coote, "Episodes," 86.

47. *London*, 1 November 1894, 691; *Liberal*, cited *London*, 17 November 1894, qtd. Pennybacker, *Vision*, 228.

48. Archer, "County Council," 319, 321, 323. On music hall history, Pennell, "Pedigree of the Music-Hall"; see also Summerfield, "Effingham Arms."

49. Archer, "County Council," 328, 323, 324.

50. Archer, "County Council," 324.

51. Kift, *Victorian Music Hall*, 68–69.

52. Bourdon, *Les Théatres Anglais*, 248.

53. Image, "Mr. Image's Speech," 261.

54. *Church Reformer*, 5 October 1889; Image, *Selwyn Image Letters*, 64.

55. Allen, "New Hedonism," 379.

56. Allen, "New Hedonism," 383, 384, 387, 390.

57. Allen, "New Hedonism," 391.

58. Coote, "Episodes," 85.

59. Shaw, "Living Pictures."

60. Etty, "Autobiography," 40.

61. Crook, review of Jenkyns, *Dignity and Decadence*.

62. Qtd. B. Bailey, *William Etty's Nudes*, 22–23.

63. B. Bailey, *William Etty's Nudes,* 33, 37.

64. Koritz, *Gendering Bodies,* 66.

65. Symons, "World as Ballet," 389.

66. Qtd. Gibbons, "Reverend Stewart Headlam," 331.

67. Anstey, "Conrad," *Mr Punch's Model Music-Hall,* 167. On Hoffman's book, see Gay, *Bourgeois Experience,* 1: 198.

68. Anstey, "Conrad," *Mr Punch's Model Music-Hall,* 168.

69. Anstey, "Conrad," *Mr Punch's Model Music-Hall,* 169.

70. Anstey, "Conrad," *Mr Punch's Model Music-Hall,* 172.

71. Anstey, "Conrad," *Mr Punch's Model Music-Hall,* 8.

72. "County Council and Public Morals," 31.

73. Image, "Mr. Image's Speech," 261.

74. Qtd. B. Bailey, *William Etty's Nudes,* 16.

75. Symons, "At the Alhambra: Impressions and Sensations," *Savoy,* no. 5 (September, 1896): 77, qtd. Beckson, *London in the 1890s,* 113.

76. Hollingshead, "Music Halls," 90. Hollingshead died in 1904, seven years before the *Britannica* brought out this piece.

77. "Mrs Chant at the Playgoer's Club."

78. "The Music-Hall."

79. Hobson, *Psychology of Jingoism,* 2–3.

80. Fitzgerald, *Music-Hall Land,* 7, 4.

81. Mackenzie, *Propaganda and Empire,* 40.

82. Desmond, *London Nights,* 236.

83. Richards, *Memories,* 323.

84. J. B. Booth, *Old Pink'un Days,* 317–18.

85. Desmond, *London Nights,* 241.

86. *DT,* 12 October 1894.

87. Wharton, *House of Mirth,* 131.

88. Veder, "Tableaux Vivants," 23. Nina Auerbach has examined amateur theatricals from a variety of perspectives in *Private Theatricals.*

89. Veder, "Tableaux Vivants," 19.

90. Guest, *Adeline Genée,* 50.

91. Koritz, *Gendering Bodies,* 23.

92. Thomas, "Double Standard," 210.

93. Qtd. Thomas, "Double Standard," 215.

94. "Women's Conference."

95. *Diary of an Actress,* 54–55. Tracy C. Davis has studied the lives and working conditions of everyday actresses in her indispensable book *Actresses as Working Women.*

96. Linton, "Modern Revolt," 148–49.

97. Drysdale, *Physical, Sexual, and Natural Religion,* 449.

98. See, e.g., Mill, *Subjection of Women*, 85–86.

99. Mill, *Subjection of Women*, 3, 45–46.

100. Blackwell, *Purchase of Women*, 27, 33–40.

101. Chant, "Women and the Streets," 128–30.

102. Walkowitz, "Male Vice," 88.

103. Thomas, "Double Standard," 209–10.

104. Qtd. Said, *Culture and Imperialism*, 103.

105. Hyam, *Empire and Sexuality*, 1.

106. Hobson, *Psychology of Jingoism*, 8–9.

107. Hobson, *Psychology of Jingoism*, 3.

108. Qtd. Hibbert, *Fifty Years*, 100.

109. Senelick, "Politics as Entertainment," 169.

110. Wilde, *Oscar Wilde's* The Importance of Being Earnest, 107.

111. Hibbert, *Fifty Years*, 88.

# WORKS CITED

## PRIMARY SOURCES

London County Council (Greater London Record Office):

    LCC/MIN 1889–1904

        10,303 Theatres Committee Papers/Empire Theatre of Varieties

        10,803 Theatres Committee Papers/Empire Theatre of Varieties

        10,920 Theatres Committee Papers/Trocadero

        10,891 Theatres Committee Papers

        10,717 Minutes. Theatres and Music Halls Committee. Vol. 7.

        10,718 Minutes. Theatres and Music Halls Committee. Vol. 8.

        10,766, 10,870 Inspection Subcommittee

Catalogue, Papers of London County Council. Theatres and Music Halls
    Committee: "LCC Minutes and Papers—Public Health Committee . . . Theatres
    and Music Halls."

London County Council. *Minutes of Proceedings.* 1894. London: For the Council,
    Jas. Truscott & Son (printer), n.d.

———. *Minutes of Proceedings.* 1895. London: For the Council, Jas. Truscott & Son
    (printer), n.d.

Newspapers and Periodicals

    *Barmaid*

    *Builder*

    *Church Reformer*

    *Daily Graphic*

    *Daily Telegraph*

    *Entr'Acte & Limelight*

    *Era*

    *Financial News*

    *Fortnightly Review*

    *Great Thoughts*

    *Guardian*

    *Harper's New Monthly Magazine*

    *Illustrated London News*

    *Illustrated Sporting and Dramatic News*

    *London*

*Magazine of Art*

*Music Hall*, cont. as *Music Hall and Theatre* (1889), then as *Music Hall and Theatre Review* (1889–1912)

*New Review*

*New York Herald*

*Pall Mall Gazette*

*Punch*

*Saturday Review*

*Sketch*

*Standard*

*Star*

*Times* (London)

*To-Day*

*Vigilance Record*

*Westminster Review*

*Woman's Signal*

Parliamentary Papers

*Report from the Select Committee on Theatres and Places of Entertainment with Proceedings, Minutes of Evidence, Appendix, and Index.* 2 June 1892. British Parliamentary Papers 3: Stage and Theatre. Rpt. Shannon: Irish UP, 1970.

*Report from the Select Committee on Theatrical Licences and Regulations with Proceedings, Minutes of Evidence, Appendix, and Index.* 1866. British Parliamentary Papers 2: Stage and Theatre. Rpt. Shannon: Irish UP, 1970.

Public Record Office, London and Kew

Theatre Programs, Empire Theatre of Varieties and Alhambra Theatre of Varieties
British Library
Harvard Theatre Collection
Mander and Mitchenson Theatre Collection

### SECONDARY SOURCES

"The Aim of the Purity Crusaders: Interview with Mrs. Ormiston Chant." *Pall Mall Gazette*, 13 October 1894, 7.

"Alhambra Theatre." *DT*, 30 October 1894, 3.

Allen, Grant. "The New Hedonism." *Fortnightly Review*, n.s., 1 March 1894, 377–92.

———. *The Woman Who Did.* London: John Lane, 1895.

Altick, Richard D. *The Shows of London.* Cambridge: Belknap P of Harvard UP, 1978.

Amos, Sheldon. *A Comparative Survey of Laws in Force for the Prohibition, Regulation, and Licensing of Vice in England and Other Countries.* London: Stevens & Sons, 1877.

Anstey, F[rederick]. "London Music Halls." *Harper's New Monthly Magazine* 82 (January 1891): 190–202.

———. *Mr Punch's Model Music-Hall Songs & Dramas: Collected, Improved, and Re-Arranged from 'Punch.'* London: Bradbury, Agnew, 1892.

Archer, William. "The County Council and the Music Halls." *Contemporary Review* 67 (March 1895): 317–27.

———. "A Napoleon of Musical Comedies." Unidentified clp. stamped [27 October 1915]. HTC.

A. S. [Arthur Symons?]. "Notes from the Music-Halls." *Sketch,* 17 October 1984, 624.

Ashbee, Henry Spencer (Pisanus Fraxi). *Index of Forbidden Books.* London: Sphere Books, 1969.

Au, Susan. "Tutu." *International Encyclopedia of Dance.* 6: 216–17.

Auerbach, Nina. *Private Theatricals: The Lives of the Victorians.* Cambridge: Harvard UP, 1990.

"Babble." *Music Hall and Theatre Review,* 12 October 1894, 9–14; 19 October 1894, 9; 2 November 1894, 9.

Bailey, Brian J. *William Etty's Nudes.* Pulloxhill, Bedford: Inglenook, 1974.

Bailey, Peter. "Custom, Capital, and Culture in the Victorian Music Hall." *Popular Culture and Custom in Nineteenth-Century England,* ed. Robert D. Storch. London: Croom Helm, 1982. 180–208.

———. *Leisure and Class in Victorian England: Rational Recreation and the Contest for Control, 1830–1885.* 2nd ed. London: Methuen, 1987.

———. "'Naughty but nice': Musical Comedy and the Rhetoric of the Girl, 1892–1914." *The Edwardian Theatre: Essays on Performance and the Stage,* ed. Michael R. Booth and Joel H. Kaplan. Cambridge: Cambridge UP, 1996. 36–60.

———. *Popular Culture and Performance in the Victorian City.* Cambridge: Cambridge UP, 1998.

Baker, H. Barton. *History of the London Stage and Its Famous Players (1576–1903).* New York, 1904. Rpt. New York: Benjamin Blom, 1969.

Banks, J. A., and Olive Banks. *Feminism and Family Planning in Victorian England.* New York: Schocken, 1964.

Bartley, Paula. *Prostitution: Prevention and Reform in England, 1860–1914.* London: Routledge, 2000.

"The Battle of the Music Halls—And After." *Vigilance Record,* 15 November 1894, 25–26.

Beaumont, Cyril. *Bookseller at the Ballet: Memoirs 1891 to 1929.* London: C. W. Beaumont, 1975.

Beckson, Karl. *Arthur Symons: A Life*. Oxford: Clarendon, 1987.

———. *London in the 1890s: A Cultural History*. New York: W. W. Norton, 1992.

Beerbohm, Max. *Around Theatres*. 2 vols., 1924. Rpt. London: Rupert Hart-Davis, 1953.

———. "An Object Lesson." *Saturday Review*, 6 May 1899. Rpt. Beerbohm, *Around Theatres*. 30–34.

Benjamin, Walter. *Illuminations*. Trans. Harry Zohn, ed. Hannah Arendt. New York: Schocken, 1969.

Bensusan, S. L. *Souvenir of London*. T. C. & E. C. Jack [1911].

Berlanstein, Lenard R. *Daughters of Eve: A Cultural History of French Theater Women from the Old Regime to the Fin de Siècle*. Cambridge: Harvard UP, 2001.

Blackwell, Elizabeth. *Purchase of Women: The Great Economic Blunder*. Pt. 1. London: John Kensit [1887].

Bloom, Ursula. *Curtain Call for the Guv'nor: A Biography of George Edwardes*. London: Hutchinson, 1954.

Boase, Frederic. *Modern English Biography*. 6 vols., 1901, 1908. Rpt. London: Frank Cass, 1965.

Boase, George C. "The Lord Chief Baron Nicholson." *Notes and Queries*, 7 January 1893, 3–5.

Booth, Charles, ed. *Life and Labour of the People in London*. Vol. 8: *Population Classified by Trades, cont*. London: Macmillan, 1896.

Booth, J. B. *Old Pink'un Days*. London: Grant Richards, 1924.

Booth, Michael R. "Soldiers of the Queen: Drury Lane Imperialism." *Melodrama: The Cultural Emergence of a Genre*, ed. Michael Hays and Anastasia Nikolopoulous. New York: St Martin's, 1996. 3–20.

———, ed. *English Plays of the Nineteenth Century*. Vol. 2: *Dramas, 1850–1900*. Oxford: Clarendon, 1969.

———, ed. *Hiss the Villain: Six English and American Melodramas*. London: Eyre & Spottiswoode, 1964.

Bourdon, Georges. *Les Théâtres Anglais*. Paris: Bibliothèque-Charpentier, 1903.

Bratton, J. S. "Theatre of War: The Crimea on the London Stage 1854–5." *Performance and Politics in Popular Drama*, ed. David Bradby, Louis James, and Barnard Sharratt. Cambridge: Cambridge UP, 1980. 119–37.

Bristow, Edward J. *Vice and Vigilance: Purity Movements in Britain since 1700*. Dublin: Gill & Macmillan, 1977.

Busby, Roy. *British Music Hall: An Illustrated Who's Who from 1850 to the Present Day*. London: Paul Elek, 1976.

"Cafe du Globe, Leicester Square." *Peeping Tom: A Weekly Journal of Town Life*, no. 1 (27 June 1859): 1–2.

Caradec, François, and Alain Weill. *Le Café-Concert*. Paris: Atelier Hachette/Massin, 1980.

Carter, Alexandra. "Blonde, Bewigged, and Winged with Gold: Ballet Girls in the Music Halls of Late Victorian and Edwardian England." *Dance Research* 13, 2 (Winter 1995): 28–46.

*Catalogue of the Drawings Collection of the Royal Institute of British Architects.* Ed. Jill Lever. Vol. T–Z. London: Gregg International, 1984.

*Catholic Who's Who & Year-Book, 1910.* Ed. Sir F. C. Burnand. London: Burnes & Oates, n.d.

Chant, L. Ormiston. "Women and the Streets." *Public Morals*, ed. James Marchant. London: Morgan & Scott [1903]. 128–34.

Chant, Mrs. Ormiston. *Sellcut's Manager.* London: Grant Richards, 1899.

———. *Social Purity Alliance: Speech of Mrs. Ormiston Chant at the Annual Meeting of the S.P.A., 13 June 1883.* Pamphlet. [1]-4.

———. *Why We Attacked the Empire.* London: Horace Marshall & Son [1895].

"Characteristic Sketches." (No. 26.) *The Town*, no. 26 (25 November 1837): 201.

Cheshire, D. F. *Music Hall in Britain.* Newton Abbott: David & Charles, 1974.

Chevalier, Albert. *Albert Chevalier: A Record by Himself.* With Brian Daly. London: John Macqueen, 1895.

Churchill, Rt. Hon. Winston S. *My Early Life: A Roving Commission.* London: Thornton Butterworth, 1930.

Clifton, Gloria. "Members and Officers of the LCC, 1889–1965." *Politics and the People of London*, ed. Andrew Saint. London: Hambledon, 1989. 1–26.

Conolly, L. W. *The Censorship of English Drama, 1737–1824.* San Marino: Huntington Library, 1976.

Coote, William Alexander. "Episodes of the Work of the National Vigilance Association." *Church Reformer* 14 (April 1895): 84–86.

Corbin, Alain. *Women for Hire: Prostitution and Sexuality in France after 1850.* Trans. Alan Sheridan. Cambridge: Harvard UP, 1990.

"County Council and Amusements." *Era*, 24 November 1894, 17; 1 December 1894, 16.

"County Council and Licensing." *Era*, 13 October 1894, 16.

"The County Council and Public Morals." *Vigilance Record*, 15 April 1889, 30–31.

"County Council Licensing." *Era*, 5 October 1895, 17.

Crook, J. Mordaunt. Review of Richard Jenkyns, *Dignity and Decadence: Victorian Art and the Classical Inheritance.* London: Harper Collins, 1992. *TLS*, 9 October 1992, 18.

Davidson, John. *The Poems of John Davidson.* Ed. Andrew Turnbull. 2 vols. Totowa, NJ: Rowman and Littlefield, 1973.

Davies, A. Emil. *The London County Council, 1889–1937: A Historical Sketch.* London: Fabian Society, 1937.

Davis, John. "The Progressive Council, 1889–1907." *Politics and the People of London*, ed. Andrew Saint. London: Hambledon, 1989. 27–48.

Davis, Tracy C. *Actresses as Working Women: Their Social Identity in Victorian Culture.* London: Routledge, 1991.

———. *The Economics of the British Stage, 1800–1914.* Cambridge: Cambridge UP, 2000.

———. "Indecency and Vigilance in the Music Halls." *British Theatre in the 1890s: Essays on Drama and the Stage,* ed. Richard Foulkes. Cambridge: Cambridge UP, 1992. 111–31.

"Death of Mr George Edwardes." *Times* [5 October 1915]. Clp. HTC.

"Death of Mrs Ormiston Chant: A Notable Social Worker." *Times,* 17 February 1923, 12.

de Lano, Pierre. *Les Bals travestis et les tableaux vivants sous le second empire.* Paris: H. Simonis Empis, 1893.

Desmond, Shaw. *London Nights of Long Ago.* London: Duckworth, 1927.

*The Diary of an Actress, or Realities of Stage Life.* Ed. H. C. Shuttleworth. London: Griffith, Farran, Okeden & Welsh, 1885.

Disher, Maurice Willson. *Winkles and Champagne: Comedies and Tragedies of the Music Hall.* London: B. T. Batsford, 1938.

Donohue, Joseph. "W. P. Dando's Improved Tableaux Vivants at the Palace Theatre of Varieties, London." *Theatre Arts Journal: Studies in Scenography and Performance* 1 (forthcoming).

———, ed. "The Empire Theatre of Varieties Licensing Controversy of 1894: Testimony of Laura Ormiston Chant before the Theatres and Music Halls Committee." *Nineteenth Century Theatre* 15 (1987): 50–60.

Donohue, Joseph, and James Ellis, comps. *A Handbook for Compilers:* The London Stage, 1800–1900; A Calendar of Performances. Amherst, MA: Privately printed, 1976.

Downer, Alan S. *The Eminent Tragedian William Charles Macready.* Cambridge: Harvard UP, 1966.

*The Dramatic Peerage, 1892.* Comp. Erskine Reid and Herbert Compton. London: Raithby, Lawrence, n.d.

[Drysdale, George]. *Physical, Sexual, and Natural Religion: By a Student of Medicine.* London: Edward Truelove, 1855.

Earl, John. "Building the Halls." *Music Hall: The Business of Pleasure,* ed. Peter Bailey. Milton Keynes: Open UP, 1986. 1–32.

Edwardes, George. "Living Pictures." *New Review,* November 1894, 461.

Ellis, Sarah Stickney. *The Daughters of England, Their Position in Society, Character, and Responsibilities.* London: Fisher, Son, n.d.

"The Empire Closed." *DT,* 27 October 1894, 3.

"The Empire Licence." *Era,* 27 October 1894, 17.

"The Empire Music Hall License." *Vigilance Record,* 15 November 1894, 26–32.

"The Empire Palace, Ltd." *Era,* 30 March 1895, 16.

*The Empire Past and Present, 1884–1905.* 20pp. Theatre Museum (London).

"The Empire Theatre: Arguments in the Queen's Bench." *DT*, 8 November 1894, 4.

"Empire Theatre License: Mandamus against the County Council." *DT*, 1 November 1894, 2.

"Empire Theatre: Scene at the Re-opening." *DT*, 5 November 1894, 3.

*Entr'Acte Annual.* Comp. W. H. Combes. London: Entr'Acte, 1895.

Etty, William. "Autobiography." *Art-Journal* 11 (1849): 13, 37–40, 99.

Farr, Dennis. *William Etty.* London: Routledge & Kegan Paul, 1958.

Farson, Daniel. *Marie Lloyd & Music Hall.* London: Tom Stacey, 1972.

Faulk, Barry J. *Music Hall and Modernity: The Late-Victorian Discovery of Popular Culture.* Athens: Ohio UP, 2004.

Fitzgerald, Percy. *Music-Hall Land: An Account of the Natives, Male and Female, Pastimes, Songs, Antics, and General Oddities of That Strange Country.* London: Ward and Downey, [1890].

Foldy, Michael S. *The Trials of Oscar Wilde: Deviance, Morality, and Late-Victorian Society.* New Haven: Yale UP, 1997.

"'La Frolique' at the Empire." *Daily Graphic*, 24 May 1894, 12; 25 May 1894, 4.

Ganzel, Dewey. "Patent Wrongs and Patent Theatres: Drama and the Law in the Early Nineteenth Century." *PMLA* 76 (1961): 384–96.

Gänzl, Kurt. *The Encyclopedia of the Musical Theatre.* 2 vols. New York: Schirmer, 1994.

Gaunt, William, and F. Gordon Roe. *Etty and the Nude: The Art and Life of William Etty, R.A., 1787–1849.* Leigh-on-Sea, Essex: F. Lewis, 1943.

Gay, Peter. *The Bourgeois Experience: Victoria to Freud.* Vol. 1: *Education of the Senses.* Vol. 2: *The Tender Passion.* New York: Oxford UP, 1984, 1986.

"George Edwardes and the Stalls." *Era*, 10 May 1902. Clp. HTC.

Gibbon, Sir Gwilym, and Reginald W. Bell. *History of the London County Council, 1889–1939.* London: Macmillan, 1939.

Gibbons, T. H. "The Reverend Stewart Headlam and the Emblematic Dancer: 1877–1894." *British Journal of Aesthetics* 5 (October 1965): 329–40.

Gilbert, W. S. *The Savoy Operas.* 2 vols. London: Oxford UP, 1963.

Glover, James Mackey. *Jimmy Glover His Book.* London: Methuen, 1911.

Grand, Sarah. *The Modern Man and Maid.* London: Horace Marshall & Son, 1898.

[Greg, William Rathbone.] "Art VII–1: De la Prostitution dans la Ville de Paris; Par Parent-Duchatelet. . . ." *Westminster Review* 53 (June 1850): 448–506.

Grubb, Arthur Page. *From Candle Factory to British Cabinet: The Life Story of the Right Hon. John Burns, P.C., M.P.* London: Edwin Dalton, 1908.

Guest, Ivor. *Adeline Genée: A Lifetime of Ballet under Six Reigns.* London: Adam and Charles Black, 1958.

———. *Ballet in Leicester Square: The Alhambra and the Empire, 1860–1915*. London: Dance Books, 1992.

———. *The Ballet of the Enlightenment: The Establishment of the Ballet d'Action in France, 1770–1793*. London: Dance Books, 1996.

———. *Dandies and Dancers*. Dance Perspectives 37. New York: Dance Perspectives Foundation, 1969.

———. *The Empire Ballet*. London: Society for Theatre Research, 1962.

Guilbert, Yvette. *The Song of My Life: My Memories*. Trans. Béatrice de Holthoir. London: George G. Harrap, 1929.

Gurr, Andrew. *The Shakespearean Stage, 1574–1642*. 3rd ed. Cambridge: Cambridge UP, 1992.

Hamlyn, Clarence. *A Manual of Theatrical Law containing Chapters on Theatrical Licensing, Music and Dancing Generally, and Dramatic Copyright*. London: Waterlow & Sons (printers), 1891.

Harrison, Brian. "Underneath the Victorians." *Victorian Studies* 10 (March 1967): 239–62.

Harrison, Charles. *Theatricals and Tableaux Vivants for Amateurs: Giving Full Directions as to Stage Arrangements, "Making Up," Costumes, and Acting*. London: L. Upcott Gill, 1882.

Hays, Michael. "Representing Empire: Class, Culture, and the Popular Theatre in the Nineteenth Century." *Imperialism and Theatre: Essays on World Theatre, Drama, and Performance*, ed. J. Ellen Gainor. London: Routledge, 1995. 132–47.

Headlam, Stewart D. *The Function of the Stage*. Lecture. London: Frederick Verinder, 1889.

Hibbert, Henry George. *Fifty Years of a Londoner's Life*. New York: Dodd, Mead, 1916.

Hichberger, J. W. M. *Images of the Army: The Military in British Art, 1815–1914*. Manchester: Manchester UP, 1988.

"The History of the Empire." *Era*, 27 October 1894, 17.

*History of Woman Suffrage*. Vol. 4: 1883–1900. Rochester, NY: Privately published, 1902.

Hobson, John Atkinson. *The Psychology of Jingoism*. London: Grant Richards, 1901.

Holder, Heidi. "Melodrama, Realism, and Empire on the British Stage." *Acts of Supremacy: The British Empire and the Stage, 1790–1930*, ed. J. S. Bratton et al. Manchester: Manchester UP, 1991. 129–49.

Hollingshead, John. "The Bumble Pest!" *Entr'Acte Annual* (1895), 9.

———. *Gaiety Chronicles*. London: Archibald Constable, 1898.

———. "Molly-Coddling Regulation and Milksop Principles." *Entr'Acte Annual* (1896), 11–13.

———. "Music Halls." *Encyclopaedia Britannica*. 10th ed., 1902. 31: 45–49. Rpt. 11th ed. Cambridge: Cambridge UP, 1911. 19: 87–90.

————. *The Story of Leicester Square*. London: Simpkin, Marshall, Hamilton, Kent, 1892.

Howard, Diana. *London Theatres and Music Halls, 1850–1950*. London: Library Association, 1970.

Hyam, Ronald. *Empire and Sexuality: The British Experience*. Manchester: Manchester UP, 1990.

Hyde, H. Montgomery. *Oscar Wilde: A Biography*. New York: Farrar, Straus and Giroux, 1975.

Hyman, Alan. *The Gaiety Years*. London: Cassell, 1975.

Image, Selwyn. *The Art of Dancing: On a Question of Dress*. London: Office of the "Church Reformer," 1891.

————. "Mr. Image's Speech." *Church Reformer* 8 (November 1889): 260–61.

————. *Selwyn Image Letters*. Ed. A. H. Macmurdo. London: Grant Richards, 1932.

"In Defence of the Empire." *Pall Mall Gazette*, 22 October 1894, 7.

*International Encyclopedia of Dance*. Founding ed. Selma Jeanne Cohen. 6 vols. New York: Oxford UP, 1998.

*Intrigues and Confession of a Ballet Girl; Disclosing Startling and Voluptuous Scenes Before and Behind the Curtain, Enacted by Well-known Personages in the Theatrical, Military, Medical and Other Professions; with Kisses at Vauxhall, Greenwich, &c., &c., and a Full Disclosure of the Secret and Amatory Doings in the Dressing Room, Under and Upon the Stage, in the Light and in the Dark, By One Who Has Had Her Share*. N.p.: N.pub., n.d. British Library, shelf mark P.C.31.h.21.

*The John Johnson Collection: Catalogue of an Exhibition*. Oxford: Bodleian Library, 1971.

Jupp, James. *The Gaiety Stage Door: Thirty Years' Reminiscences of the Theatre*. Boston: Small, Maynard, [1923].

Kennedy, Michael. *The Oxford Dictionary of Music*. Oxford: Oxford UP, 1986.

Kift, Dagmar. *The Victorian Music Hall: Culture, Class, and Conflict*. Trans. Roy Kift. Cambridge: Cambridge UP, 1996.

Koritz, Amy. *Gendering Bodies / Performing Art: Dance and Literature in Early Twentieth-Century British Culture*. Ann Arbor: U of Michigan P, 1995.

L., T. H. "A Chat with a Costumier: 'Wilhelm' at home." *Sketch*, 8 March 1893, 343–44.

Lamb, Andrew. *150 Years of Popular Musical Theatre*. New Haven: Yale UP, 2000.

Leacroft, Richard. *The Development of the English Playhouse*. Ithaca: Cornell UP, 1973.

Lecky, W. E. H. *History of European Morals*. 10th ed. 2 vols. London: Longmans, Green, 1892.

Lee, Alan J. *The Origins of the Popular Press in England, 1855–1914*. London: Croom Helm, 1976.

Lespès, Leo. *Les Tableaux Vivants*. Paris: Librarie Centrale, 1865.

Lester, Marjory. "Family Histories: Laura Ormiston Dibbin." Unpublished manuscript, n.d. [Copy in author's possession.]

*The Licensed Victuallers' Official Annual: "The Blue Book of the Trade" for the Year 1895.* Ed. Albert B. Deane. London: Licensed Victuallers' Central Protection Society of London, Ltd., [1895].

"The Licensing Question." *Daily Telegraph,* 26 October 1894, 3.

"Licensing the Music-Halls." *Pall Mall Gazette,* 11 October 1894, 7.

Linton, E. Lynn. *The Girl of the Period and Other Social Essays.* 2 vols. London: Richard Bentley & Son, 1883.

———. "The Modern Revolt." *Macmillan's Magazine,* December 1870, 142–49.

"The Living Pictures." *New Review* 11, no. 66 (November 1894): 461–70.

"The 'Living Pictures.'" *Vigilance Record,* 15 September 1894, 15–16.

"Living Pictures at the Empire." *Era,* 10 February 1894.

*London Encyclopaedia.* Ed. Ben Weinreb and Christopher Hibbert. New York: St. Martin's, 1983.

"London Music and Dancing Licences." *DT,* 11 October 1894, 3; 12 October 1894, 7; 27 October 1894, 3.

"The London Music Halls: The Empire." *Era,* 12 January 1895, 16; 2 March 1895, 16.

MacKenzie, John M. *Propaganda and Empire: The Manipulation of British Public Opinion, 1880–1960.* Manchester: Manchester UP, 1984.

Macqueen-Pope, Walter James. *Carriages at Eleven: The Story of the Edwardian Theatre.* 1947. Rpt. Port Washington, NY: Kennikat, 1970.

———. *The Melodies Linger On: The Story of Music Hall.* London: W. H. Allen, [1950].

———. *Twenty Shillings in the Pound.* London: Hutchinson, 1948.

*La Maison de Verre définé de Tableaux Vivants.* Par E. D. Paris: Aux Dépens de la Compagnie, 1891.

Mander, Raymond, and Joe Mitchenson. *The Lost Theatres of London.* New York: Taplinger, 1968.

*The Marchioness's Amorous Pastimes and Some Other Merry Tales.* London: Privately printed (Not to be sold), 1893. [False imprint; printed in Brussels.] British Library shelf mark P.C.31.f.33.

Mason, Michael. *The Making of Victorian Sexuality.* Oxford: Oxford UP, 1994.

Matlock, Jann. *Scenes of Seduction: Prostitution, Hysteria, and Reading Difference in Nineteenth-Century France.* New York: Columbia UP, 1994.

Mayer, David, ed. *Playing Out the Empire: Ben Hur and Other Toga Plays and Films, 1883–1908.* Oxford: Clarendon, 1994.

Mayhew, Henry. *London Labour and the London Poor.* 4 vols. London: Griffin, Bohn, 1861–62. Rpt. New York: Dover, 1968.

McCarthy, Justin. *John Burns*. British Political Portraits 5. New York: Outlook, 1903.

McCullough, Jack W. "Edward Kilanyi and American Tableaux Vivants." *Theatre Survey* 16 (May 1975): 25–41.

———. *Living Pictures on the New York Stage*. Ann Arbor: UMI Research, 1983.

Meller, H. E. *Leisure and the Changing City, 1870–1914*. London: Routledge and Kegan Paul, 1976.

"Men of the Day. No. MCCLXXVI. — Mr George Edwardes." *Vanity Fair*, 26 April 1911, 489.

Mill, John Stuart. *On Liberty*. Collected Works of John Stuart Mill. Vol. 18: *Essays on Politics and Society*. Ed. J. M. Robson. Toronto: U of Toronto P, 1977. 213–310.

———. *The Subjection of Women*. 1869. Cambridge: M.I.T. P, 1970.

Morton, Charles. "The Living Pictures." *New Review*, November 1894, 462.

Morton, W. H., and H. Chance Newton, comps. *Sixty Years' Stage Service, Being a Record of the Life of Charles Morton, "The Father of the Halls."* London: Gale and Polden, 1905.

"Mrs Chant at the Playgoer's Club." *Woman's Signal*, 22 November 1894, 329.

"Mrs Chant in America." *Vigilance Record*, 15 May 1890, 47–48.

"Mrs Ormiston Chant." *DT*, 24 October 1894, 2.

"Mrs Ormiston Chant in America." *Vigilance Record*, 15 July 1888, 64–65.

"Mrs Ormiston Chant in Canada." *Vigilance Record*, 15 April 1890, 32–33.

"Mrs Ormiston Chant on Music-Halls." *DT*, 26 October 1894, 3.

Munby, Arthur J. *Munby, Man of Two Worlds: The Life and Diaries of Arthur J. Munby, 1828–1910*. Ed. Derek Hudson. London: John Murray, 1972.

"Music, Dancing, and Theatre Licences." *Times*, 11 October 1894, 7.

"The Music-Hall." *Saturday Review*, 17 November 1894, 534.

"Music Hall Employees' Agitation." *Era*, 20 October 1894, 17–18.

"Music Hall Gossip." *Era*, 10 November 1894, 17.

Myers, Betty June. "Lanner, Katti (Katharina Josefa Lanner)." *International Encyclopedia of Dance*. 4: 121–22.

"The National Vigilance Association and the 'Living Pictures.'" *Vigilance Record*, 15 October 1894, 17–22.

Nead, Lynda. *Myths of Sexuality: Representations of Women in Victorian Britain*. Oxford: Basil Blackwell, 1988.

"New Ballet at the Empire." *Illustrated Sporting and Dramatic News*, 13 October 1894, 196.

Nicholson, Renton. *Rogue's Progress: The Autobiography of "Lord Chief Baron" Nicholson*. Ed. John L. Bradley. Boston: Houghton Mifflin, 1965.

Pascoe, Charles Eyre, ed. *London of To-Day: An Illustrated Annual Publication*. 10th ed. London: Simpkin, Marshall, Hamilton, Kent, 1894.

Pennell, Elizabeth Robins. "The Pedigree of the Music-Hall." *Contemporary Review* 63 (April 1893): 575–83.

Pennybacker, Susan. "'It was not what she said but the way in which she said it': The London County Council and the Music Halls." *Music Hall: The Business of Pleasure*, ed. Peter Bailey. Milton Keynes: Open UP, 1986. 118–40.

———. *A Vision for London, 1889–1914: Labour, Everyday Life, and the LCC Experiment*. London: Routledge, 1995.

Perugini, Mark E. *The Art of Ballet*. Philadelphia: J. B. Lippincott, 1915.

Pettitt, Henry, and Sir Augustus Harris. "A New and Original Drama of Everyday Life. Entitled A Life of Pleasure." Lord Chamberlain's Plays, British Library. Licensed 8 September 1893. Drury Lane, 21 September 1893.

Pierpont, Claudia Roth. "Wilhelm, C." *International Encyclopedia of Dance* 6: 397.

Pigache, Captain D. Nicols. *Café Royal Days*. London: Hutchinson, 1934.

Pinero, Arthur Wing. "Living Pictures." *New Review*, November 1894, 463.

Pratt, A. T. Camden. *People of the Period: Being a Collection of the Biographies of Upwards of Six Thousand Living Celebrities*. 2 vols. London: Neville Beeman, 1897.

"Protests of Ratepayers." *DT*, 19 October 1894, 3.

Reeve, Ada. *Take It for a Fact (A Record of My Seventy-Five Years on the Stage)*. London: William Heinemann, 1954.

Richards, Grant. *Memories of a Misspent Youth, 1872–1896*. London: William Heinemann, 1932.

*Round London: An Album of Pictures from Photographs of the Chief Places of Interest in and around London*. London: George Newnes, 1896.

Ruskin, John. "Of Queens' Gardens." *Sesame and Lilies: The Works of John Ruskin*, ed. E. T. Cook and Alexander Wedderburn. Vol. 18. London: George Allen, 1905.

Russell, Dave. "'We Carved Our Way to Glory': The British Soldier in Music Hall Song and Sketch, c. 1880–1914." *Popular Imperialism and the Military, 1850–1950*, ed. John M. MacKenzie. Manchester: Manchester UP, 1992. 50–79.

Sachs, Edwin O., and Ernest A. E. Woodrow. *Modern Opera Houses and Theatres*. 3 vols. 1896–98. Rpt. New York: Benjamin Blom, 1968.

Said, Edward. *Culture and Imperialism*. New York: Vintage Books, 1994.

Saint, Andrew, ed. *Politics and the People of London: The London County Council, 1889–1965*. London: Hambledon, 1989.

Sala, George Augustus. *Gaslight and Daylight, with Some London Scenes They Shine Upon*. London: Chapman & Hall, 1859.

Sanger, "Lord" George. *Seventy Years a Showman*. London: J. M. Dent & Sons, 1927.

Saunders, William. *History of the First London County Council: 1889–1890-1891*. London: National Press Agency, 1892.

Scott, Clement. "The Playhouses." *ILN*, 20 October 1894, 491; 10 November 1894, 587.

Scott, Harold. *The Early Doors: Origins of the Music Hall.* London: Nicholson & Watson, 1946.

Seale, Julie. "Miss Seale's Paper." Paper read at a meeting of the Church and Stage Guild, 1 October 1889. *Church Reformer* 8 (November 1889): 259–60.

Senelick, Laurence. "Music-Hall." *International Encyclopedia of Dance.* 4: 520–23.

———. "Politics as Entertainment: Victorian Music-Hall Songs." *Victorian Studies* 19 (December 1975): 149–80.

———, ed. *Tavern Singing in Early Victorian London: The Diaries of Charles Rice for 1840 and 1850.* London: Society for Theatre Research, 1997.

Senelick, Laurence, David F. Cheshire, and Ulrich Schneider, eds. *British Music Hall, 1840–1923: A Bibliography and Guide to Sources, with a Supplement on European Music-Hall.* Hamden, CT: Archon Books, 1981.

"The Shah at the Empire." *Era,* 24 December 1887, 16.

"Shares of Shows." *Music Hall and Theatre Review,* 27 July 1894, 12.

Shaw, George Bernard. "The Author's Apology." *Mrs Warren's Profession: A Play in Four Acts.* London: Grant Richards, 1902.

———. "The Empire Promenade." *Pall Mall Gazette,* 16 October 1894, 3.

———. "The Living Pictures." *Saturday Review,* 6 April 1895. Shaw, *Our Theatres in the Nineties.* 1: 79–86.

———. *Mrs Warren's Profession. The Bodley Head Bernard Shaw,* ed. Dan H. Laurence. Vol. 1. London: Max Reinhardt, 1970. 229–356.

———. *Music in London, 1890–94.* 3 vols. London: Constable, 1932.

———. *Our Theatres in the Nineties by Bernard Shaw.* 3 vols. London: Constable, 1932. Rpt. 1954.

———. "Two Easter Pieces." *Saturday Review,* 18 April 1896. Shaw, *Our Theatres in the Nineties.* 2: 98–104.

Shir-Jacob, Anita. "Staging the British Empire under Charles Dibdin the Younger at Sadler's Wells, 1800–1819." *Popular Theatres? Papers from the Popular Theatre Conference, Liverpool, John Moores University, 1994,* ed. Ros Merkin. Liverpool: John Moores University, 1996. 190–205.

*Sickert: Paintings.* Ed. Wendy Baron and Richard Shone. New Haven: Yale UP, 1992.

"A Signal Victory." *Woman's Signal,* 18 October 1894, 241–42.

"Sir Charles Frederick Gill." Obituary. *Times,* 23 February 1923, 15.

Smith, Alison. *The Victorian Nude: Sexuality, Morality, and Art.* Manchester: Manchester UP, 1996.

Smith, Alison, ed. *Exposed: The Victorian Nude.* London: Tate Publishing, 2001.

Soldene, Emily. *My Theatrical and Musical Recollections.* 2nd ed. London: Downey, 1897.

"Speech by Mrs Chant." *DT,* 16 October 1894, 5.

"Statement by Mrs Chant." *DT*, 18 October 1894, 3.

"Statement by the Directors of the Empire." *DT*, 17 October 1894, 3.

Stedman, Jane W., ed. *W. S. Gilbert's Theatrical Criticism*. London: Society for Theatre Research, 2000.

Stokes, John. *In the Nineties*. Chicago: U of Chicago P, 1989.

Stuart, Charles Douglas, and A. J. Park. *The Variety Stage: A History of the Music Halls from the Earliest Period to the Present Time*. London: T. Fisher Unwin, [1895].

Summerfield, Penelope. "The Effingham Arms and the Empire: Deliberate Selection in the Evolution of Music Hall in London." *Popular Culture and Class Conflict, 1590–1914: Explorations in the History of Labour and Leisure*, ed. Eileen Yeo and Stephen Yeo. Brighton: Harvester, 1981. 209–40.

———. "Patriotism and Empire: Music-Hall Entertainment, 1870–1914." *Imperialism and Popular Culture*. Ed. John M. MacKenzie. Manchester: Manchester UP, 1986. 17–48.

*Survey of London*. Gen. ed. F. H. W. Sheppard. Vols. 33–34: *The Parish of St Anne Soho*. London: Athlone, U of London, 1966.

*The Swell's Night Guide, or a Peep through the Great Metropolis, under the Dominion of Nox. . . .* Rev. ed. 1846.

Symons, Arthur. "At the Empire." *Sketch*, 7 June 1893, 301.

———. *London Nights*. London: Leonard Smithers, 1895.

———. "The World as Ballet." *Studies in Seven Arts*. New York: E. P. Dutton, 1906. 387–91.

*Les Tableaux vivants ou mes confessions aux pieds de la duchesse: Anecdotes véridiques tirées de mes amours avec nos libertines illustres et nos fouteuses de qualité*. Par un rédacteur de la R.D.D.M. [By Paul Perret.] Amsterdam, 1870.

Taylor, Nicholas. "Sir Albert Richardson: A Classic Case of Edwardianism." *Edwardian Architecture and Its Origins*, ed. Alastair Service. London: Architectural P, 1975. 444–59.

Taylor, Tom. *Leicester Square; Its Associations and Its Worthies*. London: Bickers and Son, 1874.

Thomas, Keith. "The Double Standard." *Journal of the History of Ideas* 20 (1959): 195–216.

Thorne, Guy. *The Great Acceptance: The Life Story of F. N. Charrington*. London: Hodder and Stoughton, [1912?].

Titterton, W. R. *From Theatre to Music Hall*. London: Stephen Swift, 1912.

Torley, Sarah A. "The Empire Theatre: An Interview with Mrs Ormiston Chant." *Woman's Signal*, 1 November 1894, 273–74.

Trotter, David. *Cooking with Mud: The Idea of Mess in Nineteenth-Century Art and Fiction*. Oxford: Oxford UP, 2000.

Turner, E. S. *Roads to Ruin: The Shocking History of Social Reform*. London: Michael Joseph, 1950.

Veder, Robin. "Tableaux Vivants: Performing Art, Purchasing Status." *Theatre Annual* 48 (1995): 14–29.

Vicinus, Martha. *The Industrial Muse: A Study of Nineteenth Century British Working-Class Literature*. London: Croom Helm, 1974.

"Views of Members of the London County Council." *DT*, 19 October 1894, 3.

Walker, Katherine Sorley. "George Jacobi and the Alhambra Ballet." *Theatre Notebook* 1 (1947): 82–83.

Walkowitz, Judith R. *City of Dreadful Delight: Narratives of Sexual Danger in Late-Victorian London*. Chicago: U of Chicago P, 1992.

———. "Male Vice and Feminist Virtue: Feminism and the Politics of Prostitution in Nineteenth-Century Britain." *History Workshop* 13 (Spring 1982): 79–93.

———. *Prostitution and Victorian Society: Women, Class, and the State*. Cambridge: Cambridge UP, 1980.

Walvin, James. *Leisure and Society, 1830–1950*. London: Longman, 1978.

Ware, Dora. *A Short Dictionary of British Architects*. London: George Allen and Unwin, 1967.

Waters, Chris. *British Socialists and the Politics of Popular Culture, 1884–1914*. Stanford: Stanford UP, 1990.

West, Shearer. *Fin de Siècle*. Woodstock, NY: Overlook P, 1994.

Wharton, Edith. *The House of Mirth*. 1905. New York: Scribner's, 1969.

*Who Was Who, 1916–1928*. 4th ed. London: Adam & Charles Black, 1967.

Wilde, Oscar. *Lady Windermere's Fan: A Play about a Good Woman*. Ed. Ian Small. New Mermaids. London: Ernest Benn, 1980.

———. *Oscar Wilde's* The Importance of Being Earnest: *A Reconstructive Critical Edition of the Text of the First Production, St. James's Theatre, London, 1895*. Ed. Joseph Donohue with Ruth Berggren. Princess Grace Irish Library 10. Gerrards Cross: Colin Smythe, 1995.

Wilhelm, C. [William John Charles Pitcher]. "Art in the Ballet." *Magazine of Art* 18 (1894), pt. 1: 12–16; pt. 2: 48–53.

——— [William John Charles Pitcher]. "Designs for the Costumes of Premières Danseuses." *Magazine of Art* 18 (1894): 16.

"Women's Conference." *DT*, 24 October 1894, 2.

Woods, Robert. "Population Growth and Economic Change in the Eighteenth and Nineteenth Centuries." *The First Industrial Revolutions*, ed. Peter Mathias and John A. Davis. Oxford: Basil Blackwell, 1989. 127–53.

Wratislaw, Theodore. *Orchids: Poems*. London: Leonard Smithers, 1896.

Yates, Edmund. *Edmund Yates: His Recollections and Experiences*. 2 vols. London: Richard Bentley and Son, 1884.

Yeats, William Butler. *The Autobiography of William Butler Yeats*. New York: Macmillan, 1953.

Yeo, Eileen, and Stephen Yeo, eds. *Popular Culture and Class Conflict, 1590–1914: Explorations in the History of Labour and Leisure*. Brighton: Harvester, 1981.

Ziter, Edward. *The Orient on the Victorian Stage*. Cambridge: Cambridge UP, 2003.

# INDEX

## STUDIES IN THEATRE HISTORY & CULTURE

*Othello* and Interpretive Traditions
By *Edward Pechter*

Our Moonlight Revels: *A Midsummer Night's Dream* in the Theatre
By *Gary Jay Williams*

The Performance of Power: Theatrical Discourse and Politics
Edited by *Sue-Ellen Case and Janelle Reinelt*

Performing History: Theatrical Representations of the
Past in Contemporary Theatre
By *Freddie Rokem*

The Recurrence of Fate: Theatre and Memory in Twentieth-Century Russia
By *Spencer Golub*

Reflecting the Audience: London Theatregoing, 1840–1880
By *Jim Davis and Victor Emeljanow*

The Roots of Theatre: Rethinking Ritual and Other Theories of Origin
By *Eli Rozik*

Shakespeare and Chekhov in Production: Theatrical Events and Their Audiences
By *John Tulloch*

Shakespeare on the American Yiddish Stage
By *Joel Berkowitz*

The Show and the Gaze of Theatre: A European Perspective
By *Erika Fischer-Lichte*

Textual and Theatrical Shakespeare: Questions of Evidence
Edited by *Edward Pechter*

The Theatrical Event: Dynamics of Performance and Perception
By *Willmar Sauter*

The Trick of Singularity: *Twelfth Night* and the Performance Editions
By *Laurie E. Osborne*

The Victorian Marionette Theatre
By *John McCormick*

Wandering Stars: Russian Emigré Theatre, 1905–1940
Edited by *Laurence Senelick*

Writing and Rewriting National Theatre Histories
Edited by *S. E. Wilmer*